The Essential Guide to Teaching

Susan Davies

The Essential Guide to Teaching

PEARSON
Longman

Harlow, England • London • New York • Boston • San Francisco • Toronto • Sydney • Singapore • Hong Kong
Tokyo • Seoul • Taipei • New Delhi • Cape Town • Madrid • Mexico City • Amsterdam • Munich • Paris • Milan

PEARSON EDUCATION LIMITED

Edinburgh Gate
Harlow CM20 2JE
Tel: +44 (0)1279 623623
Fax: +44 (0)1279 431059
Website: www.pearsoned.co.uk

First published in Great Britain in 2006
© Pearson Education Limited 2006

The right of Susan Davies to be identified as author of this work has been asserted by her in accordance with the Copyright, Designs and Patents Act 1988.

ISBN : 978-1-4058-1260-3

British Library Cataloguing-in-Publication Data
A catalogue record for this book is available from the British Library

Library of Congress Cataloging-in-Publication Data
Davies, Susan.
 The essential guide to teaching / Susan Davies.
  p. cm.
 Includes bibliographical references and index.
 ISBN-13: 978-1-4058-1260-3 (alk. paper)
 ISBN-10: 1-4058-1260-5
  1. Teaching. 2. Teachers--Training of. I. Title.
 LB1775.D26 2006
 371.102--dc22

                2006042623

10 9 8 7 6 5 4 3 2
13 12 11 10

Cartoons by Jules Mann
Typeset in 9/13 Interstate by 3
Printed and bound in Malaysia (CTP - KHL)

The Publisher's policy is to use paper manufactured from sustainable forests.

Contents

Author's acknowledgements

In my case writing books is a team effort so this book is dedicated to my very own home team:

- To Gareth my best friend who bought me my first computer 20 years ago and continues to encourage me – keeping my feet on the ground even if at times my head is in the clouds!
- For Hannah, Rachael and Alys who continue to make even rainy days sunny.
- For Anne Treharne Griffiths a teacher who made a difference and who shares a passion for looking at the stars!

And with grateful thanks to Catherine Yates and Paula Parish at Pearson for sharing the vision. Thanks also to Laura Brundell for her editorial work.

Thank you also to the following teachers who acted as the main reviewers for the book at various stages of writing:

Louise Etherington, Helen Richardson, Vickie Gale, Verity Lush and Tracey Jones.

Thank you to the following schools for their assistance and with special thanks to the Headteacher Mr P.V. Wilcox and the staff and pupils of Bishop Gore Comprehensive School, Swansea:

Haybridge High School and Sixth Form
St Thomas Primary School
Eirias High School
Langdon School
Grange Primary School
Matthew Moss High School
Gorseinon College
Brynmill Primary School

Finally, with thanks to the teachers who made a difference in my life without perhaps realising it at the time:

- Mrs James, Nottage Primary School, Porthcawl, for teaching me to read when all around had given up; and
- Mr Wyn Derrick, Mr A.C. Rees, Mr Euros and Mrs Nanette Rees and Mrs Marion Williams, all of Amman Valley Comprehensive School, Ammanford.

Publisher's acknowledgements

We are grateful to the following for permission to reproduce copyright material:

Photographs: p39 (© Janine Wiedel Photolibrary/Alamy), p49 from www.JohnBirdsall.co.uk, p78 from www.JohnBirdsall.co.uk, p104 (© Janine Wiedel Photolibrary/Alamy), p113 from www.JohnBirdsall.co.uk, p119 (©Brian Mitchell/ Photofusion), p124 from www.JohnBirdsall.co.uk, p138 from educationphotos.co.uk/walmsley, p169 (©Jacky Chapman/Photofusion), p190 (© Tom Stewart/CORBIS), p198 (©Janine Wiedel Photolibrary/Alamy), p204 (© Photofusion Picture Library/Alamy), p231 (©Christa Stadtler/Photofusion), p238 (© SHOUT/Alamy), p246 (© Jennie Woodcock; Reflections Photolibrary/CORBIS), p260 (©Digital Nation/Photofusion), p269 from www.JohnBirdsall.co.uk, p281 (© BananaStock/Alamy).

Figure 5.1 from Marsh, A. and Perry, J. in Kober, C. (ed.) *Black and Ethnic Minority Children and Poverty: Exploring the Issues* (2003), End Child Poverty; Table 6.1 and Figure 6.3 reprinted by permission of HarperCollins Publishers Ltd. ©(Strong) (2001); Figures 6.1 and 6.2 from *A Proper Bike* and *The Holiday* by Rod Hunt illustrated by Alex Brychta (Oxford Reading Tree, OUP, 2004), ©Oxford University Press, reprinted by permission of Oxford University Press; Figure 22.1 by permission from Mrs A Reeves of Fielding Primary School; Figure 22.2 by permission from City of Leicester College; extract on p24 from *A Curriculum Framework for Children 3–5, Learning and Teaching Scotland*, Learning and Teaching Scotland – originally published by Scottish Consultative Council on the Curriculum (1999); extract on p47 © Guardian Newspapers Limited 2005; extracts on pp62, 64–65, 66 from *Readability* by Kevin Johnson at www.timetabler.com; extract on p171 from *Inside the Black Box* © Paul Black and Dylan Wiliam, 1998. Reproduced by permission of nferNelson publishing company Ltd.; extract on p187 reproduced by permission of The Association for Achievement and Improvement Through Assessment (AAIA); Crown copyright material is reproduced with the permission of the Controller of HMSO and the Queen's Printer for Scotland.

In some instances we have been unable to trace the owners of copyright material, and we would appreciate any information that would enable us to do so.

List of abbreviations

ACCAC	Qualifications, Curriculum and Assessment Authority (Wales) - ACCAC are now part of DELL (Department of Education and Lifelong Learning)
ADHD	attention deficit hyperactivity disorder
AS	advanced supplementary courses
AST	advanced skills teachers
BCS	British Cohort Study
BHPS	British Household Panel Study
BSA	behaviour support assistants
CA	classroom assistants
CAT	cognitive assessment test
CC	curriculum coordinator
CCEA	The Northern Ireland Council for the Curriculum, Examinations and Assessment
COA	cover assistants
CPD	continuing professional development
CPO	child protection officer
CSA	curriculum support assistants
CSI	core subject indicator
CSM	cover support manager
CSE	Certificate of Secondary Education (no longer in use)
CV	curriculum vitae
DES	Department of Education and Science
DfES	Department for Education and Skills
EAL	English as an additional language
EBP	educational behaviour plan/programme
EMA	educational maintenance allowance
EMAG	Ethnic Minorities Achievement Grant
EMLAS	Ethnic Minorities Language Advisory Service
EO	equal opportunities
EOP	equal opportunities policy
EP	educational psychologist
EWO	education welfare officer
EWS	education welfare service
FE	further education
GCSE	General Certificate of Secondary Education

HOD	head of department
HOF	head of faculty
HSO	health and safety officer
ICT	information and computer technology
IEP	individual education plan/programme
ILP	individual learning plan/programme
IT	information technology
ITT	initial teacher training
KSM	key stage manager
LAC	looked-after children
LC	learning coaches
LEA	Local Education Authority
LSA	learning support assistant
MER	monitoring, evaluating and reviewing
MFL	modern foreign language
NCDS	National Child Development Study
NLNS	National Literacy and Numeracy Strategy
NQT	newly qualified teacher
NVR	non-verbal reasoning
NVSAS	non-verbal standardised age score
Ofsted	Office for Standards in Education
PC	pastoral coordinator
PPL	promoting positive learning
PSA	pastoral support assistant
PSHE	personal, social and health education
PSE	personal and social education
PTA	Parent Teachers' Association
QCA	Qualifications and Curriculum Authority
QR	quantitative reasoning
QSAS	quantitative standardised age score
SAT	standard attainment target
SDO	school development officer
SDP	school development plan
SEAL	social and emotional aspects of learning
SEED	Scottish Executive Education Department
SEN	special educational needs
SENCO	special educational needs coordinator
SIP	school improvement plan

SLG	senior leadership group
SMART	specific, measurable, achievable, realistic, time-related
SMG	school management group
SOW	scheme of work
ST	support teacher
TA	teaching assistants
TES	*Times Educational Supplement*
TSAS	triple standardised age score
UCAS	Universities and Colleges Admissions Service
VAK	visual, auditory, kinaesthetic
VR	verbal reasoning
VSAS	verbal standardised age score
WRE	work-related experience
YOT	young offenders team

Introduction

Teaching is a challenging and rewarding profession and one of the few careers you can choose where you really can make a difference to someone's life - a difference that will stay with them for ever. The first teacher to make a difference in my life was Mrs James. She was a primary school teacher who taught me to read when others had failed. Where, I wonder, would I be now if she had not been there to make a difference?

I have been teaching for over 25 years but still remember to this day the sheer fear of going into school for the first time and confronting a class of pupils who at the time were not a lot younger than I was. I can also remember the first day I started teaching for real in my first post. No possibility at all of handing that class back to my mentor or another teacher, they were mine - all mine! However conscientiously you study during your training, nothing can prepare you for the realities that confront you on a day-to-day basis, not just in the classroom, but in the school as a whole.

For the past ten years, I have been actively involved in mentoring, training and supporting student teachers on placement in my school, as well as supporting newly qualified teachers (**NQTs**), embarking on their first teaching role. During this time it has become obvious that the fear factor still exists and most new teachers still feel they lack essential background theory, practical skills and confidence in themselves as teaching professionals. One of the best ways to learn in those first years is to look to more experienced colleagues in your school for practical advice and tips, but you cannot rely on someone being there exactly when you need them, at all times of the day and night! This book is intended to provide you with just that type of support and help you build up your knowledge and confidence.

The Essential Guide to Teaching is intended to help you make that successful transition from new teacher to experienced leading professional. It combines tried and tested practical advice with an overview of the theory and current thinking behind the practices you will find in the schools you'll teach in today.

However, this book is much more than just a book that you will use for a year or two and then discard. The chapters on teaching boys and girls, preparing a sound lesson and using formative assessment are timeless and in many ways this is a book that you can put on the shelf in your classroom and refer back to. In fact some of the chapters have been used in my own school for staff training purposes. Therefore it is intended to serve you as a companion guide long into your profession.

The content of the book is carefully chosen and based on long conversations with many trainee teachers in both the primary and secondary sectors about their specific needs. Many new teachers enter schools having no understanding of how the school as an organisation is structured, why pupils are grouped in the way they are or why in fact we teach what we do. Though this is not maybe the most scintillating way to start off a book, it is a bit of essential information that all teachers should have. In addition, the book contains detailed and collated research on topics as varied as:

✔ How best to teach boys and girls

✔ How to mark pupils' work and set clear targets for improvement

✔ How to plan effective lessons

✔ How poverty and ethnicity affect educational outcomes

✔ What data is used in school and for what purposes

In all cases detailed references are given to enable you to read further when you feel inspired to do so or the need is there.

There is practical advice too about how to write a letter of application, produce a 'Curriculum Vitae' and prepare for an interview. Once in post this book will help you to prepare for parents' evenings, write reports and keep detailed records on pupils. There are two chapters dealing solely with behaviour management that are intended to provide you with tried and tested effective strategies to deal with difficult situations that can arise. In many ways the practical advice is material that I would have loved to have had when I started my professional life.

Many proactive schools now track pupil progress using data. Understanding what data is used in schools and how to best make sense of it is critical in today's fast changing schools. You will find detailed guidance on how to collect, interpret and store this data. As well as being a classroom teacher all teachers in both primary and secondary schools are expected to take a lead role in pastoral support for their pupils. This book is one of only a few that takes a long, hard look at this and gives you clear guidance as to what is expected of you as a class/form tutor and how to fulfil this role well. The role of pastoral co-ordinators and key stage managers in a school is clearly defined. Finally how schools link with other agencies such the Educational Welfare Services and the Educational Psychological Service to support effective learning is examined.

This is a comprehensive book intended to be, as its title suggests, that all encompassing essential guide.

How can I use this book effectively?

The Essential Guide to Teaching was written so that it could be used as flexibly as possible, to allow you to dip in and out, rather than having to sit and read through the whole book cover to cover. However, to get the best out of the guide, I would recommend starting by reading the first three chapters. These chapters are intended to give a clear overview of how a school is organised both in terms of staff and pupils and where the content we teach comes from.

It is not necessary to read the rest of the book sequentially though there are units of information that are obviously best read together.

- 'Boys and Girls are Different!' may be best read alongside 'Poverty, Ethnicity and Pupil Attainment' – Chapters 4 and 5
- The behaviour chapters are written sequentially. This provides you with an overview of how schools manage discipline and then focus on how you can manage it in your classroom – Chapters 10 and 11
- The role of the form tutor and pastoral team along with the PHSE curriculum in our schools – Chapters 17 and 18
- What data schools use, how it is collected and how to understand it – Chapters 8 and 15
- 'Readability, Reading Ages and Writing Frames' with 'Learning to Teach and Teaching to Learn', as well as 'Using Classroom Supports to Maximise Pupils' Learnings' – Chapters 6, 7 and 9.
- 'Storing Data and Organising Lesson Planning' with the chapters on what data is gathered and how schools use them – Chapters 8 and 15
- 'Assessment for Learning' with 'Reporting to Parents' – Chapters 13 and 16
- 'Promoting Inclusion in Our Schools' with 'Pupil Induction' and 'Attendance, Child Protection and Anti-Bullying Strategies' – Chapters 12, 19 and 20
- 'School Inspections' with 'Applying for a Job' and 'Continuing Professional Development' – Chapters 21, 22 and 23

In every chapter you will find the following features:

 Signposting in the margin – this icon in the margin refers you back and forth to specific, linked material in other chapters – helping you to navigate your way through the book more effectively

 Weblinks – this icon in the margin gives details of additional material to be found on the book's website (see below for details)

 Time to reflect – this feature appears at the end of each chapter and helps both consolidate what has been covered in the chapter and encourages you to relate it to your own personal role and school

 Top Tips – these appear in every chapter and can be downloaded and printed off via the book's website.

Don't forget, *The Essential Guide to Teaching* is supported by a website at **www.pearsoned.co.uk/davies** where you can access extra resources including:

- additional case studies and examples of best practice
- insights into innovative educational initiatives adopted by different schools in both the primary and secondary sectors
- weblinks to educational organisations, research findings and teaching resources
- a variety of templates taken from the book which can be customised and printed off for use in lesson planning or in class
- lists of Top Tips taken from the book

Best of luck!

Sue Davies, June 2006

PART I

School Organisation

> **MER is an acronym** for monitoring, evaluating and reviewing. The best way to know what is going on in any classroom is to look at the pupils' books or to sit at the back of a number of lessons. Trainee and new teachers do a lot of this. When planning any new initiative it is important to think about how you will monitor, evaluate and review its success. Writing down clear success criteria for the outcome of any project *before* you begin is a good place to start. We will look at this in more detail in Chapter 21. See also Chapters 13, 14 and 15.

Primary and secondary schools vary in size dramatically and this affects how an individual school is structured. Primary schools normally have a headteacher and one deputy headteacher. In addition, there are other teachers who make up the middle management team. They may have an allowance for taking responsibility for a subject area or areas throughout the school, and this may have been agreed when they were first appointed. These teachers write the scheme of work (**SOW**) and ensure that the national curriculum guidelines for the programme of study in a subject are being followed. Finally, they are also responsible for monitoring, evaluating and reviewing (**MER**) work in that subject throughout the school.

> A scheme of work (SOW) is a programme of study followed by all teachers of a subject. It takes account of all statutory needs and ensures that what is taught is the same for all pupils, ie is consistent.

How primary and secondary schools are organised

Primary and secondary schools have similar management structures, see Figures 1.1 and 1.2. Secondary schools have subject leaders called:

- head of department (**HOD**) or
- curriculum coordinator (**CC**) or
- head of faculty (**HOF**), where a faculty system operates.

Size affects organisation: the smallest secondary schools are usually as big as the largest primary schools. In secondary schools:

- there is usually a headteacher and at least one but normally two deputy headteachers
- there may be assistant headteachers who are a rank below the deputy (they are also part of the management team)
- there may be advanced skills teachers (**ASTs**, who may be paid on a similar scale to members of the leadership team). ASTs have been formally recognised as being excellent classroom practitioners.

> **An AST is paid** more and has more non-contact time. The AST will use this time to produce high-quality teaching materials, share good practice and support subject leaders with the SOW. ASTs also help teachers by acting as a critical friend.

Budgets and staffing

If a school – whether primary or secondary – is small, then the number of staff available to carry out specific tasks will be restricted.

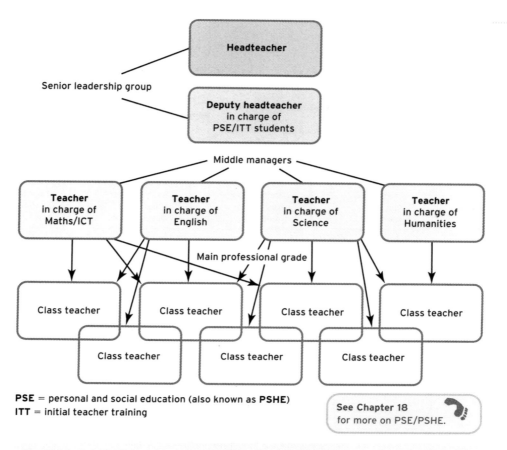

PSE = personal and social education (also known as PSHE)
ITT = initial teacher training

See Chapter 18 for more on PSE/PSHE.

Figure 1.1 Example of a primary school management structure

- Schools differ in the way they deploy staff but most are hierarchical in structure.

- Schools have a set budget dependent on the number of pupils.

- In a smaller school, particularly a primary, teachers may be responsible for two subject areas. Similarly, in a small secondary school a teacher may be responsible for physics and information technology (IT), textiles and child development, media studies and English, or English and drama, for example.

- How a school organises its staff is unique to that school and depends on the head-teacher's philosophy, the influence of the governing body and very often the budget!

- Many schools are changing the way they organise themselves and at secondary level this has meant a flattening of the management structure. Where this has occurred the deputy headteachers have been replaced by assistant headteachers, thus removing a layer of the organisation. The headteacher may have as many as seven assistant headteachers, with one normally designated senior to deputise and make decisions in their absence.

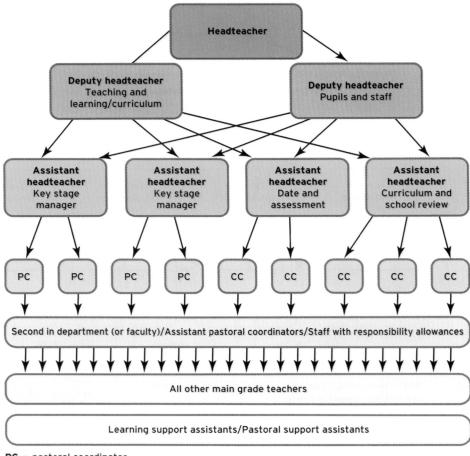

Figure 1.2 *Example of a secondary school management structure*

The senior management team

The headteacher, deputy headteachers and assistant headteachers form the senior leadership group (**SLG**) or senior management group (**SMG**) of a secondary school. In a primary school, the SLG or SMG may simply consist of the headteacher and deputy. However, in many larger primary schools this is changing and the SLG consists of staff who may be called team leaders and are responsible for a number of teachers.

See the website for an example of the team leader's job description. You could be doing this job in a short time: knowing what a team leader is looking for informs your work now.

What does a member of the senior management team do?

A team member:

- Is appointed by the governing body of the school.
- Has specific whole school responsibilities.
- May be responsible for a subject area and be formally linked to it.
- Makes decisions about the staffing and financial running of the school.
- Plays a part in writing the school development plan (**SDP**). This plan is reviewed annually but most schools now have a plan that covers three years so that longer term, more strategic planning can take place.
- Monitors, evaluates and reviews the progress of initiatives, departments or year groups.
- Chairs meetings of academic and pastoral leaders.
- Meets with the team on a regular basis, normally weekly.

What are the functions of middle managers?

To be an effective organisation the school needs to have key personnel with specific responsibilities. Middle managers play an important part in day-to-day running, ensuring that teaching and learning is effective. They check that SOWs are being followed and that pupils are making progress in line with age and ability, against targets, and in comparison to similar pupils from similar schools. They are experts in their subject, ensuring that any changes in the programme of study at any key stage are interpreted and included in their SOW.

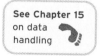

See Chapter 15 on data handling

In a secondary school the PC or head of year ensures that pupils in that year group are making the necessary progress. However, instead of looking vertically at attainment in a subject through years 7-13, as an HOD would do, a PC is interested in a specific year group's performance in all subject areas to check that attendance, attitude and behaviour are likely to ensure successful outcomes for their year.

What is expected of me and how do I fit into a school?

Mentors are appointed in primary and secondary schools to give new teachers support, whether they are students, ie those undergoing initial teacher training (**ITT**), or newly qualified teachers (**NQT**). However, you will eventually find yourself alone in front of a class.

You will have to:

- Follow the SOW set by your HOD.
- Plan lessons that are part of the programme of study.
- Follow a recognised syllabus for those pupils taking external examinations.
- Be responsible for the pastoral welfare of a class either as the class teacher or form tutor.
- Be aware of the vision for the school's future as outlined in the SDP.
- Follow whole school procedures and policies on marking, bullying, etc that you will need to familiarise yourself with and adhere to.
- Use the staff handbook to obtain information about the day-to-day running of your school and policies and procedures like those above.
- Familiarise yourself with the school prospectus. All schools must have one and the information it contains is determined by statutory guidelines.
- Work with a variety of colleagues. You may have pupils who need support and will be following specific programmes of study determined by:
  - the special educational needs (**SEN**) department or
  - a behaviour support team of educational psychologists (**EPs**).

  These pupils will have:
  - learning support assistants (**LSAs**) or
  - pastoral support assistants (**PSAs**) or
  - Ethnic Minorities Language Advisory Service (**EMLAS**) support assistants.

  You will be expected to work with these support people and take into account when planning lessons any:
  - individual learning programmes (**ILPs**) or
  - educational behaviour plans (**EBPs**).

Who will help me in my school?

The mentor

The mentor supports and helps you with any school-based problems. They can act as a go-between for you and your HOD or line manager. However, most teachers are very approachable and you can normally discuss specific issues with them directly.

The finance manager/bursar

In a small primary this may be the headteacher but in a large school there will be someone with that specific job description or role. See them for issues to do with salary and finance.

The caretaker

See the caretaker or a departmental technician for all issues to do with your classroom, for example if you need new bulbs, electric plugs, extension cables or special equipment. Science, IT and technology departments in secondary schools have technical support staff.

The health and safety officer (**HSO**)

Every school has an HSO and any issues to do with your room or the school environment in general that come under health and safety need to be recorded and submitted to them. The HSO will ensure that remedial action is taken quickly to prevent accident and injury.

Child protection officer (**CPO**)

Every school has to appoint a CPO. The CPO works with organisations such as:

- Social Services
- the Young Offenders Team (**YOT**) and with
- looked-after children (**LAC**), children who are in some form of care other than with their natural parents.

The CPO will be in charge of all multi-agency liaison that goes on and in most schools it is a deputy headteacher who takes on this role.

You must report to the CPO any concerns you have about the safety of children. Any disclosure that is made to you suggesting a crime has been committed must be immediately notified to the CPO verbally and later in writing, so that accurate records can be kept. The CPO will then make a decision about how to proceed.

The HOD or subject mentor

In a primary and secondary school there is someone who will:

- advise you about lesson planning
- give you guidance about your teaching

- suggest strategies for managing children's behaviour
- observe your lessons
- check that your class books are marked regularly and accurately
- be a critical friend.

The headteacher and deputy headteachers

Do not be afraid to approach these people for help and guidance on whole school policies that you may not fully understand. They can also help you to understand the important role that you play within the school as a front-line classroom teacher.

Other teachers and staff

Each teacher in the school was once in the position you are now in – new to the school and the job. These people can help you with discipline issues or in getting to know the school and its staff better. Every school is unique and getting to know its idiosyncratic running style is useful. Your colleagues are an invaluable source of knowledge on all sorts of issues.

Time to reflect

✔ If you are already in a school make a list of those people who make up the senior managers of the school.

✔ What responsibilities does your mentor have in addition to being a mentor?

✔ Who is in charge of Health and Safety and Child Protection? Find out from these people what their duties entail.

✔ What other information do you wish to know about responsibilities and roles?

Chapter 2

Organising Pupils for Learning

What will you find in this chapter?

✔ What is banding, streaming, setting and mixed ability teaching?

✔ What research has been done and what are the findings?

✔ How do we organise our pupils for learning?

✔ What are the problems associated with streaming and mixed ability teaching?

✔ What are the problems associated with setting pupils for learning?

This chapter provides new teachers with an overview of how schools might organise their pupils for learning. It also examines some of the major research that has highlighted the advantages and disadvantages of some of these pupil groupings. This is a huge research area and it is impossible to do it justice in one chapter, particularly when research is ongoing. So, some suggestions for further reading are provided at the end of the chapter.

You can adjust your teaching to take account of the way departments or classes are organised.

What is banding?

Banding is the placing of pupils within a class into ability groupings. It is common in primary schools and is also used in secondary schools, where it describes a slightly different teaching arrangement – a large year group is sometimes divided into two or more groupings. Pupils can be of equal ability or differentiated on criteria similar to streaming (see below).

Banding can ease timetabling problems. Look at this structure where you need ten teachers to teach a specific subject at the same time:

10D	10E	10W	10I	10DX	10S	10A	10N	10T	10X

In a secondary school this could happen when you are teaching the core subjects of English, maths and science. It would mean that all the teachers of English would be teaching at the same time, something a department might not want. Maybe not all the teachers want to teach the General Certificate of Secondary Education (**GCSE**) or maybe the department has some non-specialists who are not able to offer GCSE but are competent lower school English teachers.

Therefore, to offer the best academic experience the school may want to split the year group into two equal bands and timetable one half for English at the same time as the others have maths, for example. This would alleviate any staffing problems and ensure that the best-suited teachers are used for any particular group. In this structure you can now use staff more flexibly as you are not committed to using the whole of a department to teach a year group. From the timetable's point of view it is also easier. Let us assume that while the DEWIX band has English the SANTX band has maths:

10S	10A	10N	10T	10X

10D	10E	10W	10I	10DX

However, there are five subject teachers of English and five of maths who are not yet scheduled for any classes at that time. The school could use these 'free' teachers elsewhere. So, some of a maths or English department may be teaching lower school classes while GCSE is being taught. Likewise, they may be used to teach sixth form classes while GCSE is ongoing.

When you split the cohort the two halves may be of equal ability, but some schools have banded pupils in such a way that one half of the band contains the top 30 pupils in a year group. This means that resources can be put in place to support these very able students and that subject leaders can ensure that work set is challenging enough for these pupils. However if all your brightest pupils are in one half of the year group, then it can present problems. The obvious disadvantage to this is that it does skew the ability range of the two halves in that one contains all your most able pupils and the other half does not have the significant high flyers. Some schools like this express group system and others think that the disadvantage of one half of the year group being devoid of the top pupils is detrimental, feeling that a good spread of very able pupils can significantly pull up the standards of other students. However, it is worth remembering that banding pupils means that you can still teach in mixed ability groups or sets within that band, depending on the philosophy of the school as a whole and the subject teams.

What is streaming?

This is when pupils remain in ability-based classes for all subjects. This does not take account of the fact that a pupil may be good in one subject but struggle in another.

What is setting?

Pupils are grouped according to ability for individual subjects. This means that a pupil can be in the top set for maths but in a lower set for English or vice versa. In many schools the core subjects of English, maths and science are setted subjects but many others are taught in mixed ability groups.

What is a mixed ability group?

This is a class of pupils that are not selected in any way by ability, reading age, etc. It represents a cross-section of pupils of different abilities and if the school has pupils from a wide socio-economic base it will also reflect that mix.

What research has been done and what findings are relevant to new teachers?

Much research has been done on the effects of pupil groupings on learning outcomes but the results are not at all conclusive:

- Some evidence suggests that setting and streaming can negatively affect results attained by those pupils.

- Some evidence suggests that grouping by ability improves results.

- Some evidence is inconclusive suggesting that grouping by ability has a negligible effect.

This ambiguity occurs because this is not an easy area to research, given that there are difficulties in setting up an experiment that compares like with like. These are some of the difficulties that researchers have encountered:

- Teachers are not uniform in their approach to teaching and the teaching methods they employ. This may be even more marked now as some schools use interactive whiteboard and information technology to a much higher degree than others.

- Mixed ability classes may vary in the range of ability reflected in the group.

- Setted groups may actually have a large spread of ability within them, almost equivalent to that of some mixed ability groups.

- Class sizes may vary.

- The degree of differentiation that occurs may differ widely.

- The curriculum content may be different.

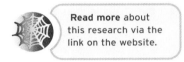 **Read more** about this research via the link on the website.

In order to get over some of the difficulties that have arisen in this area of research, Harlen suggests that we should apply the concept of 'best evidence synthesis' (Harlen in Slavin, 1986). Read more about this research via the link on the website.

In best evidence synthesis, criteria are identified for good quality research yielding the best evidence in a particular field. Research studies are then compared against the criteria and those that best match the criteria list are regarded as the most reliable.

Harlen suggests that research based solely on measurements and comparison of achievements of pupils in both ability and mixed ability groups is inadequate. In order to get a full picture, researchers need to seek the views of the learners themselves about what they think of the way they are organised for learning. This kind of study is discussed later in the chapter. Visit the website for a link to this research.

How do we organise our pupils for learning? How might my subject area be organised, and why?

In the UK there is a long tradition of grouping by ability in secondary schools. There is also evidence that in-class grouping by ability is widespread in primary schools. Streaming and setting in primary schools is only possible in large schools and therefore is not as prevalent as it is in secondary schools.

The 1970s and 1980s was a period when mixed ability teaching was more popular. This was due to the general public's concern for 'educational equality', but the pendulum swung back in the 1990s to favour ability groupings for the following reasons:

- The Educational Reform Act of 1988 required schools to adopt the National Curriculum. Many teachers felt that this programme of study made it difficult to teach in mixed ability groups.

- Schools had to be seen to be academically successful in order to attract pupils and compete in the 'league tables', and middle-class parents like setting, feeling that their children are better catered for in these ability groupings.

- The government's White Paper 'Excellence in Schools' (DfEE, 1997:38) revealed the Labour government's commitment to setting: 'Unless a school can demonstrate that it is getting better than expected results through a different approach, we do make the presumption that setting should be the norm in secondary schools.'

Reid *et al.* (1981) found that the nature of the subject could affect how pupils were organised for learning. If a subject required pupils to work through a body of knowledge in a logical sequence, the problems of teaching in mixed ability groups were thought to be insurmountable. In contrast, subjects that could be taught in a thematic or modular manner lent themselves more readily to a mixed ability approach. A further factor was the role of the teacher in the classroom context. If the teacher was central to the lesson and was the major resource, fewer opportunities existed for mixed ability teaching. It was suggested that for this reason modern linguists were less likely to be enthusiastic about mixed ability groupings. Setting is also prevalent in maths, science and English – the core subjects.

One research study in detail

What new teachers need to know about the effects of setting and streaming

The research study carried out by Boaler *et al.* (1997) is particularly interesting as it looks at both attainment and the attitude of the learners to the way they are organised for learning. The research included case studies of two year groups containing over 100 pupils in two schools. The study focused on the teaching of maths where in one school it was taught in sets and in another in mixed ability groups. The pupils were matched according to:

Visit the website for a link to this research.

- ability
- ethnicity
- sex
- socio-economic status.

Case Study

The pupils were observed in lessons and interviewed and assessed regularly. This research was different in that it took into account not only how well the children were doing but also their own perceptions of the positive and negative learning experiences that they were undergoing.

The results found that:

- In the mixed ability school the pupils attained higher GCSE grades and significantly more A-G passes. This is despite the fact that pupils were of the same ability in both schools at the start of their schooling, measured using national and standardised tests.

- In the school that used setting, the biggest determining factor upon achievement at GCSE was social class. This was a more important determinant than the ability measure taken on entry to the school. In the mixed ability school there was no link between social class and achievement.

- The effects of setting disadvantaged a significant proportion of top set pupils. A number of pupils were negatively affected by pace and the pressure put upon them because they were in a top set, and there were expectations formed within these groups of how well these pupils should do. This was shown to disadvantage girls more than boys. These girls had previously been successful in mixed ability groups at key stage 3.

- In interviews (see below) the pupils stated that working at the pace of the class was not always conducive to success. It negatively affected their understanding as they were either forced to work too fast, which led to a lack of understanding and anxiety, or they were forced to work too slowly and this led to disaffection and underachievement. In mixed ability classes when pupils worked at their own pace they reported a greater level of understanding.

- In the school that used setting, social class influenced setting, which resulted in disproportionate numbers of working-class pupils being allocated to low sets.

- Pupils who are entered for maths GCSE can enter one of three tiers of examination (this is currently under review). It was found that those pupils who were entered for examinations where they could not access the higher grades became demotivated or disillusioned. They believed that they could have done better if they had been allowed to.

What the pupils say and why new teachers should listen

- Lessons are difficult and if you can't answer he says, 'You won't be in set 1 next year - you are in set 1 you shouldn't be finding this difficult.' (School R boys, set 1)

- He explains work like we're maths teachers - really complex, I don't understand it. (School R boys, set 1)

- It's just our group who keeps changing teachers. Why? 'Cause they don't think they have to bother with us, I know that sounds really mean, but they don't think they have to bother with us, 'cause we're group 5 so if they have a teacher who knows nothing about maths, they'll give them to us, say a PE teacher. (School R girl, set 5)

🍎 You have to come in, sit down, there's stuff on the board and he says copy it. It's too easy, it's far too easy. (School A boy, set 6)

🍎 I can get high if I'm pushed as hard as I can to get up there, but it's not easy when you just do the same things over and over again. How can you move up? There is nothing you can do, he has no ideas how we're doing, he hasn't taken our book in once. (School R girl, set 5)

🍎 We have different books – high books, medium books, low books, so everyone has the right amount of work – no-one's doing nothing too hard or too easy. If you think it's too hard or too easy you just tell Miss and she gives you the right level.

🍎 I prefer groups when we're all mixed up like in form groups. 'Cause we're all mixed up, a variety of clever and dumb. So the dumb learn from the clever and then sometimes the clever can't do it, so they'll learn from people who aren't as good, 'cause sometimes they're good at some things but not others. (School W boy, set 3)

🍎 It was last week, we were doing bar charts and pie charts and all that and I think I was the third person in the class who got it properly – we had to make it into a graph, it was good. (School C girl, mixed ability)   Source: Harlen and Malcolm, 1997.

What are the problems associated with streaming and mixed ability teaching? What should new teachers be aware of?

Gregory (1984) identified the following problems with streaming and mixed ability teaching:

🍎 Lower teaching expectation is followed by poor pupil progress (Winn and Wilson, 1983, citing Tuckman and Bierman, 1971).

🍎 Teacher behaviour and school organisation respond differentially to different ability groups. Upper ability groups receive more teacher time, more praise, less direction and criticism. In contrast, teachers of low ability groups stressed basic skills, facts and drill, and used unimaginative teaching approaches. Lower ability groups had fewer science materials, poorer library facilities and less competent teachers.

🍎 Mixed ability teaching involved more work for the teacher as the burden of preparation is daunting (Wilcox, 1961; Davies, 1975; Kelly, 1975).

🍎 Many teachers were not trained to teach mixed ability groups (Collier, 1982).

🍎 Bright pupils in mixed ability classes are not being stretched academically (Wragg, 1984; HMI, 1978); in fact these researchers experienced great difficulty in finding any mixed ability teaching and reported that less able children were not being catered for.

Even teachers considered to be effective in handling mixed ability classes often resorted to whole class teaching and made no provision for the least able. They often had discipline problems. They streamed the class into ability groups and gave no evidence of any kind of selective approach to pupils of differing abilities (Kerry, 1982a, 1982b).

Gregory concluded that on the whole the problem with setting or streaming was lowered teacher expectation for the lower ability groups. With mixed ability teaching the problem seemed to lie in the fact that there was no evidence to suggest that such groupings enhanced social interactions. The need for large amounts of supplementary materials did not seem to have been met. Many teachers, despite the mixed nature of the group, seemed to resort to a whole class approach to teaching that was wholly inappropriate.

What are the problems associated with setting pupils for learning? What new teachers need to know!

The following have been identified:

- Pupils in a set are often treated as a homogenous group when the ability range in a set can be every bit as wide as that found in a mixed ability class.
- Setted lessons are often observed to have pupils tackling identical work at an identical pace and the pace is determined by a small number of students.
- Teachers of pupils in a low set have low expectations of the group and tend to set work that is too easy.
- It seems that placing pupils in a set creates definite expectations that override any need to see pupils as individuals with individual learning requirements.
- Teachers of pupils in a top group set a pace that is too fast for many in the group and the pressure to succeed makes many anxious.
- Pupils who are entered for examinations where they can access only a low grade are disillusioned.
- Teachers of low sets are often non-specialists whereas research has suggested that the low sets often benefit from the most specialised teachers. Low sets are more likely to have more teachers in the course of their studies than top sets.
- Pupils in low sets should be able to move into a higher set if they work hard. This cannot happen if the content base of work they are provided with is too easy or is not detailed enough. The gap widens between the sets and makes movement upwards very difficult. Research has shown that movement from set to set is not as widespread as it should be.
- In setted lessons teaching tends to be more restricted in style with teachers relying on chalkboard teaching and textbook work with a narrower range of attainment being catered for.

🍎 Setting does not always accomplish what it is supposed to do - to match the work set to the needs of the pupil.

There is no evidence that any particular way of organising classes or teaching groups in itself improves learning. The main determinant of effective learning is teaching which is responsive to the key needs of learners.

(Boyd, 2000)

This chapter shows a new teacher how schools organise pupils for learning. The research would seem to be inconclusive suggesting that no one system of banding, setting or streaming can be said to produce better results. However, the pupils themselves suggest that what works best for them is when the teacher is indeed responsive to their individual needs whatever they may be.

Good teachers realise that within any class whether it is banded, streamed or set there will be a range of pupils with different strengths and weaknesses. There will also be pupils who learn in different ways depending on the individual preferred learning style of the pupil. The best teachers will ensure that their lesson is differentiated so that pupils who are finding the topic easy will be able to develop and enrich their learning and not be held back. Those who find the topic or area of work more challenging will be supported so that they will in time get to a competent level of understanding. This range of ability is always present in any class taught in a school.

> There is more on lesson planning in Chapter 7.

Pupils also highlight how schools treat different groups of pupils within the school. Pupils from low sets suggest that they are given poorer teachers who are not subject specialists or are perceived to be weaker teachers. When setting works well pupils will see that hard work or aptitude will allow them to move to a higher group. Pupils clearly identified times when this could not happen. This was because they were possibly not taught the skills needed to progress upwards and were therefore disenfranchised by methods used to organise pupils for learning. Pupils are human and can perceive and feel annoyed by actions that clearly discriminate against them and prevent their progression.

Time to reflect

✔ When you were in school how were your classes grouped for learning? Which subjects were taught in sets and which subjects were taught in mixed ability groups?

✔ Did you experience the same feelings about this as the pupils who were surveyed?

✔ Ask how pupils are grouped in your primary or secondary school now.

✔ Do different subjects group pupils in different ways? If so find out why this may be the case.

References and further reading

Boaler, J. (1997), 'When even the winners are losers: evaluating the experiences of top set students', *Journal of Curriculum Studies*, 29(2), 165–82.

Boaler, J., Wiliam, D. and Brown, M. (2001), 'Students' experiences of ability grouping – disaffection, polarisation and the construction of failure', **www.nottingham.ac.uk/csme/meas/papers/boaler.htm**

Boyd, B. and Simpson, M. (2000), 'Developing a framework for effective learning and teaching in S1/S2 in ANGUS Secondary Schools', Angus Council Education Department.

Collier, F. (1982), 'A retreat from mixed ability teaching' in Sands, M. and Kerry, T. (eds), *Mixed Ability Teaching*, Croom Helm.

Davies, R.P. (1975), *Mixed Ability Grouping Possibilities and Experiences in Secondary Schools*, Temple Smith.

DfEE (1997), 'Excellence in schools', White Paper.

Gregory, R.P. (1984), 'Streaming, setting and mixed ability grouping in primary and secondary: some research findings', *Educational Studies*, 10(3).

Harlen, W. and Malcolm, H. (1997), *Setting and Streaming: A Research Review*, SCRE, **www.scre.ac.uk**

HMI (1978), 'Mixed ability work in comprehensive schools', Matters for Discussion Series 6, HMSO.

Kelly, A.V. (1975), *Case Studies in Mixed Ability Teaching*, Harper and Row.

Kerry, T. (1982a), 'Mixed ability teaching in the humanities', in Sands, M. and Kerry, T. (eds), *Mixed Ability Teaching*, Croom Helm.

Kerry, T. (1982b), 'The demands made on pupils' thinking in mixed ability classes', in Sands, M. and Kerry, T. (eds), *Mixed Ability Teaching*, Croom Helm.

Reid, M., Clunies-Ross, L., Goacher, B. and Vile, C. (1981), 'Mixed ability teaching: problems and possibilities', accessed through a summary by Upton, D. *Educational Research*, 24(1).

Slavin, R.E. (1986), 'Best evidence synthesis: an alternative to meta-analytic and traditional reviews', *Educational Researcher*, November: 5–11.

Tuckman, B.W. and Bierman, M. (1971), *Beyond Pygmalion, Galatea in the Schools*. Arlington, Virginal Computer Microfilm International Corporation.

Wilcox, J. (1961), 'A search for multiple effects of grouping upon growth and behaviour of junior high school pupils', Dissertation, Cornell University.

Winn, W. and Wilson, A.P. (1983), 'The affect and effect of ability groupings', *Contemporary Education* 54, 119–125.

Wragg, E.C. (ed) (1984), *Classroom Teaching Skills: The Research Findings of the Teacher Education Project*, Routledge.

Part 2

Teaching and Learning

Chapter 3

The National Curriculum

 What will you find in this chapter?

✔ Who decides what is taught in our schools?

✔ What is a scheme of work?

✔ What is a departmental handbook and what is a staff handbook?

✔ What are the golden rules when planning a curriculum?

In this chapter you will find information about why schools teach the subject range, content and skills that they do. This is not something arbitrary – the programmes of study and the schemes of work are based on directives from the curriculum authority for each of the four nations. Read on to find out how what we teach is determined and how consultations in our four nations work.

In every country that makes up the UK there is a curriculum authority that determines what we teach in our schools and how it is to be assessed.

- In England it is the Qualifications and Curriculum Authority (**QCA**).
- In Northern Ireland it is The Northern Ireland Council for the Curriculum, Examinations and Assessment (**CCEA**).
- In Scotland it is The Scottish Executive Education Department (**SEED**).
- In Wales it is the Qualifications, Curriculum and Assessment Authority (**ACCAC** – Awdurdod Cymwysterau, Cwricwlwm ac Asesu Cymru).

Visit the website for links to the curriculum authorities' websites.

All of these authorities have websites and it is worth visiting these to download any materials that you need.

Who decides what is taught in our schools?

The consulting committees that have provided us with a curriculum are made up of representatives of the curriculum authority but they always contain teachers or headteachers as well. In addition, representatives of teaching unions or professional bodies may be present. These committees provide schools with a framework from which to work. For example, below is an extract taken from the Scottish Office Curriculum Framework for children aged 3–5. It outlines what are considered to be the broad areas of learning that schools will need to cover in their schemes of work. The framework document is extensive and gives detailed information on exactly what is meant by each of the headings listed below.

Key aspects of children's development and learning

Each key aspect sets out a range of learning to which all children are entitled during their pre-school years.

These are:

- Emotional, personal and social development
- Communication and language
- Knowledge and understanding of the world
- Expressive and aesthetic development
- Physical development and movement.

Source: Learning and Teaching Scotland (1999).

This framework outlines how pupils should be assessed and how the schools should report this to parents. When a school is inspected, the inspection team ensures that the curriculum framework that is laid down as a statutory requirement is being taught and assessed appropriately and that nothing is omitted.

Although an individual authority's curriculum reflects commonality with the rest of the UK, it will be unique in that it is influenced by national need. For example in the Welsh curriculum outline that follows bilingualism is mentioned – this may or may not be perceived as a need by the three other nations. Over the past 20 years there have been significant changes to the curricula in schools and this is a continuing process.

Extract from the National Curriculum Guidelines for Early Learning in Wales

There are seven areas of learning that form the Foundation Phase curriculum. Emphasis has been placed on developing children's knowledge, skills and understanding through experiential learning – learning by doing and by solving real-life problems both inside and outdoors. The seven areas of learning are:

1 Personal and Social Development and Well Being

2 Language, Literacy and Communication Skills

3 Mathematical Development

4 Bilingualism and Multi-cultural Understanding

5 Knowledge and Understanding of the World

6 Physical Development

7 Creative Development.

Schools and settings where 'Language, Literacy and Communication Skills' is currently developed through the medium of Welsh will not be required to teach the Bilingualism element of the Framework. Schools and settings where 'Language, Literacy and Communication Skills' is developed through the medium of English will be required to teach the Bilingualism element of the Framework. This reflects the current situation where schools that teach through the medium of English, teach Welsh as a second language.

During the pilot project, ACCAC will be monitoring and evaluating the impact of the draft Framework for Children's Learning, producing guidance to support the development of the seven areas of learning and an assessment continuum.

Supporting documents: *The Foundation Phase in Wales – A Draft Framework for Children's Learning*

Source: ACCAC (2000)

> Key skills are now a vitally important part of the work done in primary and secondary schools. All subjects are expected to include all these key skills at certain appropriate points in the SOW. Look at your main subject SOW again and try to see where the key skills would be delivered. Are they highlighted in any way?

Key skills

Key skills now form an important part of all classroom learning.

The following are the 'hard' skills versus the 'soft' skills:

- communication
- numeracy
- information technology

- working with others
- problem solving
- improving one's own learning.

Cross-curricular links

It is expected that pupils have an understanding of environmental issues, careers guidance, study skills, economic and industrial awareness, health education, and in Wales the Curriculum Cymreig. Some of this learning occurs in discrete lessons, possibly as a part of the PSE (Personal, Social and Health Education) programme but it could occur in a subject lesson, for example:

>
> See Chapter 18 for more on PSE/PSHE.

- a lesson of English where students are learning how to answer essay questions (study skills)
- a geography lesson where pupils are studying population migration (economic and industrial awareness).

What is a departmental handbook and what is a staff handbook?

A handbook, like the SOW, is a working document and will be regularly updated. It ensures that there is consistency in operational procedures within the department and any policy documents.

Here is a list of areas that you may expect to find in a departmental handbook:

- departmental aim with a brief outline
- factual information – this will include details about staff, resources, pupil organisation, support staff and their roles
- staff arrangements for meetings, induction arrangements and training and monitoring procedures

- a calendar of important events in the school year, key assessment, coursework, reporting deadlines

- policies on presentation of work, marking, differentiation, homework, numeracy, IT, literacy

- cross-curricular dimensions like economic and industrial awareness that might form a feature of the curriculum in your country

- ethos and environment for pupils – departmental displays, discipline procedures, equal opportunities, child protection, health and safety (Note: health and safety and child protection organisation will be in line with a whole school policy and must be adhered to carefully).

- improvement planning for that subject or area of learning that should include clear success criteria and a monitoring, evaluating and reviewing strategy

- a review of the success of prior developments

- staff development

- key issues such as how pupil progress is tracked and the strategies used for improvement

- syllabus information and contact addresses

- schemes of work

- preparation for parents' evenings – what records you want available

- departmental guidelines on reporting to parents and the use of assessment for learning in everyday marking

- how quality assurance is provided within the department

- how the school contributes to extra-curricular aspects

- how the department or area contributes to the moral, social and corporate life of the school (later in your working life when applying to go through threshold you will need to show how you have contributed to the life of the whole school)

- links with other schools, other agencies, the community.

This seems an extensive list but in fact many of these areas can be covered in a short paragraph and where necessary there will be appendices. A school or departmental handbook gives a very important insight into how the school or area of learning is run.

If you are going to a school for an interview you could ask to see its handbook while you are there. It is also the case that as a new teacher you may find yourself in charge of a learning area or subject area and it would be good practice to produce your own handbook.

Many schools now produce a staff handbook, which is a reference document that explains how a school runs. It gives a list of staff with responsibilities; information about the day-to-day running of the school; lesson times; important information about school procedures, like how to organise a school trip; important forms that can be photocopied as and when required; as well as the school calendar. In most staff handbooks you will find whole school policies on child protection, bullying, assessment, homework, etc.

Some handbooks will also contain information about job descriptions. They are a really useful reference tool, especially for new teachers, so make sure that you get one and when on initial teacher training ask to see if your current school has one you could look at.

What are the golden rules when planning a curriculum?

Remember that the term curriculum refers to all the learning experiences put in place by a school to achieve determined and specified educational objectives.

- The curriculum should contain the statutory requirements set out by your curriculum authority both academically through subject teaching and through the personal and social education offered.

- It should reflect the unique nature of your school within the community. For example: if you live in an industrial area you may see engineering on the curriculum in a secondary school; in a primary school children may have visits to a factory incorporated into their programme of study; or if you live in an area of outstanding natural beauty or where tourism plays a major factor this too could influence what is included in the school curriculum.

- The curriculum should allow students to have breadth and balance to their learning. By 'breadth' we mean that pupils should have the opportunity to engage in the **nine areas of learning** (see alongside). By the term 'balance' we mean that they should all be given appropriate attention in relation to one another. Time should be evenly distributed between all areas of learning.

> **Try to identify** in your school areas of the curriculum that have been affected by the strengths of members of staff, or its location, or by the nature of the pupil intake.

> **The nine areas of learning** are:
> - aesthetic and creative
> - human and social
> - linguistic and literary
> - mathematical
> - moral
> - physical
> - scientific
> - spiritual technological.
>
> For more information, see *Curriculum from 5 to 16*, (HMI, 1985).

 It should be relevant to the pupils you are teaching and reflect their present and future needs in a rapidly changing world. This can be seen in the way that IT is being used more in primary and secondary schools. In addition, pupils are getting more adept at using IT at a younger age. This affects the way that IT is incorporated into schemes of work in all subjects and all levels, reflecting the future needs of these pupils.

 The curriculum should be differentiated and should allow children of all abilities and learning needs to achieve their potential.

The hidden curriculum

Finally the X factor within a school and the curriculum is something called the 'hidden' curriculum. It is best described as everything that happens once you walk through the door into school; not necessarily what happens in the classroom but in the corridors and social areas of the school. This hidden curriculum is what affects the ethos of the school. If a school values its staff and pupils, and teaches respect and moral responsibility overtly in its everyday dealings with one another and the community, then the hidden curriculum will be a positive one. The hidden curriculum is basically to do with the way messages are conveyed to pupils through their experience with the school. It is what they learn through overt and covert 'messaging' – what is seen to be acceptable behaviour and everyday practice.

Time to reflect

✔ In this chapter you were given two extracts from primary frameworks. Have a look at your national website for information about your own subject specialism as it applies in the secondary sector.

✔ Have a look at an SOW for another subject area in your primary or secondary school. Compare it to your own subject SOW. Are they both written in a standard format? Some schools insist that all SOWs follow a standard format and others do not.

✔ Do both SOWs contain similar information?

✔ Do you prefer one to another, and if so, why?

References and further reading

ACCAC (2000), 'National curriculum guidelines for early learning in Wales'.

ACCAC (2004), 'The foundation phase in Wales – a draft framework for children's learning'.

HMI (1985), 'Curriculum from 5 to 16: curriculum matters 2', HMSO.

Learning and Teaching Scotland (1999) – originally published by Scottish Consultative Council on the Curriculum, *A Curriculum Framework for Children 3 to 5*.

England (The Qualifications and Curriculum Authority) **www.qca.org.uk**

Wales (The Qualifications, Curriculum and Assessment Authority) **www.accac.org.uk**

Scotland (The Scottish Executive Education Department) **www.scotland.gov.uk**

Northern Ireland (The Northern Ireland Council for the Curriculum, Examinations and Assessment) **www.ccea.org.uk**

Chapter 4

Boys and Girls are Different!

What will you find in this chapter?

✔ What do we know about boys and girls?

✔ Why are boys and girls different?

✔ How are boys and girls doing academically?

✔ Proven strategies to enhance progress in the learning environment.

This chapter suggests ways in which good teaching can help narrow the gap in attainment between boys and girls. It is now recognised that boys and girls have different learning preferences and different strengths and weaknesses. To narrow the attainment gap it is important to identify the differences in learning styles and skills as well as suggesting strategies that will definitely benefit both sexes, thus enabling boys to achieve more in line with girls.

What do we know about boys and girls?

Gender is only the fifth most important factor that will influence educational achievement. A child's socio-economic background, ethnicity and the prior learning that they bring to school will have more to do with their success than their sex. So why focus so publicly on this area of concern? In truth, because we know that the strategies that are available will make a difference and are easier to identify and consistently implement within a school. Chapter 5 considers strategies that have brought about improvement in performance in children from ethnic minority groups or from underprivileged backgrounds.

The following is a generalisation – there will always be girls and boys who will be different. However, for the most part the following differences between the sexes are true.

See Chapter 6 for information on how linguistic background can affect learning.

See Chapter 12 on inclusion – how ethnic background can affect learning.

The average boy

- Solves mathematical problems non-verbally.
- Is better at mental rotation and does not need to turn the map upside down to follow the route!
- Likes data, systems and facts.
- Is more likely to read non-fiction than fiction.
- Is a risk taker and a doer.
- Is highly influenced by his peers.
- Requires more space.
- Learns by doing and by experience, so is an experiential learner.
- Is more likely to be left-handed.
- Has a larger right brain hemisphere (for mathematics and spatial skills) in contrast to the left (for language).
- Talks and plays more with inanimate objects.
- Is less able to follow linear processes and pay attention to detail on the way.
- Has a shorter concentration span and is easily bored.
- Is more likely to be disruptive.
- Is more likely to need help with his reading.
- Is three times more likely than the average girl to be dyslexic.
- Is more likely to need special educational support.
- Is more likely to be excluded permanently.
- Is less able to think reflectively but more willing to think speculatively.
- Has weaker planning and organisational skills.
- Likes subjects such as maths, physics, technology, IT, business studies and physical education.

The average girl

- Plans out tasks.
- Is more organised.
- Spends more time on homework and coursework.
- Is a reflective thinker.
- Balances her school work with her life outside school.
- Likes relationships and people.
- Dislikes taking risks and is overly cautious.
- Is less influenced by peer pressure.
- Has better listening and oral skills and is more likely to talk while solving mathematical problems.
- Is a natural student.
- Has a larger left brain hemisphere.
- Is less likely to be dyslexic or myopic.
- Learns by adopting a step-by-step approach.
- Suffers fools in the classroom and tolerates poor delivery more readily.
- Underestimates her ability and often lacks confidence.
- Is slow to anger.
- Is more likely to smoke.
- Is less likely to take up teacher time or receive praise in the classroom.
- Likes English, modern languages, drama, dance, textiles, religious studies, PSE, humanities, art, music, biology, chemistry.

Why are boys and girls different?

Current brain research asserts that many of the differences between boys and girls are pre-ordained. What happens to the foetus in its early weeks in the uterus is crucial. At six or seven weeks of age, a surge of testosterone begins changing the embryos that have inherited the male chromosome into boys. This change in the sex hormone levels affects the way that male and female brains develop.

- A boy's brain is larger than a girl's. However, the girl's brain is more dense and the *corpus callosum* is larger. (The *corpus callosum* is the bundle of nerves that connects the right- and left-hand sides of the brain.)

- The girl's brain develops before the boy's and this gives her certain advantages over him.

- In both boys and girls the left side of the brain controls thinking and develops later than the right – this is the part that deals with spatial relationships. In boys this time

Proven strategies to enhance progress in the learning environment

Research has shown that there are a number of strategies that can be used to narrow the gap in attainment. Look at the Top Tips boxes for some ideas to try with your classes.

> Remember, because the strategies will work for both boys and girls the gap in performance will still exist; but you will have gone some way towards narrowing it.

 In my classroom I could...

✔ Have a seating plan and ensure that boys and girls work together.

✔ Use the data available on a pupil to set clear individual targets. Teachers now have detailed information from Cognitive Tests (**CATs**) and Standard Assessment Tests (**SATs**), etc about a pupil's potential. They also have reading and spelling ages.

> **See Chapter 13** for assessment for learning strategies.

✔ **Assessment for learning strategies** are highly successful.

✔ Ensure that the lesson has a clear structure and that all tasks are time related. Boys need to be set challenging tasks.

✔ Try to make pupils compete against themselves rather than each other. Boys would rather 'opt out' than fail. Try the approach of 'In this lesson you need to focus on your . . .'

✔ Remind everyone that they are in competition with other schools – this makes the contest important but avoids competitiveness within the class itself.

> **Geoff Hannan** (2000) suggests a 'Going for 5' strategy. This can be used in any subject and involves asking the pupils to write down five things they have learnt about, for example, erosion, the circulatory system or Romeo.

✔ Mentor individual pupils within your class by monitoring them closely and telling them that you are watching their progress: this could be over a week or a half term. Do not try to go for a longer period as pupils need short-term goals and successes to build up confidence. Set a target and suggest a reward. Some pupils actually like a phone call home to tell parents they are doing well. For some it is a welcome change from the other type of call!

✔ Use questioning techniques that encourage boys to develop reflective skills where they need to speculate and hypothesise within a time regime.

✔ Encourage mixed pairs to discuss answers collaboratively as this improves the oracy of boys but also encourages girls to develop risk-taking strategies.

✔ Have clear behaviour rules. Avoid rudeness, disrespect, sarcasm and unfairness, all of which ruin the atmosphere of a classroom. Use your eyes and facial movements to control a class and not your voice except when absolutely essential.

> **See Chapter 6** for examples of writing frames.

✔ Use writing frames – these are plans that pupils can follow in order to complete a piece of work. Many contain key words and paragraph openings that help pupils. These 'scaffold' a pupil's writing.

In my department we could...

✔ Teach boys and girls in separate classes. This has been done in a number of schools. (*See the Case Study below.*)

✔ Ensure that all staff concentrate equally on boys and girls as research shows that boys dominate teacher time. Boys also answer more questions in class than girls if allowed to.

✔ Review the specifications that examination boards offer to ensure that the testing suits both boys and girls. In one Shropshire school the geography department moved from a board that assessed mainly through essay-based questions (a task boys find difficult) to one that used a number of different techniques, including multiple choice. This brought about significant improvement in departmental results.

✔ Modular examinations have improved the performance of boys. The short-term goals and positive feedback encourage them to work.

✔ Departments with strong tracking systems for detecting underachievement and promoting learning succeed better with boys.

The single-sex classroom experience

In one school this strategy was used in an English department with a Year 8 cohort. Two equally matched classes of only boys or girls were taught by a teacher of the same sex as the class. The average examination mark was noted for both classes prior to the experiment, and the aim was to see a rise in both classes' performance in the next round of examinations. The results were interesting: the boys' performance actually worsened while the girls' improved.

Questionnaires were used to find out what the boys and girls thought of the arrangement and whether they wished to stay in their present class without the opposite sex. The responses were unanimous.

The girls' response

The girls preferred to be taught away from the boys. Reasons cited included:

 able to hold discussions in a mature fashion and have their say

 able to have more teacher time

Case Study

- preferred the literature they chose to study as it interested them and was 'girly' in subject matter
- preferred a girls-only class in general.

The boys' response

The boys hated the whole experience of being taught in an all-male group. The teacher of the boys' group also begged to be allowed to teach girls again; the experience of having an all-male class had not been a pleasant one for him either!

The outcome

Due to the fact that this strategy was intended to narrow the gender gap and not widen it, a decision was made to revert to mixed class teaching. This was by no means a strictly 'controlled' experiment but it does echo an article in the Accelerated Learning newsletter (2002) suggesting that although we know there are differences between boys and girls 'it is a bold leap to say that they are so different we should teach them in different ways', and in this case in different classrooms!

At a whole school level we can...

✔ Adopt a consistent approach to seating plans for boys' and girls' learning.

✔ Put in place mentoring schemes for those pupils (whether in primary or secondary schools) who are not going to achieve without intervention. Traditionally schools put together a list of pupils who would not achieve five A*– C grades without a tutor who could negotiate strategies with them for success. This scheme does not have to be applied solely to pupils in Year 11. In fact many staff would say that this is too late and early identification of pupils at risk is better practice. It is possible to identify children at age 8 who would benefit from help and as time progresses this age could be reduced even further.

✔ Use mentoring schemes to provide equal opportunities and be accessible for any pupil who needs them. Mentors can be teachers, pastoral or senior staff, or professionals from outside the school who agree to meet with their mentee on a regular basis.

✔ Use rewards to celebrate all kinds of achievement.

✔ Ensure that an ethos of learning is cultivated within the school and targets are shared with the pupils. For example: this year we want to get x percentage of five A*– C grades; or this year we want all pupils to improve their reading age by *x* months. This sets a clear agenda for learning success. It is also important to share the performance of boys and girls in the school and gender differences.

✔ Hold boys-only assemblies to discuss the factors that will prevent boys achieving and put in place clear strategies to see they are minimised.

✔ Have strong pastoral teams that set clear targets for the pupils and have clear expectations about behaviour and learning outcomes.

✔ Encourage pupils to take responsibility for their own learning and contribute to their own success.

✔ Have a consistent policy about feeding back information to pupils on their attainment and how they can improve.

Curriculum areas all play a significant part by putting in place schemes of work that present pupils with a challenge, particularly from one year to the next or from one key stage to the next.

Time to reflect

The whole point of this chapter is to ensure that teachers are aware of the strategies that can be used to narrow the gap between boys' and girls' attainment. With that in mind and taking Geoff Hannan's advice on board, consider the following:

✔ Rank five things that you could use in your classroom that you think might improve boys' attainment.

✔ Think about the department you are in at present or, in the case of a primary school, the subject area you are particularly involved with. What strategies, if any, are being used to narrow the gender gap? What is proving to be effective?

✔ Which of the strategies mentioned in this chapter might work in your department/subject area?

✔ Write down any strategies that your school is using. Which is the most effective? Are there any listed above that you think could be effective?

References and further reading

Accelerated Learning newsletter (2002), April, **www.alite.co.uk**

Bradberry, M. (2002), 'Boys and girls', *ParentLife*, October, **www.lifeway.com**

Curtis, P. (2003), 'Miliband pledges to tackle boys' failure in schools', *The Guardian*, 11 July.

DfES, (2000), 'Raising boys' achievement', a report by Homerton College, *Cambridge*,
www.standards.dfes.gov.uk

DfES, (2002), 'Youth cohort study', **www.statistics.gov.uk/STATBASE**

Gurian, M., Henley, P. and Trueman, T. (2001), *Boys and Girls Learn Differently: Action Guide for Teachers*, Jossey-Bass.

Hannan, G. (2000), *Raising Boys' Achievement*, Heinemann.

Mansell, W. (2003), 'Gender gap widens in teenage years', *Times Educational Supplement*, 7 February.

Sammons, P. *et al*. (1996), 'The impact of background factors on pupil attainment and progress in Scottish schools', ISEP, Policy Paper No. 1, SEED.

The Scottish Office (1999), 'Raising standards: setting targets', *Primary school support pack: gender issues in raising achievement*, SOED.

Ward, H. (2004), 'Reading proves harder for boys', *Times Educational Supplement*, 21 May.

Wylde, D. (2002), 'Different learning styles of boys and girls', 20 June,
www.gradnet.wits.ac.za

Chapter 5

Poverty, Ethnicity and Pupil Attainment

What will you find in this chapter?

✔ The effect of poverty on attainment.

✔ Ethnicity and educational attainment.

✔ Best practice to reduce the attainment gap.

In the previous chapter gender was identified as one of the causes of poor attainment in schools. Whilst not the most significant, the fact is that gender differences in attainment can be markedly reduced by intervention strategies that a school or a teacher has control over. The same is not strictly true of attainment gaps that are caused by poverty, ethnicity and social background. Research has suggested that cohesive government socio-economic and education policies are needed for strategies to be successful to combat these causes. However there are strategies that schools and teachers can use that will help all pupils, particularly those whose educational outcome could be affected by their parent's income or ethnicity. Listed overleaf are some examples:

It is important that schools avoid becoming schools for one ethnic minority or another – schools should be representative of society both in the economic and ethnic mix of pupils who go there. Research has also suggested that poor white children are actually underachieving significantly, as are boys and certain ethnic minority groups.

With this in mind we should specifically track and monitor:

- performance of boys versus girls
- performance of children who are eligible for free school meals versus children who are not
- performance of ethnic minority children versus other ethnic groups in the school. Research has shown that it is possible that some ethnic groups will strive in some schools and not in others and identifying trends is vital.

Comparing all of these children's potential against final achievement and ensuring they are on track to achieve that target is essential to ensure a successful outcome for all children irrespective of background. It is also necessary for LEAs to take a lead on this and work with schools to ensure that all schools set targets to ensure that these groups do attain. At the same time the targets that schools are setting should be rigorous so that over time Black Caribbean and Bangladeshi children actually manage to close the widening attainment gap.

Schools that are making a difference

Blair and Bourne (1998) researched primary and secondary schools in a number of LEAs who seemed to be making a difference to the ethnic children in their areas. They visited 11 primary and 18 secondary schools; all schools had over 10% of students from Bangladeshi, Black Caribbean or Pakistani communities. The schools were:

- all attaining at or above the national average for A–C grades obtained, or at or above the national average for key stage 1 and 2 results, *or*
- though not yet at national levels were making significant movements towards the national average, *or*
- were out-performing similar schools with similar free school meals, EAL students and levels of attendance.

Blair and Bourne found that where schools were making a difference there were common identifiable features that could be contributory to these results. They also suggested that these initiatives are transferable between schools with different intakes and in different contexts.

Initiatives to follow and adopt

- The headteacher provides a strong lead on inclusion and equal opportunities.
- Pupils and their parents are listened to by the school and the school makes an effort to learn from experiences with families.
- There are strong and careful links made with the communities.
- There are clear procedures for dealing with racist incidents and racist bullying and these are carefully investigated and dealt with judiciously.
- Work progresses on strategies to prevent exclusions.
- There are high expectations of the teachers and students and clear systems for targeting, tracking and monitoring individual students.
- Monitoring by ethnicity is embedded and ensures that the schools know whether all pupils are achieving in line with expectations.
- The schools all value the diverse mix of pupils in their midst and make an effort to promote their culture, language and ethnicity.
- The schools that are successful also value the white children and ensure that there are equal opportunities for all.
- Schools have strong behaviour policies that are consistently applied.
- Schools encourage children to set their own targets or assess their own progress.
- Schools encourage a range of after-school and lunchtime clubs intended to support those who might be least motivated.
- Mentors are used to encourage children in the schools.
- Schools use all the help available from the LEA to support their vision and make it a reality.
- Schools have induction and intensive language and literacy programmes for beginners in English.
- Schools offer a broad range of modern languages including languages spoken in the local community at secondary school level.

Source: based on Blair and Bourne (1998)

Time to reflect

Look at the above initiatives:

✔ List the initiatives that a teacher in a classroom could apply.

✔ Which would need to be whole school?

✔ Which need to be LEA and which rely on national strategy?

References and further reading

Ashworth, A. *et al*. (2001), 'Education maintenance allowance, the first year: A quantitative evaluation', DfEE 257.

Bennet, R. (2005), 'Labour failed poorest children', *The Times*, 25 February.

Bernstein, B. (1971), *Class, Codes and Control*, Vol. 1, Routledge and Keegan Paul, London.

Blair, M. and Bourne, J. (1998), *Making the Difference: Teaching and Learning Strategies in Successful Multi-Ethnic Schools*, The Open University.

Cassidy, S. (1999), 'Wealth wins top marks', *The Times Educational Supplement*, 21 May.

EAL, 'Ethnic minority issues and poverty, literacy and social inclusion: The impact of poverty on schools', **www.literacytrust.org.uk**

Gillborn, D. and Safia Mirza, H. (2000), 'Educational inequality mapping race, class and gender: a synthesis of research evidence', Ofsted.

Gregg, P. and Blanden, J. (2004), 'Family income and educational attainment: a review of approaches and evidence for Britain', *Oxford Review of Economic Policy*, Vol. 20, No. 2, Oxford University Press and the Oxford Review of Economic Policy Limited.

Kober, C. (ed) (2003), *Black and Ethnic Minority Children and Poverty: Exploring the Issues*, End Child Poverty.

LSE, 'Policies towards poverty, inequality and exclusion since 1997'. A study of findings by members and associates at the London School of Economics, **www.jrf.org.uk**

Mansell, W. (2003), 'Deprived white pupils bottom of teenage pile', *The Guardian*, 4 July.

Marsh, A. and Perry, J. (2003), in Kober, C. (ed) *Black and Ethnic Minority Children and Poverty: Exploring the Issues*, End Child Poverty.

Ofsted (1985), *Research and Analysis*.

Joseph Rowntree Foundation (1999), 'Rowntree report on child poverty', December.

Secondary Headteachers Association (2005), 'Pupil achievement in secondary education'.

Ward, L. (2005), 'Catch-up lessons to help bridge class gap in school', *The Guardian*, 27 July.

Chapter 6

Readability, Reading Ages and Writing Frames

What will you find in this chapter?

✔ What is readability?

✔ How do we assess reading age?

✔ What are text types and writing frames?

It is important that all teachers, irrespective of their subject specialism, understand about readability and reading ages, as over time, every teacher will present their classes with a variety of materials and resources. Some will come from textbooks, examination or test papers and some you will make yourself. In this chapter we explore the importance of matching materials to the individual pupil and the positive effect that this can have on their learning experience.

If a teacher is to plan individual instruction to meet specific needs, the first task is to assess the attainment level of every child and provide each with reading material of the right level of ability. **(DES, 1975)**

All teachers need to understand what a specific reading age means in terms of the children and the individuals being taught within the classroom. A pupil's reading age will significantly affect their ability to engage in your subject whatever it might be. Remember it is the responsibility of all teachers to help pupils overcome obstacles that prevent their learning, whatever that obstacle might be.

Finally, this chapter looks at text types and writing frames. Teachers need to be able to categorise the different writing that pupils are expected to undertake in the classroom. In the primary school much work is done to ensure that pupils understand different text types. This is developed further in secondary school where pupils write in the style of journalists, report writers, advertisers, and so on. Writing frames have traditionally been used to 'scaffold' pupils' own writing and have proved to be very useful tools for learning.

What is readability?

Readability refers to all the factors that affect a pupil's success in reading and understanding a text and include:

- the motivation and interest of the pupil
- the way the material is presented, the font size, the legibility, use of illustrations, layout, visual impact and clarity
- the complexity of the words used in relation to the reading ages and the experience the reader brings to the text, ie its conceptual level.

How can you interest and motivate pupils to read?

It is true that pupils have little chance of avoiding using the materials presented to them. However, there are ways that we can encourage pupils to read and encourage compliance. We can use praise, merits and rewards and ultimately their own success in the subject to promote greater interest. In addition, we can make sure that the materials we provide have been chosen carefully, that the reading material is matched to the reader and that where possible the material is visually attractive and produced on good quality paper.

How can you ensure resource material is appropriate?

Research has shown that pupils find it more difficult to read non-fiction than fiction and therefore it is helpful if the reading age of a non-fiction text is slightly lower than the average of a class. If your class is aged 12, the reading age will probably vary between

8-16 years with the average being clustered around the 12 mark. (How to gauge the reading level of a text is discussed later in the chapter.) Remember though that the reading level of a text is a break-off point for a reader of that reading age. The break-off point means that pupils who have a reading age of 10 are at their outer limit of reading capability and reading comprehension when they read an extract that requires a reading age of 10. This is because most readability formulae are based on a correct answer score in a comprehension test. If a book has a reading level of 10, an average 10 year old would score only 50% on a test of comprehension on that text. If our class only scored 50% on a comprehension test would we then assume they had fully understood the text? Probably not!

Take the following passage in the box below as an example. What is wrong with it?

> Gingnahc Smoor.
> Over the last few years there has been a gniworg tserestni in srevoekam of all kinds not just snedrag, but slaudividni and homes. This has meant that the noisivelet skrowten have jumped on the bandwagon and have provided a elohw egnar of new semmargorp designed to cater for our curiosity. A whole new breed of seitirbelec has been born who are on these semmargorp, we want to know everything about them. These seitirbelec have become dlohesuoh seman and their lives fascinate us. One of the most suomaf is from the ginnedrag dlrow, eilrahc kcommid is a well known erugif and her face is familiar to us all. I am now an Xtreme expert on all sorts of srevoekam and I am not the only one this is true of sdierf, sevitaler and sruobhgien. What will the next mad ezarc be I wonder!

Finding it hard to read and understand? Then reverse the letters for the unfamiliar words so that the heading becomes *Changing Rooms*, and so on.

See if you agree with these criticisms:

- The font is too small at point 10 and research suggests that point 12 suits fluent readers. The less fluent the reader the more likely it is that a larger font is more appropriate. At the secondary level though, older pupils do not want to be labelled as 'slow' and this often happens when 'big' print is used. Teachers need to be sensitive to this issue. Comic Sans is one of the most legible fonts for use on worksheets and for pupils of all ages, and is the one favoured by a lot of 'literacy across the curriculum' schemes. However, you may want to vary the font throughout your worksheet. Research also suggests that using a variety of fonts throughout the text aids learning as it breaks the material up into 'visual' units.

- The line length is too long: 10-12 words is the suggested optimum length.

- The words used are unfamiliar to a reader and hinder understanding.

- The spacing between the lines is too narrow.

- There is a lack of visual illustrations, which might help understanding.

The sentence structure is quite complex and the numbers of words that are polysyllabic raise the reading level considerably. For instance:

- This short sentence needs a reading age of less than 9 years.

- This longer sentence, which contains an adjectival clause and polysyllabic words, has a reading age of more than 16 years.

(Source: based on 'Readability' by Keith Johnson, **www.timetabler.com**)

Below are some questions about the passage. You will be able to answer them – yet you may not have understood much of what you have been reading.

1 What has happened over the last few years?

2 What has jumped on the bandwagon?

3 What has been born?

4 What is this person an Xtreme expert in?

This can happen in your classroom. You have presented your class with new terminology that they may not understand. You include a task like this with all your unfamiliar words. You ask questions, as has been done above, and the pupils answer them correctly. The exercise merely proves that they can locate an answer *not* that they understand it.

The readability game: version 1

One of the most important factors affecting readability is the language that is used. Key words should be clearly explained to the class and where possible definitions of these words should be displayed around the room.

One technique for doing this that has been successful is to give the pupils a passage containing a number of words they should know but may not. In pairs, ask them to underline any words they are not sure of. Then ask them to get into groups of four. In the group of four look at the underlined words. If anyone in the group can explain any of the underlined words then they do so. The group of four now identify a new group of words made up of any they still don't know and get rid of any that they have had explained to them. The group now is doubled and becomes eight. The process is repeated. Finally, the teacher goes through any words that are still unknown and checks that the ones the pupils do know have been properly understood.

Health warning. Do this only in a class where you have good control!

The following version can be used as an alternative to the above for a change or with a class who are more difficult to control:

The readability game: version 2

Make a set of cards for each pupil – one red, one amber, one green.

Read the passage aloud pausing over new or unfamiliar words. Ask the class to hold up a card to show their level of understanding of the word.

- Green – I know this word and can use it correctly and understand what it means in this subject.
- Amber – I think I know what this word means.
- Red – I haven't got a clue.

The cards allow the teacher to see at a glance the numbers of pupils in the class who understand the key words used. It also keeps a firm hand on what is going on in the classroom and ensures that all pupils are involved in the lesson. No time for messing about! Choose someone with a green card in their hand to explain what the word means. Go through the passage in this way until all words are explained. Sometimes you may wish to choose someone with an amber card to explain what they think the word means.

See Chapter 7 for examples of lesson starters

To check that this information has been retained, this exercise can be attempted at the beginning of a future lesson as a quick **lesson starter**. This works well at primary and secondary level.

Making your own worksheets

✔ **Ensure that your worksheets are legible. The font size should be at least 12pt and you should be sensitive to the font you are using. Comic Sans is easy to read** whilst others are not so easy for some pupils especially if they are written in small point size. *Remember that pupils in secondary schools do not want to be stigmatised by* **having worksheets that look like they were prepared for much younger pupils.**

✔ **Ensure that the paper quality is good. This seems a minor point but the paper quality affects legibility and the motivation of the pupils reading it.**

✔ **Ensure that headlines are used to mark off sections of the text and change fonts to provide visual blocks of work that can be easier to recall.**

✔ **Ensure that illustration is used where possible. However the illustrations need to be relevant to the subject and placed appropriately in the text.**

✔ **Ensure that the readability level of the text allows pupils to fully engage with the material. Ensure that key words or unusual words are clearly explained. This can be done on the worksheet.**

Choosing resource material

✔ Pupils find non-fiction more challenging to read and therefore the reading level of the text should be carefully matched to the level of the class. Non-fiction texts that are going to be used without teacher support, ie without you reading them aloud for pupils or explaining the text as you go along, should be *two* years lower in reading level than the average of the class.

✔ Where you are responsible for choosing set books for your class choose wisely. Order inspection copies and get pupils to review them for you. Whatever the age of the pupils you teach they will have something to say about a book you show them – so ask for their opinions.

✔ Ensure that the layout and look of the book is good and that where possible colour has been used. Not only do these illustrations aid visual learners but also most non-fiction books benefit from having clear illustrations to support the text.

✔ Active verbs are easier to read than passive verbs. For example: 'the books were taken by the pupils' is more difficult than 'the pupils took the books'.

✔ Modal verbs such as 'could', 'should', 'might' and 'may' cause comprehension difficulties for poorer readers in a class.

How do we assess reading age?

Reading ages can be determined by conducting various tests with pupils. Some determine the skill a child has in decoding a text and by this we mean their ability to read aloud the passage as it is printed on the page. Some tests will determine not just this mechanistic decoding ability but will also seek to ascertain whether the pupil can 'understand' what they have read and at what level this understanding is, ie comprehending the meaning contained within the passage not just reading it aloud.

Currently, there are a number of objective measures of reading ages available. In order to use these tests you need to follow a few basic rules:

🍎 Count the syllables in a word. If you are not sure how to do this, say the word aloud to help you hear the different sounds: delay = 2; different = 3; dissident = 3; laces = 2; aloud = 2; some = 1.

🍎 When counting any dates, symbols or initials count one syllable for each number: 2006 = 4; 6.33 = 3.

🍎 Abbreviations count as one syllable: for instance km, kg.

🍎 Ignore headings and sub-headings.

🍎 Formulae are usually ignored but probably increase the reading age.

Here are some well-known tests you can use but there are plenty more to be found. Just type in a search for readability tests on the web to get to a relevant site (eg **www.timetabler.com**)

> **Printable versions** of these tests are available on the website.

Gunning FOG Readability Test

Select samples of 100 words, normally three such samples is adequate.

- Calculate L, the average sentence length (number of words divided by number of sentences). Estimate the number of sentences to the nearest tenth where necessary.
- In each sample count the number of words with three or more syllables. Find N, the average number of these words per sample.
- Then the grade level needed to understand the material $= (L + N) \times 0.4$
- So the reading age $= [(L + N) \times 0.4] + 5$ years.

This FOG measure is suitable for secondary and older primary age groups.

Flesch-Kincaid Formula

This is a US Government Department of Defense standard test:

- Calculate L, the average sentence length (number of words divided by number of sentences). Estimate the number of sentences to the nearest tenth where necessary.
- Calculate N, the average number of syllables per word (number of syllables divided by number of words).
- Then grade level $= (L \times 0.39) + (N \times 11.8) - 15.59$
- So reading age $= (L \times 0.39) = (N \times 11.8) - 10.59$.

Powers-Sumner-Kearl Formula

This is the only one suitable for primary age books and is most suitable for books in the 7-10 age range.

- Select samples of 100 words.
- Calculate L, the average sentence length (number of words divided by number of sentences).
- Estimate the number of sentences to the nearest tenth, where necessary.
- Count N, the number of syllables per 100 words.
- Then grade level $= (L \times 0.0778) + (N \times 0.0455) - 2.2029$.
- So reading age $= (L \times 0.0778) + (N \times 0.0455) + 2.7971$ years.

Many schools assess pupils' reading ages as standard practice. Schools use well-established standardised reading tests like those produced by the National Foundation for Educational Research. By using a standard test schools are able to reassess pupils year on year and see the reading gain made by pupils who may or may not be having reading support of some kind. In this way, schools can also compare one intake of pupils with another to assess pupil profile. If the intake is markedly different, either with more able readers or weaker readers, then the school can put in measures to take account of this. They could challenge stronger readers further or put in place more support for the weaker readers. The reading ability of a pupil cohort can seriously affect the lesson planning and teaching materials used every day by teachers in a school.

It is important to know the reading ages of pupils in your class so that you can make appropriate materials for them. Below is a list of reading ages of materials that will be familiar to you.

Title	Reading age in years
Financial Times	17½ years
Times Educational Supplement	17
A Tale of Two Cities (Dickens)	13
To Kill a Mockingbird (Lee)	11 ½
Lord of the Flies (Golding)	11
Kes: A Kestrel for a Knave (Hines)	10½

In addition you can look at the National Literacy and Numeracy Strategy's (**NLNS**) lists of words for those pupils should be made familiar with during their primary years (**www.standards.dfes. gov.uk/literacy/publications/framework/**).

However, just because pupils are made aware of these words it does not mean they understand their meaning or how to use them in sentences. Figures 6.1 and 6.2 are extracts taken from the Oxford Reading Tree scheme. This gives you an awareness of exactly what a pupil with a reading age of 8 or 9 is likely to feel comfortable reading. You may want to compare this to some of the textbooks or worksheets that you use on a regular basis in your classes.

Using reading levels to group pupils for learning

It is common in primary school classes to find pupils grouped according to ability in a class. Sometimes the teacher may put children of similar ability in a subject together on one table so they can support each other's learning. This can be done with reading as well so that able readers can work together on a common text that challenges them. However, it may also be useful to put **a strong** reader or two in amongst less fluent readers, encouraging them all to read aloud within the group. This can work in a primary or secondary setting and allows the teacher to use strong readers to aid the development of less fluent readers.

Grandmother told Wilma about the Jump Up.
"Back home you'd call it a carnival," she said.
"Can we be in it too?" asked Wilma.
"Yes, I should think so," said Grandmother.
"Shall we try and make you some costumes?"
"Yes please," said Wilf and Wilma.

Figure 6.1 *A Proper Bite – average reading age 8*

The next day they set off on the picnic. Wilma's dad took them out of town in his car. He put the bikes in his trailer and he put Anneena's bike on the roof rack.

"Where are we going?" asked Biff. "It seems funny to go for a bicycle ride in a car."

Wilma's mum laughed.

"We are going to Kingswood Forest," she said. "When we get there we can ride our bikes and stop whenever we like for our picnic."

"We can't go too far," said Chip, "if Anneena has to ride that old bike."

Figure 6.2 *The Holiday – average reading age 9*

Source: Pages from A Proper Bike and The Holiday by Rod Hunt illustrated by Alex Brychta (Oxford Reading Tree, OUP, 2004), © Oxford University Press, reprinted by permission of Oxford University Press.

Try to get all pupils in your class to read aloud at some point but ensure that what you ask a poor reader to read aloud is manageable for them and not obviously very easy to the rest of the class.

Knowing the reading ages of your pupils enables you to be flexible about the way you group pupils in your class. It also ensures that you do not ask a less fluent reader to read aloud a passage that is clearly beyond them, thus possibly damaging their confidence immeasurably.

Some teachers shy away from asking anyone to read aloud who doesn't volunteer. It is a sensitive issue and one that you need to feel comfortable about. However, whatever your subject area, you should ensure that reading is encouraged and where possible reading aloud occurs whether it is by you or volunteers in your class.

What are text types?

Primary schools spend a lot of time teaching pupils the different types of writing that make up the text types found in non-fiction. They are clearly identified and pupils are given a clear formula to use in order to write in that genre.

In both primary and secondary school we expect pupils to be able to:

- recount (accounts of observations and experiences, visits, anecdotes from everyday life)
- report (produce a factual account or description; this could be of an experiment in science)
- explain (the how and why of an event or occurrence)
- be procedural (give instructions, possibly how to make something in technology or give directions)
- persuade (opinions, promotional literature, advertisements, leaflets, political speeches)
- discuss (how they feel about an event or subject). This will contain balanced arguments and will call for pupils to analyse and evaluate their response to the subject giving a point of view supported with evidence.

What are the main types of writing required by my subject?

Table 6.1 helps you to identify what types of writing are used in your subject area and what skills are being developed. Provide examples of the types of writing that are commonly found in your subject in the third column. In the fourth column list any writing tasks within your subject that fit this category. Fill in the final column (Where taught?) and then complete the specific skills column, some of which has been started for you.

Table 6.1 Identifying types of writing

Text types	Typical examples or locations in my subject	Key examples in my subject	Writing tasks within my subject	Specific skills within my subject	Where taught?
Narrative	Novels, myths, ballads, short stories, folk tales, plays			Note taking	
Recount	Autobiography, biography, newspaper articles, journals, travel books, blurbs			Comparing and contrasting information	
Procedural	Recipes, rules, instruction manuals			Selecting information	
Explanation	Parts of an encyclopaedia, manuals, sections of many textbooks			Summarising information	
Report	Sections of many textbooks; official reports; sections of reference books			Single sentence, short paragraph, evaluative writing	
Persuasion	Adverts, brochures, political propaganda, editorials			Establishing evidence providing information to support a point of view	
Discussion	Formal essays, opinion pieces, evaluation and analysis			Structuring information	
Other				Writing key sentences using the appropriate connecting phrases or scanning	

Source: Strong (2001 : 134)

What are writing frames?

A writing frame is basically a plan that pupils follow which enables them to complete a piece of work to the best of their ability. Figure 6.3 shows the processes involved in using a writing frame.

Here is an example of two writing frames one simple and one more complex. Pupils find persuasive writing the most difficult of all the text types and therefore these frames cover that genre of writing.

> **Teacher models the process of using a writing frame**
> Explains and demonstrates.

> **Joint activity with teacher and class working on writing frame together**
> Teacher leads class in how to fill in frame.

> **Scaffolding activity**
> Pupils use a frame of their own to support their writing. These can be differentiated to support able or less able pupils.

> **Involve pupils in the process**
> Get pupils to create their own frames that will structure their writing. They can work in pairs, groups or as a class to do this.

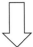

> **Independent activity**
> Pupils can now structure their writing without the help of the frame.

Figure 6.3 *Using a writing frame*
Source: Strong (1999: 87)

Writing frame examples

Printable versions of these writing frames are available on the website.

The task

Write down the advantages (good things) and the disadvantages (the bad things) of keeping animals in a zoo. Explain whether you think it is a good thing or not.

Version 1: A simple writing frame

In my essay I am going to write about _____

I think there are three advantages to keeping animals in a zoo.

First, _____

Secondly, _____

Thirdly, _____

I think there are three disadvantages to keeping animals in a zoo.

First, _____

Secondly, _____

Thirdly, _____

However, I think that overall we should/should not keep animals in a zoo because

_____

Version 2: A more advanced writing frame

In this essay I am going to _____

Some people are of the opinion that _____

They also believe _____ because _____

However, _____

On the other hand, there are some people who are of the opinion that

_____

They disagree with the idea that _____ because

_____

They suggest that _____

They also state that _____

I believe that _____ because _____

In addition, I believe that _____ because _____

To conclude, _____

Writing frames help to improve the quality of a pupil's work by helping them to get organised. However there are advantages and disadvantages to their use.

Writing frames can help pupils by:

- Curing the 'I don't know how to start' syndrome.

- Providing them with a sense of what they are writing and how to write it.

- Encouraging them to avoid using repeated phrases such as 'and then, and then'.

- Giving them an understanding of the different genres of writing and what each should contain.

- Encouraging them to work confidently and independently.

- Encouraging them to achieve their potential by allowing them to express their ideas.

However, writing frames can be a disadvantage, particularly for able pupils, for the following reasons:

- They limit creativity. Writing frames were developed to help pupils write non-fiction. Pupils should be encouraged to use the frames for guidance only and able pupils may want to write without them or use them for loose guidance only. You can help by ensuring that the frames are flexible and varied.

- Pupils can become too reliant on the frame. They should be encouraged to plan their own work using their own frames.

- Like anything, pupils get bored doing or using the same thing all the time, so limit their use.

 Time to reflect

This chapter has been about readability, reading ages and writing frames. With that in mind:

✔ Think about what you have learnt about readability and how you can make resource material that will best match your pupils.

✔ How could you organise your class more effectively over time by using the reading ages of the pupils to inform your decisions?

✔ Think about the language complexity of the material that you present to the class both when you are supporting their learning and when they are left to use materials alone, possibly for homework.

✔ Think about how you can use writing frames to support your pupils' learning and aid them to achieve their potential.

Now read Chapter 7 on lesson planning where you will need to use your knowledge from this chapter in a practical context.

References and further reading

DES (Department for Education and Science) (1975), 'A language for life', *The Bullock Report*, 17.19.

Johnson, K. 'Readability', **www.timetabler.com**

Strong, J. (1999), *Literacy at 11-14: A Practical Guide to Raising Achievement Through Whole School Literacy Development*, Collins.

Strong, J. (2001), *Literacy Across the Curriculum: Making it Happen*, Collins.

CHAPTER 7

Learning to Teach and Teaching to Learn - Planning Lessons

What will you find in this chapter?

✔ What makes a good lesson?

✔ Preferred learning styles.

✔ Starting the lesson: lesson starters and brain gym.

✔ Using mini whiteboards to engage all learners.

✔ Using games to engage learners and consolidate learning.

✔ Using interactive whiteboards in lessons.

✔ How do we use videos in lessons?

✔ The four-part lesson.

This chapter consolidates your knowledge from Chapter 5 by applying it in a practical context. You will learn how to plan and structure lessons to give pupils variety, keep them interested while learning, and consolidate their knowledge.

What makes a good lesson?

This question is often asked in an interview for a teaching post especially when the short-listed applicants are new to the profession. It is a question that is intended to ascertain if you have the basic knowledge required to plan and deliver good lessons, time and time again.

Figure 7.1 shows the constituents of a good lesson. Research over the last decade and a half has changed our view of how a successful lesson should be planned and recent research has concentrated on the preferred learning styles of children. We all learn differently and if you are going to become a successful teacher and ensure that pupils in your class succeed, you need to be aware of preferred learning styles. In addition, schools use data to tell them how individual children are performing in reading and spelling as well as cognitive abilities tests that predict how a child might perform at the end of key stage 4.

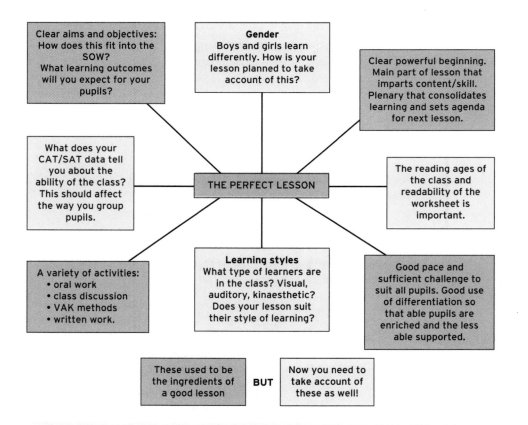

Figure 7.1 Lesson planning for successful teaching

LESSON INFORMATION SHEET

DATE	PERIOD	SUBJECT	TEACHER	LSA/EMLAS/ANO

GROUP	NUMBER OF BOYS GIRLS TOTAL	TYPE OF GROUP

TOPIC/UNIT OF WORK/learning styles used in this lesson

TOPIC OF THE LESSON AND LEARNING OBJECTIVES

MAIN ACTIVITIES OF THE LESSON

CONTENT OF PRECEDING LESSONS

CONTENT OF LESSONS TO FOLLOW

REVIEW OF THE LEARNING AT THE END

KEY SKILLS TO BE EVIDENT IN THE LESSON

HOMEWORK TO BE SET

SUPPORTED STUDENTS

Figure 7.2 A sample lesson information sheet

A lot of research has also centred on how boys and girls learn and this has resulted in teachers using different classroom techniques in order to get the best for all pupils.

In Chapter 14 the need for differentiating lessons is also emphasised. It ensures that all learners in the class are catered for and that the able are enriched and the less able supported.

Even in subjects where pupils are set there will be huge differences in the most and least able in the group. There is clearly a lot of thinking to be done before a teacher plans a lesson suitable for the whole class. Look at the lesson information sheet (Figure 7.2). Many colleges and universities produce sheets that may be similar to this, and they are useful in helping with lesson planning. Study Figures 7.1 and 7.2 carefully and then read the rest of the chapter before thinking about planning your own lessons.

Sample lesson plans from a recent NQT and the Lesson Information Sheet template can be found on the website.

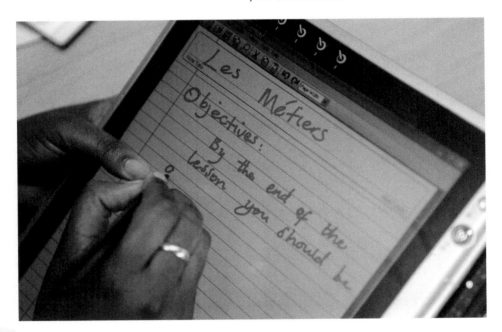

Preferred learning styles

You will hear people talk about **VAK** learning methods. Most pupils prefer one of the following learning styles to another.

- **V is for Visual**. These learners need to see the teacher's body language and facial expression. They may prefer to sit near the front of the class. They may also think in pictures and learn through visual displays such as diagrams, illustrated textbooks, overhead transparencies, interactive whiteboards, flipcharts and handouts.

🎴 **A is for Auditory**. These learners learn through verbal lectures, discussions, listening to audiotapes, the teacher, etc talking things through and listening to what others say. Auditory learners interpret the underlying meaning of speech through listening to the tone of voice, pitch, speed and other nuances. Written information has little meaning unless it is also heard.

🎴 **K is for Kinaesthetic**. These pupils learn by doing. They prefer the hands-on approach and enjoy actively exploring the physical world around them. They may prefer role-playing or hot-seating exercises.

> **If you want** to know more about planning lessons using VAK methods then look at *The Teacher's Toolkit* by Paul Ginnis. For more on learning styles look at Howard Gardner's *Frames of Mind: The Theory of Multiple Intelligences.*

Look at Figure 7.3: it shows you how you can work out what type of learner *you*

When you	Visual	Auditory	Kinaesthetic and tactile
Spell	Do you try to see the word?	Do you sound out the word or use a phonetic approach?	Do you write the word down to find if it feels right?
Talk	Do you talk sparingly but dislike listening for too long? Do you favour words such as see, *picture* and *imagine*?	Do you enjoy listening but are impatient to talk? Do you use words such as *hear, tune* and *think*?	Do you gesture and use expressive movements? Do you use words such as *feel, touch* and *hold*?
Concentrate	Do you become distracted by untidiness or movement?	Do you become distracted by sounds or noises?	Do you become distracted by activity around you?
Meet someone again	Do you forget names but remember faces or remember where you met?	Do you forget faces but remember names or remember what you talked about?	Do you remember best what you did together?
Contact people on business	Do you prefer direct, face-to-face, personal meetings?	Do you prefer the telephone?	Do you talk with them while walking or participating in an activity?
Read	Do you like descriptive scenes or pause to imagine the actions?	Do you enjoy dialogue and conversation or hear the characters talk?	Do you prefer action stories or are not a keen reader?
Do something new at work	Do you like to see demonstrations, diagrams, slides or posters?	Do you prefer verbal instructions or talking about it with someone else?	Do you prefer to jump right in and try it?
Put something together	Do you like to look at the directions and the picture?		Do you ignore the directions and figure it out as you go along?
Need help with a computer application	Do you seek out pictures or diagrams?	Do you call the help desk, ask a neighbour or growl at the computer?	Do you keep trying to do it or try it on another computer?

Figure 7.3 What is your primary learning style?
Source: Adapted from Rose (1987)

Look at Chapter 15 that deals with data in detail and how teachers, departments and schools use data to set effective targets for progress.

might be. It can also be used with your pupils to build up a profile of the preferred learning style of the class.

Read the word in the first column and then answer the questions in the successive three columns to see how you respond to each situation. Your answers may fall into all three columns, but one column is likely to contain the most. The dominant column indicates your primary learning style.

In schools where teaching and learning is high on the school development plan, pupils' preferred learning styles are identified and the teachers use the data to inform their lesson planning. Where a class has a high number of pupils who prefer to learn kinaesthetically and visually, the teacher may use this information to plan lessons that will better enable these pupils to engage in the learning and attain their potential.

Pupils may not fall neatly into one preferred learning style or another. To ensure that pupils all get a chance to learn most effectively, the challenge for the teacher is to plan a series of lessons that include these different learning styles. This is one major way that lesson planning has changed. Now for a lesson to be successful, it should not be viewed as a one-off performance but as one in a series of lessons that a teacher is producing for that class.

The following are some techniques that can be used to make lessons more engaging and easier to recall. Study them carefully in conjunction with Figure 7.1 before deciding what is going to go into your lesson and completing your plan.

Starting the lesson

Some schools have adopted a whole school approach to lesson planning in which all teachers follow a similar pattern/structure.

Lesson starters

A popular method is using a lesson starter. Lesson starters are exactly that – a quick-fire beginning to the lesson. Here are some ideas that can be adapted to any subject area.

Lesson starter 1

In a modern foreign language (MFL) lesson get pupils to write down:

- the numbers from 1-10
- the days of the week
- the months of the year
- ten words to describe things to do with a house
- ten words to describe people and their appearance.

Get pupils to listen to you when you give them numbers in the foreign language and ask them to add them together, multiply them, etc. This fits in with numeracy work that should be occurring across the school.

When taking the register ask pupils to answer with a word that you have been using over the last two weeks. No one is allowed to repeat a word that has been used before.

When taking the register ask pupils to answer with a word that you have been using – the next person must listen to the letter at the end of the word. Their word must start with that letter.

Lesson starter 2

In an **English** lesson, take a long word like Constantinople. If the pupils are very young then give them five minutes to find as many words as they can from its letters. If they are older ask them to find as many words with five or more letters. Give a small prize to anyone who comes up with words of seven or more letters, except 'constant'!

Give pupils a list of words with definitions that are mixed up. Get them to match the definitions as this can extend vocabulary knowledge.

As an introduction to a poetry lesson, give pupils a list of key words and ask them to match definitions to a key word.

When reading a story put a list of words on the board that describe a character – this can be adapted for any age or ability. Get them to write down the name of the character.

Lesson starter 3

In a **science** lesson, put a list of symbols on the board. This can be an interactive board or an ordinary whiteboard. Get pupils to write down the full name for the symbol.

Give pupils a list of key words (eg atoms, molecules, solutions) and a list of definitions or constituents. Get pupils to match the key words to the definitions, etc.

Put pictures of laboratory equipment up on the board. Give pupils a list of names which match the equipment and get them to pair these up.

Give pupils a spelling test. Write five words on the board, get them to memorise the spelling and then wipe them off and test them. This can be used as a mini whiteboard activity and or in any other subject. It also brings literacy into science.

While lesson starters ensure that pupils become engaged immediately, thus imposing class control and hence behaviour, they must be used with care:

- If they are used at the wrong time, for instance when a start to a lesson is going to be disrupted by pupils arriving later than normal as can happen after an assembly, they can be more disruptive than beneficial.
- If everyone uses lesson starters pupils will become bored with them. Pupils, like teachers, enjoy variety.
- They can take too long and dominate the lesson so diminishing the main learning intention.
- Preparing lesson starters takes time and effort and sometimes they do not fit neatly with the learning intention.

No matter how you plan your lesson it is most important to:

✔ Share the learning intention with the class. It is not a secret.

✔ Explain what you are learning and why.

✔ Explain how the lesson fits with the rest of the work that they are doing. Pupils are entitled to share THE BIG PICTURE.

Look at Chapter 14 for more information on learning intentions as this is integral to good lesson planning.

Brain gym

Another technique similar to lesson starters is something called brain gym where teachers pose a question that pupils have to problem solve.

Brain gym

Question: If you are in a room with a candle, a wood stove and a gas lamp and you have only one match, what do you light first?

Answer: *The match*

Question: Would you rather a crocodile attack you or an alligator?

Answer: *I would rather the crocodile attack the alligator.* (Read the line again)

Question: Add a single straight line to make this equation true: 5 + 5 + 5 = 550

Answer: *5 + 545 = 550* (You have added a line to + to make it into a 4)

Question: You have a barrel filled to the top with water which weighs 150 pounds. What can you add to the barrel to make it lighter?

Answer: *Holes!*

> **Many brainteasers** can be downloaded from the web but permissions may apply in some cases! See **www.brainbashers.com** for example.

There are plenty of brainteasers that teachers can use. They do get pupils thinking and can be good for getting brains activated and ready to learn. However, like lesson starters they can be overused and pupils get fed up when every teacher is using the same techniques. Also, the danger is that in a short lesson too much time may be lost in the warm up and little real time may be left for the learning intention to be clearly stated and delivered. It is better to use all these different techniques little and often – variety is the spice of life!

Using mini whiteboards to engage all learners

Mini whiteboards are today's equivalent of the little blackboards with a few sticks of chalk that you used to be able to buy. Now whiteboards and felt pens are used with a cloth to wipe the boards over. Pupils in a class are given these and the aim is to ensure that all pupils are engaged in the learning activity. No one can escape as they all have to produce the answers and hold the boards up. Mini whiteboards can be used in any subject as the following ideas suggest.

Mini whiteboards 1

This works for any age, primary or secondary. Depending on what you are doing you can get pupils to:

- Add/subtract/multiply/divide checking that they have sound basic mathematical skills and know their tables.
- Look at a sum on the board with its answer and ask the class if the answer is true or false.
- Change a fraction into a decimal.
- Work out the area of a shape that is given.
- Work out the degree of an angle.

Mini whiteboards 2

- Give pupils a time in a foreign language and ask them to write down the time in numbers.
- Give pupils the names of buildings and people, asking them to write down the meaning in English (eg school/house/church/station/policeman/teacher/nurse/footballer.
- Ask pupils to write down the meaning of a word that you give them.
- Read out a passage in a foreign language. Ask questions and get pupils to write down one- or two-word answers.

Mini whiteboards 3

- Ask pupils to write down three key words that have been used in the lesson. Choose one of the key words (eg photosynthesis) and write down three things about it. Compare what the class has written to see if they have written the same things and then discuss the responses.
- Jumble up a set of numbered pictures that show how species rely on one another for survival. Get pupils to put them in the right order by putting the numbers of the pictures in the right sequence on their boards.
- Write the definitions of a word on the main board and ask pupils to write down the word being defined on their boards.

Using games to engage learners and consolidate learning

Games are fun and engage pupils but as in all activities they need to be kept under control.

There are many methods that can be used to consolidate learning but it is best when the activity is given a rigid time frame. Like anything new, pupils need more time when they first get to play but this can be reduced as they improve.

Dominoes for maths

Make cards that have the names of mathematical shapes on them or the shapes themselves. This helps pupils learn the spelling and recognise the shape, so introducing literacy into maths lessons.

Dominoes can be adapted and used in many subjects:

- In chemistry match symbols to the names of elements that appear in the periodic table.
- Match OS symbols in geography to their names.
- Match health and safety symbols in laboratories to their meanings.
- Match the shapes of land masses to the names of countries.
- Match capital cities to countries.
- Match dates to events in history.
- Match fractions to the decimal equivalent.
- Match a sum to the answer.
- Match a definition to a word to improve and extend vocabulary.

Work like this can be used at the end of a lesson to consolidate learning or in the middle of a lesson before a transition to a new task or aspect of the lesson.

Guess the lesson

Put a word on the board. Tell the pupils that this lesson has something to do with the word on the board and that they will get a maximum of five words to help them. This is good for oracy work as the pupils have to give a reason to support their answer. It is important that key skills are integrated into all subject lessons.

History

mud   barbed   wire   1914   poppy   trenches

Answer: World War I

This could be supported by music playing from that era as the pupils walk in and by an interactive video showing clips from World War I. Copies of the poem 'In Flanders Fields' by Dr John Macrae could be given out. The words could also be substituted by pictures.

Jerusalem   quest   pilgrimage   journey   duty

Answer: The Crusades

longboats   Norway   axe   horned helmets   blonde hair

Answer: Vikings

Geography

Play a piece of music with Luciano Pavarotti singing.
Have an Italian flag.
Have a packet of spaghetti.
An outline shape of the country.

Answer: Italy

Washing lines

These can be used in a lesson to show a sequence of some kind. Stretch a line of string across the room by either getting pupils to hold ends or put two hooks in the wall and keep the line ready for when you want to use it.

Mathematics

Give out large cards, each with a number on it. You might want to explore number size for example so pupils would have to pin the cards on the line in ascending or descending order.

| 0.0067 | 0.063 | 0.05 |

Science

- Use the line to display the most acidic and the most alkaline chemicals or match pH levels to chemicals. Hang up the pH values and put the right chemical next to each one.
- Use the line to show the sequence of events in a reaction between two chemicals and the results and conclusion.

Geography

- Use the line to show a journey from one place to another, especially useful for small children. For example, 'What would I see if I left school and walked to the post box?' Put the items in order of appearance on the journey.
- Put a set of given countries in order from east to west along the latitude line. Then order them from west to east.
- Biggest countries and smallest countries can also be ordered.

History

Make timelines of events in history or the topic that is being studied. Or consider events in the life of a well-known historical figure.

English

A sequence of events in a story and the plot outline can be hung on the line.

Can we play a game?

In this game groups of pupils have a set of cards and they are all given an equal share face down in front of them. They must not tell their opponents what is written on their card.

The aim of the game is to get pupils to guess what is being described without using any of the three words written below the main word.

Ocean
Large
Body
Water

Simile
As
Like
Comparison

This idea can be used in any subject and can be good for encouraging understanding and knowledge of key words, and ensuring that key skills such as oracy and literacy are being embedded within all subject areas.

What is the word?

Ask for a volunteer and get them to sit at the front. On their forehead put a sticker that they have not seen. This should be a key word that has been used in the lesson. You may wish to demonstrate by allowing a reliable pupil to choose a sticker that you have not seen from a number that are face down.

The aim is for another person to use questions to find out what the unknown word is. This again ensures that oracy skills are being developed. Extend this further by having a list of definitions, etc on the board or on a sheet and ask pupils to match a definition to the key word. This is a good way to consolidate learning.

Using interactive whiteboards in lessons

Interactive whiteboards can be powerful educational tools when used well. However, there are still many teachers who have no access to them. Ensure that you have watched lessons where these are being used. In many secondary schools nearly every teaching room has a whiteboard and teachers have made, bought and shared

See the Case Study on the website.

valuable software. They are used to introduce the learning intention by having an example of the day's work on the board for all to see.

There are many ways to use this resource.

Examples from an English lesson

Example 1: Teaching a poetry lesson

- Put the poem on the board without the title. Ask the class to think about what the title could be and to give reasons. To do this they have to think carefully about the content. Ask them to date the poem.
- Allow 10 minutes for a discussion.
- At the appropriate time put the title on the board and then the date.
- Begin to discuss the content of the poem and allow pupils to come up and annotate the text on the whiteboard.
- At the end of the lesson save the annotations and print out a copy. This then forms the basis of the next lesson.

 See the website for an example.

In addition, photos can be used to link with the theme of the poem or biographical information about the poet can be built into the lesson. Software is also available for all subject-specific areas of learning.

Example 2: For any text

- A PowerPoint presentation was used to introduce the text 'View from the Bridge' by Arthur Miller. The text is set in the USA and deals with immigrant workers from Italy. It is important to give a lot of background information to pupils so that they understand the context.
- The same presentation was then put onto the school network and in the next lesson pupils were asked to log on and fill in the worksheets that they were given. These were differentiated into 'higher' and 'foundation' worksheets, as this was a key stage 4 mixed-ability English class.
- Pupils filled in the worksheets independently were then allowed to work in pairs. This was to allow pupils to pair up and share their work.
- Eventually the worksheets were taken in and the pupils' research skills and understanding were assessed.
- All the data compiled by the pupils were collated onto two final worksheets that the pupils were given to keep and use as a reference tool.

How do we use videos in lessons?

For teachers who do not have access to interactive whiteboards, the use of a video can work well in all subject areas to engage pupils and improve attainment. The major TV channels produce some excellent resources that can be used as the basis of many lessons. Large schools with their own libraries might have a stock of these. In schools without a librarian there may be someone responsible for recording programmes. LEAs have library services, which might also be involved in supporting learning, and many schools have a funding allocation for books and learning resource materials like videos and DVDs.

In subjects like English literature adaptations of the texts certainly aid understanding and help to bring the text alive for many pupils. In many cases, world events such as the tsunami of 2004 can be used to support pupils' understanding of the effects of natural disasters on the environment and mankind, and current affairs programmes provide much valuable resource material enabling informed discussions about complex issues.

In some cases teachers may show a video and then re-show it with pupils being expected to respond via a worksheet, or it may be used as an integral part of a lesson to reinforce a theme.

The four-part lesson

In some schools, as with lesson starters, a standard format for the way lessons are planned has been implemented (see Figure 7.4).

Phase 1

Learning atmosphere established.

Previous lesson is reviewed and the present one is set in the context of the BIG PICTURE.

Clear lesson intentions and objectives are given.

A sense of challenge and excitement in the learning is generated.

Phase 2

New information is provided but in small amounts.

Teacher asks closed questions then open questions that elicit greater understanding.

This part of the lesson is characterised by tasks and activities.

Key words are being used.

Phase 3

Success criteria are being tested.

Have the pupils understood at a basic level and a more complex level?

Oral questioning and written tasks explore this.

Tasks that require thought, understanding and verbalisation of understanding are provided.

Pupils transfer information into a format that suits their learning style.

Phase 4

This phase is vitally important and is, in effect, a plenary session with pupils actively reviewing the learning objectives.

Pupils think about what they have learnt.

The teacher may use questions and encourage pupils to work in pairs to discuss and consolidate their learning.

Pupils may think about what activities they have participated in and what learning techniques have been successful for them.

The plenary should also lead into the next lesson.

Figure 7.4 *The four-part lesson*

Differentiation

Differentiating the work you plan to use in class is important. In all lessons you must expect different pupils to learn at different rates and some pupils in all classes will finish work before the others. If these pupils have completed the work well and you are confident they understand the work then you need to supply them with extension work. This could be an extra written question or an extra diagram that they are expected to interpret. The task is not there to occupy the pupil but should develop the pupil's learning further so that you are enriching their learning experience. Pupils like to be challenged!

Differentiation is a term used to describe the way teachers plan work to suit a particular group of pupils. An English teacher could set an essay entitled MY BEST HOLIDAY. This task would differentiate by outcome. All ages and abilities of pupil could undertake this task but an A* pupil will write a piece commensurate with their ability. The task differentiates by outcome.

However, a teacher covering circulation in biology may have to alter the materials used to suit pupils of different abilities by altering the readability of the material, the type of tasks they set to test understanding, and so on.

The data that schools now provide on pupils and their prior learning allow teachers to group pupils in a class effectively. Teachers use these data in a number of ways. Sometimes they group the most able students together so that they can challenge them with a task that the average pupils in the class might find too hard. In this way they can enrich their learning and push them on a little more. However, at times it may be useful to put an able pupil in a group with weaker pupils in order to develop that group and to move them all forward. Pupils learn most effectively from each other and teachers need to harness that and use it to good effect.

Remember that whenever you set a task you must make it time related. In Chapter 4 you should have noted the need for setting time-related tasks. Boys definitely need a tight structure to their learning and enjoy an element of competition in their lessons. You will also need to refer to Chapter 6 on reading ages and readability when you are planning your worksheets. It is important that you make your materials accessible but do not dumb down the work or make it too easy. Your aim must be to extend pupils' vocabulary and learning. Children need to be exposed to a rich language experience in the classroom, this is particularly true of those who have come to this country and are learning the language.

Look again at Figure 7.1 on page 76 and think about what you should be considering when you are planning your lesson. The different ideas given above also provide a teacher with ways to engage the attention of pupils and appeal to a range of learning preferences. Then use the following checklist to ensure that you have accounted for all aspects.

Checklist

Your lesson should take account of all of the following:

✔ **Clear aims and objectives.**

✔ **A well-planned lesson that can be delivered in the time allowed.**

✔ **Good pace and challenge.**

✔ **Groupings identified (pupils must realise that you are in charge of the layout and seating for the class – no discussion is allowed on this.) Use data to group the able together when you want to enrich their learning and set them a challenging task. Put able children with average pupils to bring the whole group performance on.**

✔ **Seat boys and girls together to improve the oral work of boys and when you want to encourage risk taking – girls can be overly cautious and boys too hasty. Put them together to find a good, balanced approach to tasks.**

✔ Variety of tasks – all clearly timed to ensure that pupils remain focused and on task.

✔ Differentiation may be achieved through the type of questions that you ask the most able in the class versus the average or less able, or through the written kinaesthetic tasks set and through the groupings you identify (see checklist on page 92).

✔ Learning styles should take into account what VAK methods were used in the last lesson and the teacher should aim to produce lessons that recognise these different preferences.

✔ Refer to 'Reading ages and readability' in Chapter 6 to ensure that worksheets are pupil friendly.

✔ Clear learning outcomes and success criteria are identified for the pupils.

Time to reflect

✔ The acronym VAK is used to describe different learning styles. What do the letters represent?

✔ What eight factors should you think about when planning the perfect lesson?

✔ What is a lesson starter and can you think of one you would use in your own subject and classroom?

✔ How would you use one of the games suggested in a lesson?

✔ How could you use photos, videos or an interactive whiteboard in your lesson?

✔ Plan a lesson that is structured as a four-part lesson.

✔ How would you differentiate this lesson to suit three distinct ability groups: the most able, the average child and the less able in a year group?

References

Gardner, H. (1993), *Frames of Mind: The Theory of Multiple Intelligences*, Basic Books – The Perseus Books Group.

Ginnis, P. (2002), *The Teacher's Toolkit*, Crown House Publishing.

Hughes, M. with Potter, D. (2002), *Tweak to Transform*, Network Educational Press Ltd.

Rose, C. (1987), *Accelerated Learning*, Accelerated Learning Systems Ltd.

Chapter 8

Storing Data and Organising Lesson Planning

🍎 **What will you find in this chapter?**

✔ What data do you have access to?

✔ How should data be recorded?

✔ Storing resource materials and lesson plans.

In order to become an excellent teacher it is not enough to deliver high-quality lessons. Teachers must be good markers of pupils' work and be able to give good diagnostic feedback to pupils about how they can improve (see Chapter 13). They must also be able to track pupil progress comparing it with the data that they have available to them (see Chapter 14). As a teacher you will have access to a lot of base-line information on any pupils you teach. This chapter is concerned with how you keep that data. It aims to make you a much more effective and efficient teacher, one able to use the data so that you are both data *and* knowledge rich. Having the data and not using it to best effect makes it redundant! This chapter is also about how best to organise your lesson plans and any resource materials you have produced for future use and ease of reference.

What data do you have access to?

Here is a limited list of the data you may be given:

- reading ages and spelling ages
- Standard Assessment Test (SAT) levels
- teacher assessment from the prior year, reports, etc
- Cognitive Abilities Test (CAT) results.

Only reception class teachers will lack this data and they will begin the 'data gathering' process by compiling profiles on pupils on entry to primary school. All teachers need to keep this important data in their markbooks or in a suitable file. Teachers should also record classwork and homework performance on a regular basis.

How should data be recorded?

All schools should have detailed marking policies and some will instruct you as to whether you should record in levels, grades or marks. However, most have a whole school policy that is interpreted by individual departments. The recording of classwork in a practical subject may be very different from the recording of pupils' work in a maths lesson, for instance. Make sure you record pupil progress appropriately using detailed guidance from your line manager or subject leader. Some schools now insist that only a comment is recorded in a pupil's book and that this comment identifies the strengths and weaknesses of the work. The comment must also identify how the pupil can progress to the next stage of learning. If this is the case and you are in a school or department like this then it does not mean that you can't record the level, grade or mark achieved in your own markbook.

A markbook of some kind is mandatory for all staff and teachers must keep detailed records of pupil attainment to inform their report writing and enable them to report orally to parents during parents' evenings. Some schools provide loose-leaf files in a standard format for all areas of learning; others provide purpose-made markbooks. It is useful to have all the data on pupils available in one place and not to have to move between different files.

Figure 8.1 illustrates an extract from a markbook showing part of a sample page of data on a pupil group.

What is an individual learning plan (ILP)?

Some pupils have special needs and these children may need support of some kind. Pupils with dyslexia for instance will have an individual learning plan (ILP). In some schools they are called individual education plans or **IEPs**.

Names	Form/Class	M/F	Reading age	Spelling age	CAT verbal	CAT numerical	CAT non-verbal	SAT English	SAT Maths	SAT Science	ILP/EMLAS
Wasima Ali	7A	F	11.6	11.0	100	110	102	5	5	5	EMLAS
Josh Anderson	7A	M	10.6	9.0	94	107	108	4	5	5	ILP

Figure 8.1 Extract from a markbook

> **See Chapter 5** on poverty and ethnicity factors and how they affect teaching and learning outcomes.

EMLAS stands for Ethnic Minority Languages Advisory Service. Some children may speak English as a second language and need additional language support. They could well be very able and their language difficulty should not prevent them being in top sets if the school uses a setting system.

Some pupils may have a school health plan. These enable a school to put in place a plan for managing children who have individual health care that a school needs to take account of. For example:

- a child who has to be allowed to leave the room immediately they want to go to the toilet
- a child with hearing or visual impairment of some kind
- a child with severe epilepsy or asthma.

For secondary teachers/some primary teachers

These are for secondary teachers or teachers in a primary school who teach a number of classes for a subject. Look at the 'Top Tips' on page 100 if you are a primary teacher in an early years class or if you teach a class for every subject. You may want to take ideas from both sets of tips and adapt them to suit yourself.

In your markbook:

- ✔ Allow at least five double pages for each year group.
- ✔ Trim down the last four pages, cutting off the area where you would put names. This will mean that the names written on the first page are seen whichever page you happen to turn to.
- ✔ On the first page write the names and all the current data you have, as seen in Figure 8.1.
- ✔ Put classwork marks on one page and homework marks on another (see

98

Names
Wasima Ali
Josh Anderson
Charlotte Bedwell
Hannah Davies
Rhys Davies

Figure 8.2 *Adapting your markbook*

Figure 8.2). This makes it easy to see how well pupils do without class support. It also ensures that you can see at a glance the homework record of a pupil. Compare the marks between classwork and homework. Parents can make a big difference to homework marks! However, children may also be distracted in class and work more effectively at home.

✔ If you are a teacher with no form of electronic marking and you have a number of different classes, record attendance on a separate page. This is an important piece of data and can affect pupil performance significantly.

✔ Keep one double page for making notes. An English teacher would make notes about oral work, spelling, punctuation skills, quality of imaginative writing, persuasive writing, and so on.

✔ Make up your own shorthand to help you remember certain pieces of work for good or bad reasons! You may wish to refer to these marks/grades/levels in a

ENGLISH	C	L	A	S	S	W	O	R	K	06
Names Year 10 / 2	CW Comp 2005 /20		Writing /20		Oral work					
Wasima Ali	16	A (M) ↑	14	B–	14	B–				
Josh Anderson	13	C–	TBF		15	A ↑				

Figure 8.3 *Example of a 'shorthand' system*

comment for a report. For example: **ND** = not done, **EXC** = excellent, **M** = merit awarded, **D** = detention given, → average, ↑ better than average, ↓ lower than average, **TBF**, to be finished, and so on. Leave a column next to the level/grade/mark to enable you to do this (see Figure 8.3).

✔ Add up the marks or look across at the levels or grades awarded for a period of time – a half term for instance. Award an average for that period of time. It is useful to do this from time to time to see the rank order for the class. In this way you will not overlook a bright child who is quiet and does not demand your attention and yet is near the top of the class. It is often the case that the ones you think are doing well and demand your time are not the best! Some schools have a reward system. Use this as a reference for awarding **rewards/merits**, etc.

See Chapter 13 for more on rewarding good work.

✔ Some teachers use computers as markbooks and put the data onto an Excel spreadsheet. This has obvious benefits for ranking the class, etc.

✔ You may want to put exam/test and term grades on a separate page. Record the level of examination that a pupil is to be entered for: higher/ intermediate/foundation or the appropriate level.

✔ Record the identifying numbers of the books that pupils may have on loan from the department or learning area so that you can get these returned at the appropriate time.

✔ Remember that markbooks should be used at parents' evenings and that pupils' books should also be in evidence so parents can see the quality of learning and marking.

One school's use of its website

In Eirias High School, Colwyn Bay, a maths teacher, Patrick Morrow, now puts his classes' classwork, homework and test/examination results onto his website. Pupils have a password and they can only access their marks. In this way they are able to see how they are performing. For each piece of work the average mark awarded to the class is shown. This means that if they scored 4.5 on a piece of work and the average is 3.7 then they may have done well. If the opposite is the case then the pupil needs to improve in that area of learning. Pupils can relate their progress to that of the rest of the class. Pupils who miss work can also access lesson and resource material, which they download and use to catch up on.

Patrick Morrow is also keen to show attendance and can show how poor attendance often affects performance in that area of learning – highlighting depressed scores. This

Case Study

See the website for more on how attendance affects performance.

is very obvious in a subject like maths where topics are studied sequentially and end-of-topic assessments show how poor **attendance** might have affected the ability to do well in this area.

For primary teachers

This idea has come from a newly qualified teacher (**NQT**) who struggled in her first year to keep detailed records on her class of five year olds who she taught for every subject.

✔ Prepare a file with enough dividers for every child in the class.

✔ Write their names in alphabetical order leaving a space for each child.

✔ Write out a master marksheet for each subject.

✔ Add in the learning outcomes for the subject that the child has to achieve during the course of the year and the levels these correspond to. If you do this on a computer it is then easy to update and print out spares if you need them. Leave a space so that notes can be added.

✔ Highlight and date each time a child achieves a learning outcome in the file.

✔ Keep all ILPs and additional important data on that child in their file space.

✔ Keep any parental letters at the back of the assessment data so that you can refer to them if necessary.

✔ Have a sheet in the appropriate space for extra-curricular achievements and make a note of any on this.

Storing resource materials and lesson plans

Over the course of your teaching career you will amass a lot of material. In order to be efficient, and not, have to repeat work unnecessarily, organising this material is essential. Here are some ideas.

A lesson planner

Many schools provide these. Some make them in-house and they are customised to suit the school. The advantage of a purpose-made planner is that it may include important calendar dates as well as lesson times, important whole school policies, LEA contact numbers, and so on. Bought lesson planners come in A4 and A5 sizes and enable you to keep lesson notes. In your first year of teaching you may want to make more detailed plans to supplement these. Some teachers keep a file for each academic year as well.

A year file

Divide this into the classes you teach, or if you are working in the primary sector divide the file into subjects or learning aspects. In each space keep detailed lesson plans. You should also keep copies of any worksheets in a poly pocket and date it. In this way you can keep spare work ready for anyone absent on a specific day for a specific lesson. This system ensures that you always have 'spare' worksheets for those who missed the work or who mislaid the worksheet. It also avoids disruptions that can cause behaviour difficulties for relatively inexperienced teachers.

At the end of each academic year file your materials using the method suggested below.

The big files and IT backup

An English teacher can organise files neatly according to literary texts they will have taught that year:

- *Romeo and Juliet*
- *Lord of the Flies*
- *Carrie's War*
- *Charlotte's Web.*

Does your subject lend itself to this? Can you organise your work into topics? If so you could adapt the suggested idea to suit your subject(s).

Put all the information in envelope wallets that are clearly labelled on the outside. On the cover, list the sheets that are contained inside. Use poly pockets to divide up the contents of the wallet so that you can see at a glance the resource material available to you. Save all work produced on a computer onto labelled discs/CDs, etc so you don't lose material owing to computer failure. Look at the examples on the next page for suggestions on how to organise lesson topics from key stages 2 and 3.

Geography key stage 2

My town
History of the town
Why towns grow up in locations, eg
crossroads, source of rivers
Map of the town
Pictures of different types of housing
List of streets
Worksheets mark route from home to
school

Science key stage 3

Worksheets on different types of soil
Lesson starter video clip from Internet
The rock cycle
Notes on
sedimentary/metamorphic/igneous
rocks
Game to help pupils remember
Diagrams

Large lever arch files are useful for storing one-off items such as exam papers, SAT papers/tests/assessment tests. Divide the file by subject/year group taught. On the divider list the contents - this means it is easier to see at a glance what the file contains. Again put worksheets together in one poly pocket. This makes it possible to see at a glance if you have just a few or enough ready for a class. Over the years it is easy to forget just what you have produced and finding an already tried and tested good work-sheet is a pleasant surprise for a busy classroom teacher!

Finally, look carefully at the good practice of experienced teachers around you and ask them how they organise their work.

Time to reflect

✔ Do you have a mark book?

✔ What additional information has been made available to you about your pupils?

✔ How are you storing this data?

✔ Is it ordered as well as it could be?

✔ How does your mentor store data on pupils?

✔ What materials have you already prepared for lessons?

✔ How have you ordered and filed this material?

✔ Is it going to be readily re-useable?

Chapter 9

Using Classroom Supports to Maximise Pupils' Learning

What will you find in this chapter?

✔ What type of support staff will you find in classrooms today?

✔ What can you expect teaching or classroom assistants to do?

✔ Establishing best practice.

✔ How classroom assistants and support staff will be used in future.

This chapter looks at the variety of support that is available in many areas of the UK. Many schools have particular requirements and this is reflected in the amount and type of support staff they use. Remember that each school is different. The chapter then discusses the best ways of working alongside all additional adult classroom support.

What type of support staff will you find in classrooms today?

Many teachers both in primary and secondary schools will find that they have with them a support teacher (**ST**) or a teaching assistant in the classroom either on a full- or part-time basis. An ST is a member of staff who may be employed by the local education authority to support the learning of children with specific needs. One common use of a ST is to support children who have English as an additional language. These teachers have got specific expertise and will work on a one-to-one basis or with a group of children to improve their language skills and allow them to engage fully with the school curriculum.

Another common use of STs is with pupils who have specific educational needs like dyslexia. These teachers usually come from a special needs background and will come into mainstream classrooms to support average ability or able pupils who have been identified as having specific learning difficulties. These children can cope well in the mainstream, have a good level of understanding and with support will access GCSE and GCE qualifications.

Finally, STs may also be members of staff who have spare contact time and this needs to be used effectively to support those pupils who are identified as needing extra help.

Over the past ten years the number of teaching assistants (**TAs**) or classroom assistants (**CAs**) who have no formal teaching qualification has grown considerably. This is due in part to the number of initiatives that have been introduced, such as the NLNS. Another valid reason is the inclusion into the mainstream of pupils with very many widespread needs. Recently, the workforce re-modelling on-going in schools and the reduction in administrative tasks that teachers are allowed to carry out has meant a further increase in the use of support staff.

The specific titles of TAs vary. In one school they are given one title and this may be different to the school next door where a TA is doing exactly the same job. In order to provide some clarity it is more useful to suggest the range of roles and responsibilities that assistants may carry out by looking at a fictitious case study.

How High Cross Secondary uses its support staff

The following describes the way in which TAs work alongside other staff in High Cross School (this is a secondary school but primary schools, depending on their size, can also use support staff in this way). Their titles were carefully selected to suggest the types of work they do and areas of the school they work in.

Learning support assistants (LSAs) (pupil)

These are attached to individual children who have statements of educational need. These pupils have help on a one-to-one basis for a designated number of hours a week depending on the assessed need of a child. The LSAs know what work the child is doing and visit the same subject lessons on a timetabled basis. Where LSAs are attached to individual pupils, if a pupil is not in school the LSA is not required officially on that day. LSAs (pupil) normally move through the school with the individual named pupil. Where pupils have needs caused by physical or mental disability the LSAs usually have a higher degree of training and this is specific to the needs of the pupils. Some LSAs will be able to change catheters for children for instance.

Learning support assistants (group)

These are also employed by the school to work with children who do not have an individual statement but need some form of extra support that has been identified. This is normally referred to as School Action. These LSAs may have specific subject expertise – where this is the case they will be used in this subject as support where possible.

It is likely that although one member of staff is specifically employed to work with a named child they will in fact end up supporting the group of children who sit near the named pupil. Working with one is difficult to achieve as other pupils who sit near the pupil or who are friends will also ask the LSA for help if they need it. This is common practice.

Behaviour support assistants (BSAs)

These assistants work with pupils who are identified as having specific learning difficulties that are more closely allied to their behaviour than their ability. In some cases pupils may have low ability and poor behaviour. These assistants work with the pupil and support learning. They may be involved in counselling the pupil about poor behaviour and will be used to remove a pupil from the room if their behaviour threatens to disrupt the whole lesson and get them into trouble. Some of these BSAs will have attended further training devised to help them cope with those whose behaviours can be challenging.

Teaching assistant's generic job specification

This job specification may be amended at any time following discussion between the headteacher and member of staff, and will be reviewed annually.

Purpose

To support/enrich the teaching and learning of pupils in curriculum areas, pastoral areas and classrooms and maintain positive attitudes towards learning, achievement and behaviour.

Key areas of responsibility and tasks include the following:

- Strategic direction and development of year group/groups of pupils/individual pupils
- In cooperation with and under the direction of the headteacher, deputy headteachers, SENCOs and, where appropriate, the curriculum and pastoral coordinators and class teachers to:
  - support the vision, ethos and policies of the school and promote high levels of achievement
  - support the pastoral or curriculum teams, SENCO and class teachers to deliver the development plans in operation in those areas
  - contribute to strategies that positively impact on teaching, learning, behaviour management and attendance in collaboration with key personnel, including those mentioned and the attendance officer and Education Welfare Officer (**EWO**).

Teaching and learning

To:

- Assist the teacher with delivering good-quality lessons
- Deliver good-quality lessons prepared by the teacher where appropriate
- Prepare lesson material and resources to support learning where appropriate
- Use ICT effectively to support learning activities and develop pupils' competence and independence in its use
- Assist the teacher with the development of suitable classroom resources and where appropriate mount displays to enhance the learning environment
- Support the teacher in managing the behaviour of named pupil(s)
- Work with the class teacher to identify valid learning targets for individual pupils
- Work with the class teacher to deliver the individual educational plans for pupils who are targeted for classroom support
- Work with the class teacher to ensure effective use of time and provide clear structures for learning by maintaining pace and focus and ensuring that pupils remain on task

- Work with the SENCO and class teacher and other designated staff to assess a pupil's changing needs on a regular basis
- Use specific specialist skills such as behaviour management training, counselling skills, dyslexia training, etc to support the needs of pupils to ensure positive outcomes for their learning
- Support the classroom teacher by working together to use a variety of teaching approaches and a range of strategies to help their learning needs
- Develop knowledge of a range of learning support needs and to develop an understanding of the specific needs of the pupil(s) to be supported
- Work with small groups of pupils to deliver literacy/numeracy/computer-aided learning or other specific lessons as determined by link staff and with the agreement of the SENCO
- Support the physical needs of pupils ensuring that effective teaching and learning can occur
- Develop a supportive relationship with pupils in order to promote effective teaching and learning
- Mentor specific pupils, supporting them and helping them to learn effectively.

Monitoring, assessment, recording, reporting

To:

- Keep a record of the teaching and learning of pupils in their care
- Monitor pupil progress
- Contribute to the reporting process to parents and other staff about the learning of pupils
- Aid in the assessment of pupils where applicable and to contribute to the routine assessment systems
- Track the progress of named pupils in consultation with relevant teaching staff
- Assist the teacher in assessing pupils' work
- Assist in setting challenging targets for pupils
- Be familiar with reading and using school data as and when applicable
- Administer and assess/mark tests and invigilate exams/tests.

General

To:

- Take on specific tasks related to effective teaching and learning and support for pupils
- Operate within the stated policies and practices of the school
- Establish effective working relationships and set a good example through their presentation and personal and professional conduct

- Endeavour to give every pupil in their care the opportunity to reach their potential and meet high expectations
- Contribute where appropriate to the corporate life of the school through effective participation in meetings and extra-curricular activities necessary to the life of the school and specific individual pupils
- Participate in performance management processes and use the process to improve professional and personal effectiveness
- Contribute to the out-of-school learning activities where appropriate within guidelines established by the school
- Line manage other teaching assistants where appropriate
- Hold regular team meetings with managed staff
- Undertake recruitment/induction/appraisal/training/mentoring for other TAs.

It is important to identify why the classroom assistant is in your classroom. If the CA is there for an individual child then the teacher needs to be aware of the reason. Children who are supported will have ILPs and these need to be used by the teacher and the CA to support the pupil's learning. The CA may have worked with the pupil for a number of years and will have a good understanding of the problems that prevent them from learning. It is useful to find out as much as you can about pupils with support from the CA.

Make an effort to get to know the CAs you work with. Where possible try to arrange a meeting so that you can negotiate the ground rules for working as a team with pupils in the classroom. This is difficult if you work with a number of different CAs but is important.

The following list is an example of *specific* activities that CAs might be expected to undertake in any classroom situation:

- Read materials aloud to the pupil explaining any words that are difficult or that the pupil does not understand.
- Ensure that the pupil is able to use specific equipment and materials available and give help where appropriate.
- Assist the pupil in any areas of weakness or difficulty (eg spelling, reading, behaviour, handwriting and presentation).
- Restate the task if necessary to allow the pupil to engage with it.
- Help the pupil to focus on work and ensure task completion.
- Help pupils who have specific physical disabilities to learn effectively.
- Work with small groups of pupils either in the classroom or, if the school policy permits, in another workspace on specified tasks set by the class teacher
- Liaise with the class teacher about individual education plans
- Help to monitor and track progress and contribute to class teacher reports.

Establishing best practice

Tensions can arise if there has been no discussion about how to manage situations that can arise in the classroom. The class teacher is in charge of overall discipline and therefore should support the CA if the latter has difficulties with poor behaviour. In some cases the CA may remove a poorly behaved pupil or pupils at the discretion of the class teacher. The CA is there to support the learning of a child or a group of children, and in some cases may have specific expertise with behaviourally challenged children. However, even though it is important that the teacher and assistant learn to work together as a mutually supportive pair of adults, the class teacher needs to retain ultimate responsibility and take decisive action where it is called for.

'**A day in the life** of a classroom assistant' can be found on the website.

Liaising about work

The class teacher is also the professional in charge of the teaching and learning room and as such will plan and deliver the lesson and this will be part of a scheme of work (**SOW**). Therefore, sharing the SOW and the lesson plans and materials beforehand is important. Providing a pack of the materials that you are going to use during that week or over the course of a half term makes it much easier for the CA to direct the work of the pupil or pupils they are helping. The CA, with their knowledge of their pupils, will be able to suggest ways of adapting the work to suit the pupils' needs. Part of their job specification, depending on their status and salary, might well be to help differentiate the teaching materials to make them suitable to the needs of the pupils they support. Even when the CAs are not able to differentiate the written materials, they may want to find other resource materials to support their pupils' learning.

A CA may read the materials with the pupil, explaining any difficulties and restating the task if this needs doing, possibly simplifying the language and the task if this is necessary. CAs should also ensure that pupils are on task and might be involved in checking and correcting work. In some cases, CAs will be involved in assessing pupils. They may help them to complete exam papers, observe them in lesson situations and might contribute information to behavioural and learning reports that could be used by an educational team.

Establish with the CA their expected role in the classroom and if necessary use the school job specifications as a basis from which to work. In many schools the SENCO will line manage the CAs and will be able to help staff develop an acceptable system for working as a team.

Liaising about behaviour

As well as managing the work, the CA and the teacher need to discuss how they will manage the behaviour in the classroom. It is usual for the teacher to retain whole class control but to delegate some level of responsibility to the CA, who is the one sitting next to a pupil or group of pupils and as such is in a position to know what is happening in that area of the room. It is important that the teacher delegates some responsibility to the CA, allowing and indeed expecting them to manage the behaviour of the pupils nearby. However, the teacher will need to step in to manage serious breaches of discipline and show that they support the CA. One of the most common issues that can arise is when a supported pupil refuses to work for the CA or is rude to them. It is important to listen to the CA and support them when this occurs. On rare occasions it may be necessary to separate the pupil and CA, seeking help from an on-call system or the SENCO.

Classroom assistants are familiar with the school rewards and sanctions systems and should have some autonomy to use them. The class teacher should reinforce this practice. The pupils in the class need to know that both adults in the room have power and the teacher needs to be seen to support the CA. Pupils can be very good at playing one adult off against another as they do sometimes with parents! In all cases of indiscipline you must find out exactly what happened and be fair and consistent in the application of sanctions.

Establishing ground rules

In some cases the CA removes pupils from the class during the lesson and it is important to establish that the CA will take control of the behaviour of those pupils while they are with them, ensuring that pupils follow school behaviour rules. The ground rules should also include the following expectations of CAs:

- Like teachers they should have high expectations of the pupils and show respect for their social, cultural, linguistic and religious differences
- Treat pupils with respect, ensuring the development of the learner
- Work as part of a team
- Ensure that pupil's health and well-being is protected in line with legislation
- Provide support for teachers, pupils and the school
- Act as role models using language and behaviours that are commensurate with their duties in the school and with young people.

Some teachers work with pupils with profound learning difficulties and may have two or more CAs in the room. Where this occurs it is important to seek advice from line managers and from the SENCO about best practice in this situation. Make time to see others teach who have experience in this type of situation. New teachers are not expected to know everything and making use of mentors and their expertise is vital. Teaching is like skydiving: it is better to get it right first time if you can; or at least live to fly another day!

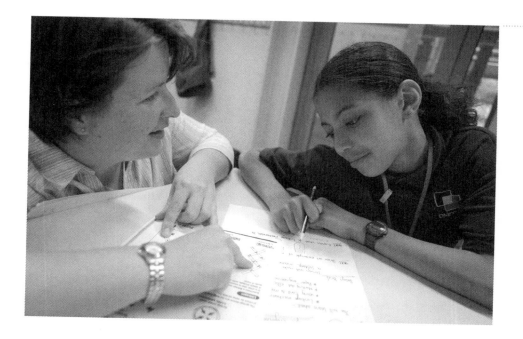

The future for classroom assistants and support staff

In future, schools will undoubtedly use TAs in more and more diverse ways. The continuous professional development that is already in place for teachers will be further extended and assistants will be further involved in school-based training as well as training provided by specialist deliverers. The challenge will be to use all assistants so that they effectively and significantly support the teaching and learning that goes on in school to improve standards.

Ofsted (2002 : 4-5) indicates:

Teaching assistants play an important part in the implementation of the NLNS by supporting teachers and pupils in the classroom ... Section 10 inspections show that the presence of teaching assistants improves the quality of teaching. This improvement is most marked when the teaching assistant and teacher work in close partnership or when the teaching assistant is following a tightly prescribed intervention or catch-up programme.

Time to reflect

- ✔ How many teaching assistants are there in your school?

- ✔ What roles do they fulfil?

- ✔ Does your mentor have any that work alongside him/her?

- ✔ How do classroom assistants record the work that they have done with pupils in your school?

- ✔ Does the classroom assistant meet with the teacher to discuss the work that will be done prior to the lesson or is this done informally in the lesson?

- ✔ Note any effective classroom practice involving teachers working alongside classroom assistants.

References and further reading

Dragonfly Training Ltd, 'How to maximise the effectiveness of teaching assistants in schools', **www.dragonfly-training.co.uk**

Lee, B. (2002), 'Teaching assistants in schools: the current state of play', National Foundation for Educational Research LGA educational research programme, Local Government Association, Research 34.

Ofsted (2002), 'Teaching assistants in primary schools: an evaluation of the quality and impact of their work', HMI report 434, 23 July.

Part 3

Behaviour Management

Chapter 10

Behaviour: Let's start at the very beginning

What will you find in this chapter?

✔ What is a behaviour policy?

✔ What strategies can be used to prevent poor behaviour? The education behaviour plan.

✔ Promoting positive learning: sanctions and rewards.

✔ Preparing to face a class.

✔ Body language, voice and eye contact.

✔ First steps in achieving class control.

The next two chapters deal with one of the biggest issues facing teachers today – that of controlling the behaviour of unruly pupils. This chapter outlines how schools manage pupils' behaviour and apply consistent measures to ensure that all staff play a part in this. It also explains how exclusions work and why certain pupils may have educational behaviour plans. It is intended to get you to think about how you will prepare for taking control of a group of pupils. No matter how good the school or how academically bright the pupils are; they all have the capacity to wreak havoc and chaos when confronted by a teacher who clearly does not know how to control a class. This is where you can start to get it right!

Why is this important

Remember that good teachers develop their management skills over time and very often reflect on a poor lesson in order to ensure that it improves the next time. These two chapters are not intended to be fully comprehensive; they are a starting point. In order to become a good classroom manager you will need to seek advice constantly, watch good classroom managers at work, read extensively about strategies you could use and objectively review your own practice. You will also need to understand how schools work in relation to managing behaviour so that you have an overview of where you will fit into this.

Before you go any further it may be useful to look at a checklist of possible reasons that prevent pupils from learning in a classroom:

- poor attitude to learning
- low self-esteem of a pupil or a whole class
- poor classroom management of the pupils
- ill-prepared lessons with a lack of clear instructions for pupils to follow
- lack of differentiation of work: it is too easy or hard
- lack of variety within work
- poor attitude and relationship of a teacher with a class
- lack of consequences from poor behaviour
- boredom.

If you know the likely causes then these can be avoided or strategies put in place to minimise them.

What is a behaviour policy?

Most secondary schools and an increasing number of primary schools have written policies on behaviour. This should go some way to ensuring a consistent approach throughout the school to such an important issue. A *behaviour policy* outlines the discipline procedures that are in place for dealing with all pupils in the school. It should explain the standard operating procedures of the school and it will be explicit about how pupils should behave in class and the expectations the school has for them. It also suggests the code of conduct for staff and, in some cases, lays down ground rules for the way that a classroom should be kept (eg all chairs placed under desks at the end of a lesson). It could also indicate how pupils might be expected to enter and leave classrooms. In some schools pupils are still expected to stand when any member of staff enters the room. It might refer to rewards and sanctions and refer to on-call staff or time-out procedures. It will refer to a list of behaviours that might occur in your classroom and suggest ways of dealing with them in a structured and hierarchical fashion.

Some schools have a three-strike system:

1 The first strike is a verbal warning for poor behaviour, failing to follow instructions, being mildly rude/answering back, etc.

2 The second strike will result in a written punishment or a punishment meted out by the classroom teacher.

3 The third strike is a formalised detention that is recorded. This will occur in a lunch hour, after school or even on a Saturday morning in some cases.

The on-call system

More extreme poor behaviour could result in an on-call where another teacher is called in to intervene. An on-call system is common in a secondary school. It is where senior staff and members of the pastoral team are on an on-call timetable/rota and will be available to support any staff who may require help with a difficult pupil or class at that time. The on-call system also means that if there is another type of emergency where staff might need support there is someone available. This on-call system might occur formally in a large primary school but in many smaller schools primary staff work closely and informally to support each other.

An on-call member of staff will normally remove the pupil from the classroom and either place them with another teacher in the department (normally the head of department or faculty) or they may take them to a designated place. In some schools pupils are made to sit outside the office of the senior member of staff on call where they carry on with work given

Referral to an educational psychologist and the EBP

In some cases the school may decide that a referral to an educational psychologist (**EP**) is advisable. When this occurs it is important to call a meeting of the pupil, parent, EP and relevant staff to put in place an EBP that will be followed. This is similar to a contract that is negotiated between all parties. Although schools try to avoid exclusions, if a pupil is seriously undermining the ethos of the school there may be no alternative. If an exclusion is to be successful the school has to show that it has put in place strategies like this to support the pupil but that, despite these, the pupil has failed to conform to the demands of the school.

It is important that the pupil understands the seriousness of an EBP and that it is not a normal occurrence within a school, but something that has had to be devised and implemented for them exclusively. In some cases where pupils are behaving so badly that they are at the point of exclusion, it is normal to limit the timetable of the pupil to a few days or sessions a week. This puts a lot of pressure on the family who have to arrange transport to and from school at inconvenient times but may be essential, as the child cannot behave for sustained periods of time at that stage of the EBP.

While this is one way of managing a serious behaviour problem within a school, pupils do not have to see an EP to have an EBP. Some pupils who have emotional problems caused by their home circumstances coupled with poor behaviour may also have similar plans and maybe involved with Social Services through family group conferencing or with other groups who support pupil learning.

Read the school behaviour policy

The above information is intended to give you an overview of how behaviour problems may be dealt with in a school. In most schools the majority of children come to school ready to learn and will cause few behaviour problems. Before you begin in your school it is important to read any behaviour policy and make sure that you are fully aware of any rewards or sanctions that are in place. Discuss fully with your line manager how pupils who misbehave are dealt with. In a secondary school each department may operate its own detention for pupils who misbehave or fail to complete homework, as well as being part of a whole school system. Primary schools, especially large ones, may also have similar systems to those in secondary schools to ensure that order and good behaviour are maintained.

Schools that are successful in terms of achieving the best results for their pupils and enabling them to attain their potential will have clear and established behaviour policies that will be applied consistently by the staff. Pupils therefore have a clear idea of what is expected of them while they are in school and clearly get the message that poor behaviour is not allowed to interfere with learning.

Promoting positive learning: sanctions and rewards

Many schools, both primary and secondary, have realised that they need to do more to encourage pupils to want to learn. Some have adopted a system called promoting positive learning (**PPL**). This system relies on mutual respect between staff and pupils and on staff working positively with pupils to ensure good learning outcomes. Staff involved in the system are encouraged to use positive praise to reinforce good behaviour and ensure that maximum learning occurs. As a guideline, it is suggested that in any lesson a teacher should be trying to use positive praise three times more often than they use negative reprimands or comments. In schools where this system has been adopted staff have agreed rewards for attendance, sustained good effort and good learning outcomes. In a primary school these could be stars on a chart in the classroom, in a pupil's book, and so on. It may also be a merit/star based system where pupils gain so many merits/stars, which will entitle them to a small reward of some kind (eg free pens, pencils, entry into a prize draw). In some secondary schools funding has been sought and this finances end-of-term merit draws for a bike, DVD player, and so on. This is sometimes coupled with a commendation system where teachers/departments identify pupils who have worked well and these pupils receive a letter home to their parents highlighting their achievement. However, many schools have found that pupils like the commendations but not the publicity that accompanies it!

As is the case with so many systems, schools will adopt and adapt a system that best suits their own ethos and needs. In one secondary school the merit system is used for the first three years and then in Years 10 and 11 pupils are awarded credits in card form. The subject teacher signs these credits and the pupil hands them in to their head of year. At the end of each term there is a prize draw so the more credits a pupil has, the higher their chance of winning the star prize is. Star prizes have included a holiday for four to Disneyland, France, as well as a chauffeur driven limousine for the end of Year 11 leavers' ball.

Pupil planners

Pupil planners have also become popular in secondary schools as a way of keeping parents informed about behaviour and merits gained. Pupils are given a planning diary for the year – usually a weekly diary with additional room for comments which parents and form teachers sign every week. In it parents record reasons for absence and teachers record merits awarded or information about behaviour, concerns about homework, and so on. These planners can also be purpose-made for the school and a school calendar of events is normally included as well as information for parents about school policies. Many schools also include the **home/school agreement** in planners as well as information regarding the school's expectations about the conduct of its pupils.

> The home/school agreement is a statutory contract between pupils/parents and the school outlining what each party agrees should occur throughout the year. Ensure that you are familiar with its content.

Planners are a useful way of keeping in touch with parents to share any concerns a teacher has about a pupil's progress.

Preparing to face a class

Having familiarised yourself with the school behaviour policy, found out as much as you can about the class you are about to teach and prepared the lesson well, you are now ready to think about entering the classroom. However, you are not quite in the door yet!

Some experienced teachers suggest introducing a set of rules and regulations over the first few days or lessons with a class. It is important that all teachers think about what is going to be appropriate in their class. Teachers who teach a practical subject might impose different rules to others who do not. Think about how pupils will enter and exit your lesson. How will you start the lesson and how you will end it? Try to make that a standard routine. Good practice suggests that the opening of a lesson should involve a clear statement of the learning intention which could be written on the board, given to each child on a piece of paper or merely stated. Good practice also suggests that a plenary session at the end of a lesson to consolidate the learning is important. Planning a lesson to include time for a good introduction and a good summary is going to be an important contributor to instilling good classroom management. However, in the first lesson it is important to make your expectations explicit to pupils.

These **rules are** available on the website to download and customise for use in your own class.

Here are some rules that are important in any lesson. They should be shared with pupils and could form the basis of your code of conduct.

Rules for sharing with your class

Pupils must:

- turn up with the necessary equipment. In primary schools much equipment may be provided, even so specialist kit may be needed on specific days (eg for PE or games) and ensuring this happens is important.
- behave appropriately at all times without nudging each other or distracting others from working.
- enter and leave the classroom in an orderly fashion.
- sit down and get equipment and books out ready for learning to begin.
- not speak while the teacher is talking.
- not shout out.
- not make sounds that are distracting whilst others are working, like whistling, tapping pens, etc.
- not answer back.
- do what the teacher says – if a pupil is asked to move, then they should follow that instruction, as there will be a reason for it.
- complete learning work to the best of their ability.
- complete homework on time.

The teacher is in charge of the teaching and the organisation of the classroom – pupils need to be clear about this.

Clearly outline the sanctions that you will use if pupils do not comply. This may include a reference to school sanctions. Knowing the school behaviour policy, and reminding pupils that you know it, sends out a powerful message about how efficient and prepared you are. Finally, behave well as a teacher and as you would expect others to behave.

Body language, voice and eye contact

Now having prepared your lesson and thought about what rules and regulations are appropriate it is important to think about what impression you are likely to have on a class. First impressions are important. Imagine if you went to a doctor's surgery and the doctor was dressed in a scruffy pair of jeans and dirty crumpled shirt, there were documents strewn everywhere and your notes could not be found. What impression are you gaining of their expertise and professionalism? Imagine if when they talk to you they mumble a lot, repeat themselves and do not maintain eye contact – what would you think? The way a teacher dresses, addresses the class and their body language tells pupils of all ages a lot about them.

Conducting a lesson is very much like giving a performance and needs initially to be practised. Try starting your lesson looking closely at yourself in a mirror. Look at your body language. Do you look confident? Imagine that you are looking at a class of 30 pupils spread out in a room. Keeping control is about having eyes everywhere and that is why getting used to scanning a room as you speak is vital to success. Immediately you are able to spot the pupil who is not listening to you and looking at them intently for a few seconds, until you have their attention, you will be able to say to them without uttering a word, 'I have you in my sights, watch it.' Eye contact is a powerful tool. Practise holding that gaze and think about what else needs to happen when you make eye contact. Your facial expression is going to change slightly. You are going to be conveying your annoyance/disappointment/displeasure that someone is not listening to you. Practise that look while looking in a mirror. Earlier it was suggested that you clearly announce to the pupils your rules and regulations. Where teachers are good classroom managers these rules became a woven part of the fabric of a lesson and pupils are overtly reminded of them when the need arises.

You will also need to practise using your voice. Good classroom managers rarely shout – bad ones do it all the time, to no effect. Teachers must have a good, clear voice and the intonation of the voice needs to be varied. Many well-known politicians have used a voice coach to retrain them into how to change a monotonous voice that can be boring and non-effective into a powerful tool for persuasion. In the case of a teacher, the voice is used to impart information and to maintain control: it needs to be clear and loud, and teachers have to project their voices. (This need to project the voice and the strain it puts on vocal chords is the reason why new teachers suffer so much from sore throats and husky voices in the first year or so of teaching.) It is the change in tone, coupled with eye contact and, if necessary, an additional verbal direction that tells a child that they have overstepped the mark. Raising the voice is unnecessary when a teacher knows how to change the tone of their voice successfully.

If you are currently in training, then it is helpful to work with other new teachers to practise starting lessons and using eye and voice control. Discuss with each other how successful you feel you have been.

First steps in achieving class control

Make sure that you have what you need for your lessons:

- a lesson plan
- worksheets/resource material – plenty of these and copies of worksheets from previous lessons if this is not the first lesson with the class
- a register of names
- a contact if you need help or support in the lesson
- spare equipment for pupils who may not have a pen or pencil
- spare paper and exercise books
- a list of your own rules and regulations.

If you are a newly appointed teacher and have a classroom of your own remember that in addition to all the above you will want your classroom space to give out a powerful message about the type of teacher you are. Interesting posters, key words and teaching materials kept in an orderly fashion are all important in creating the right impression. Finally, areas on the wall that are ready to showcase pupils' work are essential. Pupils of all ages like to see their work displayed: it suggests to them that their work is valued and that you care.

The next chapter is about how to avoid certain situations developing in your classroom as well as how to cope with the ones that you can't avoid.

Time to reflect

Before you read the next chapter consider the following questions:

- ✔ Have you read your school's behaviour policy?
- ✔ Has the school got one or is it an informal system operated in an *ad hoc* fashion?
- ✔ What have you learnt about the exclusion process in a school?
- ✔ Why is exclusion a step that should not be taken lightly?
- ✔ Are there any strategies referred to that you feel might work well in your classroom?
- ✔ What rules are going to be important in your classroom?
- ✔ Think back to when you were in school. Who were the teachers who made a good or bad impression on you? What did they do to influence you in this way? What lessons can you learn from their practice?

References and further reading

Audit Commission, 'Misspent youth', available from: **http://www.audit-commission.gov.uk**.

Chapter 11

Behaviour Management – Teachers Rule, OK!

What will you find in this chapter?

✔ The cardinal rules of classroom management.

✔ Why is the first lesson so important?

✔ What else matters in your classroom?

✔ How to cope with the 'hard' class.

✔ Using a notebook to record misbehaviour.

✔ Mentoring pupils who need help.

✔ Tackling pupils who bully teachers.

✔ Consolidating what you have learnt.

This chapter will help you win the battle of the classroom, take control of your pupils and establish an ethos where learning can take place. No matter how fantastic your lesson plan and how well you have differentiated the materials for your class – without discipline and good standards of behaviour it will all amount to nothing! As well as giving you clear guidelines about how to cope with your initial meetings with classes the chapter also outlines some common misdemeanours that can occur. Look at the scenarios and how they have been dealt with. These are intended to provide you with clear strategies that have been tried and tested and have proven successful. Now begin by reading the cardinal rules.

The cardinal rules of classroom management

Try to be in the classroom before the pupils. In a secondary school it may be possible to stand by the door and wait for the pupils to line up outside the classroom. The benefit of this is that it allows the teacher to control the entrance to the classroom and the way pupils enter the space. Do not block the entrance allowing just a small space for pupils to squeeze by, as some staff do: this is intimidating and pupils resent it. Instead greet the pupils confidently, then stand back telling them clearly to line up sensibly and then enter the classroom and sit quietly at the desk. In some schools pupils might not line up outside the room but come straight in. Whatever is the norm, teachers must control that entrance, as it is part of implicitly stating that the space belongs to them and the behaviour within it is subject to their control. Allow the pupils to come in but make sure that they enter in an orderly manner; any nonsense should be dealt with firmly.

Rule 1

The *first rule* of any classroom is not to allow any misdemeanour to go unnoticed or unchecked. If teachers let the small things go, the big things will occur all the more quickly and be twice as hard to eradicate. In a secondary teaching practice, student teachers will have a variety of classes to work with from different year groups, whereas in a primary school a teacher may work with a class for an extended period. Primary teachers may already be in the class with the normal classroom teacher and the transition from the usual teacher taking the class to the ITT student taking it may not be as evident as it is when pupils are moving from one class to another and the school day is timetabled rigorously. However, it might not be as necessary to establish such rigorous control in a primary classroom where pupils are in closer proximity to their normal class teacher and know this. In a secondary school, passing on information about misbehaviour to the normal class teacher is sometimes delayed because of the timetable and the movement within a school day around the school. This could mean that a class plays up a new teacher, feeling that punishment is further away, or indeed that they may get away with it.

Rule 2

Pupils are normally keen to see how new teachers perform and will want to settle so that they can weigh them up. At this point the teacher may want to formally introduce themselves by writing their name on the board. The *second rule* is never to enter into a dialogue about where you have taught or not taught before. If you do, you will need to lie - if they think you are new and inexperienced they are quite likely to treat you accordingly. In addition, the pupils will know that you can be distracted away from the classroom task and they will have displaced the lesson plan with one of their own. If the class does not seem ready to settle then that is your cue to ask them to face the front, stop talking and listen. If this does not work the first time, then you will have to use a sterner, louder and deeper voice tone. In most cases this will be enough.

The next step is to share with the class your individual classroom rules. By establishing your rules early you suggest to your class that you are an efficient classroom manager.

Rule 3

The *third rule* is one of the most important rules to establish – punctuality. Late pupils can seriously damage the start of any lesson and undermine the classroom discipline that teachers are trying to instil (see page 133 for detailed advice on how to deal with latecomers). A very good deterrent to lateness is to punish pupils by keeping latecomers behind during lunchtime or a breaktime. If a pupil was 5 minutes late then the teacher can 'fine' them 10 minutes. Do not do this the first time but warn them that this will happen if they are late again.

If lateness persists then increase the punishment and take the matter further. Primary teachers may not need to worry too much about punctuality, as the pupils are captive within one space for most of the time.

Remember that any punishment that a teacher suggests will be given must be carried through. Pupils who are threatened but not punished will soon become more and more disruptive as they know you bark but don't bite!

Rule 4

The *fourth rule* has got to be that pupils do not talk when the teacher is talking. You must be able to teach without a background of noise provided by pupils.

What if pupils call out in your class?

What do you do when pupils persist in calling out in your lesson or even talking across the class to one another?

Action

Re-establish firm rules about pupils who call out or hold conversations across the room. Some pupils will do this and will blithely ignore the teacher. Explain that the first person who does this will be punished. If you know this is a continuous problem and you do not think you can deal with it alone then ask for help. This may be by arranging with your mentor to remove the first offender from the class. This acts as a huge deterrent. Do not send the pupil out of the room but send a trusted pupil with a note to your mentor. Arrange for them to pick up the pupil.

The reasons

The presence of the mentor lends you further credibility and gives out a powerful message that you are in charge and you have others to support you. If you don't know who called out or made noises explain that the whole class will be kept in if the offender is not identified. It seems unfair but it is the only way to impose your will on the class and eventually the children who are innocent will force the offender to own up.

The sanctions

In addition to the child being removed it is important that you impose your own sanction. As the child is removed explain that you will expect them to return to see you and state a time.

For young children a few, short, simple rules will normally suffice, but it is still important that they are stated and that you draw your line clearly.

Rule 5

The *fifth rule* is that you must clearly assert that as the teacher you are in charge. This gives *you* the right to decide where pupils sit. You can explain how this might work. Sometimes you may allow them to sit in friendship groups, you may group them according to tasks in specific groups or you will move pupils who are not on task to prevent them disrupting others. This rule is one of the most important as pupils very often react adversely to being told to move or sit with other pupils they are not used to. However, if you remind them enough that you are the teacher and that this is your right – due to your role – then they are more likely to comply. The classroom teacher must have the sole authority to determine who sits where in any classroom without question. The younger the class the less likely it is that you will have to be too strident in outlining your rules.

Rule 6

The *sixth rule* should be that pupils answering questions learn to put a hand up and not to shout out. Pupils who are allowed to shout out will soon use this as a weapon against the teacher and oral work becomes a nightmare. Again the message has got to be one of orderliness and structure.

Why is the first lesson so important?

During the first lesson it is important to show that, as the teacher, you are aware of the rules that normally apply in the school and its sanctions and rewards. Knowledge of this kind is power and it suggests to pupils that the new teacher is part of the organisation.

This association with the establishment confers power on you that pupils will understand. In Chapter 10 you were asked to think about rules that you would establish in your classroom: now would be the time to include any of those in the list of cardinal rules suggested above. For example, another useful rule to apply is that pupils only move around the classroom when they have permission from the teacher to leave their seats. This avoids a lot of poor behaviour erupting simply because pupils are out of their seats to cause mischief.

In the first lesson it is also important to tell pupils what they can expect to learn over the week or weeks that you will be teaching them. In a primary school class it may be relevant to talk about the work for the day. However, as children get older teachers are likely to talk about the learning that will occur over longer periods of time. It may be necessary to link your scheme to a summative assessment such an external examination that they may be working towards.

Schools operate different systems and some schools will insist on all teachers starting their lessons with a **lesson starter**. The advantage of this is that all pupils come into the lesson and work immediately. This can be particularly effective with a disruptive class or in a school where behaviour is an issue. It is a useful tool for young teachers to use with difficult classes. In some schools teachers use **brain gym** to get pupils ready for undertaking the learning task for that lesson. Whatever the system operating in a school it is important to ensure that once the lesson starter is completed or the brain gym finished the learning intention is clearly shared and that pupils are ready to start on the main part of the lesson.

See Chapter 7 for lesson starters and brain gym.

What if pupils are late?

What do you do if pupils arrive late to your lessons?

Action

Do not stop the lesson except to say, 'You are late and I will need to find out why at the end of the lesson. Sit down please.'

The reasons

If you stop to find out where latecomers were then you will stop your other pupils learning. It also leaves the latecomers in a vulnerable position as they know that at the end they will have to account for where they were. Remember to tackle them or they will think they can do it again.

You are giving an overt message to all – lateness is unacceptable.

The sanctions

If it is the first time and there is a valid reason just remind them that lateness disrupts the lesson and it must not happen again. If it has

Remember, in all cases the pupils need to see you act and impose sanctions; not rely on a line manager who has already established their position.

happened before then you need to impose some sanctions in line with school policy or have some of your own ready:

✔ Write in a pupil planner for a parent to see.

✔ Give the pupil some extra work – this may be lines.

✔ Keep the pupil in for twice the amount of time they were late.

✔ If this continues report it to your line manager and seek help.

What if a pupil is passing a note?

What do you do if you spot a pupil passing a note to another pupil?

Action

Take the note away from the child but *do not* open it. Just say that you will not have people passing notes in your lesson. Tell the pupil that you will speak to them at the end of the lesson. The pupil will probably want to know if you will give the note back. The answer – 'I will think about it, depending on your behaviour for the rest of the lesson.'

The reasons

If you read the note it is likely that you will have to deal with the consequences so it is probably better to avoid this. If you tell the pupil that you will think about it then the pupil will avoid any further disruption as they know they will not get the note back, and if you read it they could be in worse trouble.

The sanctions

A verbal warning may be enough to ensure that this does not happen again. Sometimes it is useful to hold certain things over pupils by saying, 'If you are caught doing something like this again the punishment will be twice the normal, as you have been warned.' In this way you are almost forcing a pupil to behave for a while. In a difficult class this can be very useful.

What if your class has not done their homework?

What should you do if pupils have not done their homework by the deadline you have set?

Action

In all cases the class has to have some form of punishment for failing to do something that had to be done.

The reasons

This is a real test of your resolve. If the bulk of a class have failed to do homework then you have to act appropriately. This scenario can seriously impact on your effectiveness in the long term.

The sanctions

A good sanction is to try to find a time when you can keep the whole class behind for a while. This might be at a breaktime or lunchtime depending on when a lesson occurs. If it is a primary class it is easier to find a time as they are normally in one place and can be kept in more easily. A secondary class may have a different subject before break or lunch. If the timetable does not give a convenient point when the whole class is together then it will have to be told to return at a specific time you have set. In order to ensure this is taken seriously by the class it is worth stating that their form teacher or pastoral coordinator will also be told about the detention and if they fail to attend then a more serious sanction will be given.

A letter could also be put into an exercise book with a space for a parental signature, or you can use the planner to inform parents of your detention.

In a primary school a teacher may have access to parents when they pick up pupils at the end of the day. However, it is important to ensure fairness – it would be unfair to tell one parent while another pupil whose parents do not come to the school remain unaware of their child's failure to complete homework. Sanctions need to be carefully thought through.

What if a pupil you teach is on report?

What do you do when the pupil presents the report card to you at the beginning of the lesson?

Action

Sign it with the highest mark/grade/comment you can and say that you expect them to live up to that comment or you will change it.

The reasons

It suggests that high standards of behaviour are expected in your lessons as the norm. Pupils live up to the expectation if you have faith in them: if they don't the sanction is predetermined!

The sanctions

There will not normally be any because most children will want to live up to your high expectations of them. If, however, despite you writing a great comment they then disrupt the lesson, change the comment and let the person who has put them on report do the rest. Reports are usually monitored on a daily basis and the reporter and their parents will see any adverse comments and act accordingly.

What if you ask a child to move and they refuse?

What should happen if a pupil refuses to obey an instruction?

Action

Pupils have to realise that you are the lead professional in the classroom and will decide where people will sit. Remind the pupil that one of your rules is that you decide seating arrangements. Do not shout but say this very firmly and indicate with your eyes and facial expression that you are not happy. Remind the pupil that you have asked them to move and that you are not discussing it or negotiating but telling them to move. The next statement is: 'I am waiting – this is your final warning. You are now wasting my teaching time and the other pupils' learning time.' If the child refuses to move then you need to state that they are now in serious trouble and will be punished. If at this point the pupil *does* move, ask them to stay behind at the end of the lesson. At that time explain that though you were pleased they finally did act as you had expected them to, you do not expect that type of behaviour. Suggest that you are not going to punish them at this point but you are recording the incident and if there is a repeat of it, then serious actions such as contacting home and detentions will occur. However if they do not move and your school operates an on-call system, now is the time to say: 'You are already in serious trouble with me and will have to complete a punishment – but this is your last chance. If you still fail to obey instructions than you will be punished by the on-call teacher.'

The reasons

Sometimes children have bad days, as we all do. A child may refuse to act straight away and occasionally it is possible to get them to review a hasty decision and move. When they do this you are in a win-win situation as you can now praise their good sense but also use their first poor reaction to you in the future, if necessary. You do not always have to punish there and then. It is useful to say that if they continue to behave and there is no repeat of this situation you will forget about it. If they behave badly again then both misdemeanours will be recounted! In the case of the pupil who flatly refuses, they have to learn that there are rules and that they have to obey them. They will need to be encouraged to comply with a teacher's reasonable request to sit where instructed.

The sanctions

If your school has an on call system now is the time to use it. If it does not, then you will need to get your line manager to work with you. The child should really be removed from the class and an example made of them. The parents should also be informed as refusing to follow an instruction like this is a serious breach of discipline. The child may also be expected to complete a detention for you personally and in some cases they may be kept out of mainstream classes all day or even sent home. When pupils behave this badly the individual class teacher should be able to rely on whole school support from middle and senior managers.

What else matters in your classroom?

Teachers who are firm but fair and have a sense of humour are those who are most likely to win the hearts and minds of pupils. Some books on behaviour suggest that you have to make a choice between being scary and firm, or firm but fun. The reality might be somewhere between the two where a good classroom manager is firm initially, so that they establish clear boundaries and do not suggest that they can be manipulated. They may even show a hint of the scary if a pupil misbehaves. Finally, with good structures in place a teacher can introduce a little more of their personality into the teaching to show a sense of humour and a more human aspect. This comes with a health warning. If a teacher comes across as too funny initially this can be confused with being easy-going and a pushover. A teacher's job is not to try to be top of the popularity stakes. Teachers whose classrooms are orderly, safe places, where the ethos is laden with teaching and learning, and where pupils are treated with respect and can succeed, will win those stakes hands down. Pupils like teachers who teach and to be where the pupils learn!

Other things to consider:

- Being fair and unprejudiced. Pupils know when a teacher is 'talking down' to them or feels that they are superior.
- Motivating pupils by showing that you want them to succeed inside and outside your classroom and care about them as individuals, but not being too familiar.
- Not making unfair comparisons between one class and another, or one pupil and their sibling or friend, and not being influenced by others who do.
- Applying the same sanction for the same misdemeanour.
- Not backing a child into a corner so that a confrontation is inevitable.
- Not losing your temper. Most good classroom managers shout at some point for effect – not because they are 'really' mad! Most good classroom managers would be worthy Oscar winners.
- Using your head to manage, not your heart, and remembering that you are the adult and should behave accordingly. What pupils want from you is an expert who is in control of the class and sets boundaries.
- Showing through your lesson planning and marking that you are working hard for the good of the pupils. They are more likely to play up a teacher who is making no effort.
- Convincing pupils that increased good behaviour will be in their own interest.

Good clear transitions make a difference.

Lessons can go wrong when teachers are moving the pupils on from one learning task to another. It is important to make it very clear that you are moving forward. It may be that pupils have written some answers and now you want them to mark the answers as a class, or for pupils to work in pairs to assess their work. With younger classes, or when you are still establishing yourself, it is useful to halt the lesson and ask all pupils to stop what they are doing and face the front ready for the next instruction. Once the instruction has been given it is important to ensure that all pupils know what they are expected to do and a question like 'Is everybody clear what we are doing next?' is posed. There is a joke that suggests that teachers stand out in a crowd because they are the only ones to repeat an instruction three times. Hopefully, twice should be enough!

Don't forget that setting timed tasks is important for keeping pupils focused and on task.

What if a child is caught using a mobile phone in the classroom or listening to an MP3 player?

What do you do when a pupil is texting or talking on a mobile, or using headphones?

Action

Some schools have rules that apply to this and you will have to follow them. Normally it is expected that the object is taken away from the pupil. This can cause problems:

✔ If a teacher confiscates an object and it is stolen from their possession – from a drawer that they put it in for instance – then that puts the teacher in an awkward position.

✔ Many pupils can become quite confrontational if they think that their property is being taken away.

The reasons

The pupil knows that you are alert and that you do not miss anything going on in the classroom. This in itself gives a powerful message about your control. If you state that you are going to do them a favour this time but in the future you will show no mercy then you are being human/fair, but you are also warning of the potential consequences while avoiding the confrontation that might have occurred. However, if the pupil ignores your warning then you need to come out the next time all guns blazing!

The sanctions

If it is the first time, give the pupil a verbal warning. Suggest that if the object is seen in the classroom again or is being used then a school sanction will follow. The object will be taken and because they have been warned beforehand this sanction will be increased.

What if a fight breaks out in your classroom?

Sometimes, with the best discipline in the world, pupils will be overtaken by emotion and a fight will flare up.

Action

If there is a problem as the pupils enter the room and before anything starts then insist that pupils sit far away from each other and warn them about your classroom rules. Later in the lesson try to find out discretely from each of them what the problem is. Prevention is better than cure. If necessary, involve another member of staff to ensure that when they leave your room to go elsewhere they will not fight.

The reasons

Your aim must be to ensure the safety of your pupils. If it is too late for that you will need to get between the pupils and break up the fight. If this proves impossible then you will need to send for support from a nearby classroom. If the pupils are older then you will normally find that other pupils will be there to help.

The sanctions

For such a serious breach of conduct someone in authority within a primary or secondary school normally applies the sanction. This could be a deputy headteacher or a pastoral coordinator in a secondary school. In a secondary school, sanctions can include fixed-term exclusions. The term will be determined by the pastoral coordinator in consultation with a senior member of staff and will depend on the severity and reasons for the fight.

What if a child truants your lesson and you find out?

What do you do when you realise a pupil is missing?

Action

Do not let pupils get away with it. You should be omnipresent and omnipotent. Good classroom managers know everything there is to know about a pupil's behaviour.

If a school suspects that a child is truanting they must inform the parent or guardian straightaway. If it fails to do this and a pupil is then injured or worse, then as the school is *in loco parentis* it could end up in court.

The reasons

You are in charge of the pupils on your register at the time you are supposed to teach them and it is important that you check who is in school and who is absent. Secondary schools sometimes operate a system where pupils are registered in every lesson and internal truancy can be picked up. Primary pupils can be easier to check up on as the class teacher usually has a close relationship with the class. However, in both primary and secondary schools, pupils who are in school often like to let a teacher know about other pupils who are not.

The sanctions

Most schools operate a standard punishment for truancy with parents being informed, and often in a secondary school a detention or report system for being implemented. It is important that you as the class teacher show that you feel they have let you down.

Dealing with persistent truanters

Dealing with pupils who persist in truanting can be very time-consuming for staff and very stressful if you are concerned about their well-being. Three methods that have been used effectively:

- Insisting that a parent/guardian accompanies their child to school and walks them from class to class to ensure they get there safely. Parents who are supportive will do this and those who are not may be persuaded when you remind them that it is their duty to ensure that their child attends school. Usually the warning that this will occur can be enough for some pupils.

- Warning a pupil that if they leave the premises and the school is not aware of where they are and feels they are at risk then the school will report the child as a missing person to the police. This is very effective.

- Using the educational welfare officer to support school sanctions and liaise with parents.

How to cope with the 'hard' class

In your career you will inevitably come across a class that is particularly difficult. This can be because the class has learnt how to work really well together to disrupt. In a class of this kind it is normally difficult to pick on one individual who can be disciplined seriously enough to make an example of them. This is usually because pupils have become adept at moving the disruption around the class so that no single person is wholly responsible. In a situation like this it is difficult to break this cycle. Normally, it is the golden rule *not* to punish a whole class for the misdemeanours of a few but in this situation it might be the only way to stop the nonsense.

As a new teacher it is important to ensure that you have discussed any problems of this kind with a line manager. Discuss the problem pupils and the sanctions that have been put in place already to try to ensure better behaviour. It is important that there has been a strategy to encourage the class to comply and that any pupils have been punished where possible. In a school with a three-strike type system this might mean that pupils have already had some form of low-level sanction. The trouble with a class like this is that because the pupils move the disruption around the room constantly, what you are left with is a persistent low-level disruption that becomes a disaster zone for the teacher.

In a situation like this the teacher has to confront the class and discuss what has been decided to bring them back into line and ensure that learning takes place. This should be done with a line manager present for support and to give your plan more organisational backing. Before meeting the class, think about how the meeting might be handled. There are two options:

- A closed meeting – where you as the teacher are going to be autocratic and 'close down' the meeting so that you talk and they listen.
- An open meeting – where the class is allowed to put forward views of their own. However, this needs very tight handling so that they do not dictate the terms.

If the class is lacking maturity and is really difficult then the closed option is preferable.

Follow these steps:

- Explain to the class that their behaviour is unsatisfactory and that it is disrupting their learning.
- Explain that it can't go on and that the whole class is on probation.
- Pick out the pupils who usually disrupt and explain that if their misbehaviour continues their parents will be contacted.
- Explain to the class that you are now going to treat them as a team. The team has to work together to ensure that learning takes place and that it hasn't happened. Learning is going to take place from now on – or the team will be punished.
- If necessary, and as an example, arrange to have one of the key troublemakers removed from your class. They will be allowed back only when they can guarantee their improved behaviour. Explain this to the pupil concerned in private; but the class will soon know who is moving and it will act as a warning to others.
- Go over the class rules that you have established and re-establish them, ensuring that you all agree what will happen if they are not followed.
- Think about reorganising where pupils sit to ensure that no pupil is next to someone who is likely to get them into trouble. This can be negotiated; but at the end of the day you are the teacher with the ultimate say.

- If necessary, arrange for known difficult pupils to be put on report for that lesson. A report can be very simple and will allow you to put down a few comments about behaviour/attitude/amount of work completed/punctuality, etc. This can be done in both primary and secondary schools through a line manager or pastoral coordinator, or through your NQT or ITT mentor.

- Ensure that the class realises that if the behaviour does not improve then you will have no option but to punish the whole class. This may seem unfair but what happens is that the behaving pupils then become your allies in that they do not want to be punished. They will call it unfair and complain and your answer will be, 'I sympathise and understand but I have warned you what the consequences will be.'

A **printable version** of this sheet is available on the website.

Give the pupils who are the main troublemakers the '**I own my own behaviour**' sheet shown in Figure 11.1 to fill in. This makes them focus on what they have done wrong and how they have broken the rules. If they do not fill it in correctly then photocopy their response and send that to their parents with a covering letter. This action often prompts a focused response from pupils.

The form can be adapted to suit any age group and on the bottom you could include other sanctions/punishments that the pupil might get if they continue misbehaving.

Some schools already have behaviour referral forms and teachers may be expected to use them. However, it does not prevent you using the upper part of the form as a way of getting the pupil to face up to what they have done.

Using a notebook to record misbehaviour

Bill Rogers, in his book *Cracking the Hard Class*, suggests that teachers keep a notebook in which they list those who have misbehaved in a lesson. Then ask them to stay behind at the end of the lesson to discuss their behaviour. Following up interventions is the most important thing any teacher can do. If you work in a school that has a cover team in place then this strategy can work well for them. If they all keep a notebook they can periodically compare names and identify pupils who are causing trouble on a regular basis. A strategy can then be put in place to deal with these pupils; this might be designed with the help of a mentor, line manager, pastoral coordinator or senior member of staff (eg a deputy headteacher), depending on your school's structure.

When you keep pupils back it is important to think about how you will handle the situation. Pupils of any age can be surly and aggressive when they are kept behind. If you go in all guns blazing you will end up with a classic stand off which neither you or the pupil will win. Relationships will take time to mend and further sanctions will be needed depending on how the pupil has behaved.

I OWN MY OWN BEHAVIOUR

NAME OF PUPIL

CLASS

TEACHER   SUBJECT

DATE

In this lesson I broke the following class rules

....

....

....

Pupils in my class could not learn for . . . . . . minutes because I broke our class rules.
I did this because...

....

....

....

In the next lesson I will do the following to make sure I do not do this again

....

....

....

....

If I do not behave in the next lesson then my teacher is going to

....

....

....

SIGNATURE OF PUPIL ....

Figure 11.1 A sample behaviour declaration sheet

Start off by explaining that you know that their breaks are precious but that you enjoy a break as well. Explain that if you did not care about the class and their progress you would not be prepared to give up your time so readily. When you do keep pupils behind remember to leave the door open and ensure that you follow protocols for seeing pupils alone. Finally, explain what you will expect from the pupil in the next lesson and get them to agree to this. If you are using the notebook or making notes in a teacher's planner, that some schools provide as a standard document, then make sure you record this agreement. Keeping a record means that you can refer to it when writing a report on a child. It also means that you have your own record of class behaviour that you can refer to. Sometimes when you refer to a list of pupils who have misbehaved it is surprising to see who has got the most recorded misdemeanours.

What if you tell a pupil to stay behind and they refuse to follow the instruction?

How do you respond when a pupil defies you?

Action

Do not follow the pupil down the corridor but make a note that you need to see that pupil.

The reasons

If you do follow them, tempting as it is, it is likely they will not accompany you back and you will be in a situation that you cannot win at that time. You cannot manhandle a pupil physically and other pupils will see you with a pupil who is refusing to do as you ask – not at all good for your reputation.

The sanctions

Find out where the pupil is going to be at a time when you will be able to visit them. Go to the class and ask the teacher if you can see the named pupil. Teachers are normally supportive of other staff and will rarely refuse. Take the pupil outside and state that you were disappointed that they did not stay behind, as now they are in more trouble for failing to follow out an instruction that you had given. If your school uses planners, record the information in the planner. Get the pupil to have this signed by a parent. Fill in a behavioural referral form (if they exist in your school) because the pupil's failure to behave initially and then to follow your instructions needs to be shared with a line manager either verbally or in writing. Explain to the pupil that a detention is owed and that you will expect it to be done. (If pupils fail repeatedly to abide by the rules, exclusions can be put in place that are sanctions for not one misdemeanour but an accumulation of smaller ones).

In the next lesson after the follow up it is important that the class realise that you did see the pupil and that you have carried out your sanction. This is so that they are aware that you are committed to ensuring high standards of behaviour in your classroom.

Teaching pupils and managing classes is hard work. Establishing firm classroom rules takes time and a lot of effort. However, allowing the pupils to get away with things is in the end demoralising, stressful and eventually utterly exhausting. Trust in the fact that your efforts will pay off and classroom discipline for good classroom managers becomes easier as their reputation precedes them.

What if a pupil comes back from a senior member of staff to apologise to you for previous poor behaviour?

It is often hard for pupils to admit that they were wrong and for them to apologise can be a big thing.

Action

As a lead professional, however the teacher feels within, the right thing to do is to accept the apology and to suggest that in the future you trust there will be no repeat of the behaviour you have just witnessed.

The reasons

The idea of a pupil thinking that they can carry on behaving badly and that an apology can get them out of it is something that cannot be tolerated.

The sanctions

If the behaviour and the apology are events that are being repeated for the second or third time then hoping for improvement is clearly a waste of time. This needs to be discussed further and a strategy put in place. The whole issue of their behaviour has to be confronted and the sanction taken to a higher level. Pupils need to see the stakes getting higher as their behaviour fails to meet the required standard.

Mentoring pupils who need help

Mentoring schemes are common in some schools where they are used proactively to help targeted pupils with their learning. They are used for pupils who:

- need behavioural support to help them concentrate, control anger and/or focus on learning tasks
- have an education behaviour plan and some or all may have had some form of outside agency intervention from the educational psychologist. Pupils with a diag-

nosed disorder like Attention Deficit Hyperactivity Disorder (**ADHD**) may also be on medication.

Mentors meet with mentees to discuss what has gone well and what might still need working on. They can arrange for pupils to be supported in areas where they may be likely to behave badly, also ensuring that when things do go wrong there are strategies in place to limit the potential for damage on individual and class learning.

Some schools use staff (teaching or non-teaching) to help pupils manage their own behaviour and therefore improve the level at which they engage with learning. This can work well.

Tackling pupils who bully teachers

Though it is rare, it is true that there are pupils who are quite capable of running a terror campaign against a teacher. When this happens there is normally an identifiable group who between them intimidate the teacher concerned. Bullying of staff should be treated with the same degree of rigour that a school treats pupil bullying. Incidents of bullying should be logged and the culprits have to be brought to justice. Pupils can be guilty of all sorts of misdemeanours. They may knock on a door or classroom window on a regular basis, they may snigger or laugh as the teacher walks by, they may name call and, in severe cases, physically intimidate the teacher. The teacher may actually teach the pupil or they may not. Whatever the circumstances the teacher and the bullies can be brought together and the teacher then has an opportunity to explain to the pupil(s) the harassment that is being caused. A record of the meeting should be kept and the sanctions then clearly spelt out. Many schools refer to the bullying of teachers as psychological harassment and this is what it is. If the harassment persists then the teacher should expect that the matter is dealt with at a higher level with parents being called into the school and governors becoming involved. In some cases the teacher may be too upset to meet the pupils face to face and in such cases a senior member of staff will see the pupil(s). There should always be a time when progress can be assessed and the situation should be monitored on a regular basis for an extended period of time to ensure that the pupils realise that there is a zero tolerance to this type of harassment in your school. Like pupils, teachers have a right to feel safe, secure and valued in a workplace.

Mentoring the teacher

Mentoring can also work for teachers who may feel that they need help in coping with a difficult class or pupil, for example if they feel pupils may be starting to bully them. Here the teacher may have additional classroom support. An experienced teacher may work alongside the teacher, coaching them as to how to get the best out of the class. This can be an effective way of learning the tricks of the trade before a situation becomes threatening. In other cases the class teacher could discuss scenarios that may in future occur – such as being bullied by pupils – and, working with an experienced colleague, examine how best to deal with this in the future.

Consolidating what you have learnt

Managing pupil behaviour is a skill that is acquired over time and most teachers build up a repertoire of responses that they have used successfully. However, no teacher would ever say it was an easy skill to learn and it is certainly a skill that has to be used for the whole of a teacher's career. Managing behaviour is a bit like ironing – the pile gets smaller and the minute you think you have finished you have to start all over again! The following information may help to consolidate what has been discussed in this chapter.

In my classroom I could:

✔ Plan lessons well, differentiating them to suit the needs of the pupils.

✔ Control the classroom entry and exit and any movement around the room.

✔ Ensure that pupils are aware of the classroom rules and refer to them regularly so that they become part of the classroom ethos.

✔ Ensure that all sanctions threatened are carried out or pupils will not take classroom management seriously.

✔ Have a zero tolerance policy on disrespectful behaviour to anyone in the class – everyone deserves respect.

✔ Be assertive and confident in the classroom and look carefully at the scenarios and responses highlighted in this chapter.

✔ Seek help and advice if there are problems with a class.

✔ Strive not to lose temper with pupils. (If the lead professional can't control their temper, how are pupils supposed to learn to control theirs?).

✔ Aim to gain credibility from other staff by being able to control the class and carry through sanctions.

In my department or area of the school we could:

- ✔ Have a clear departmental policy for behaviour.
- ✔ Share explicit rules/rewards, sanctions with pupils.
- ✔ Support people within the department or teaching area when they are having difficulties by removing pupils where appropriate. Assisting through mentoring if necessary as the lead professional.
- ✔ Share good behavioural strategies and practice.
- ✔ Share innovative teaching techniques and good lessons – this can help reduce poor behaviour.
- ✔ Have a reference library of books that support good practice on behaviour management and teaching and learning.
- ✔ Develop staff through good staff development and inset. Encourage applications for grants, etc.
- ✔ Inculcate a no-blame culture so staff feel they can ask for help.
- ✔ Encourage staff to share responsibility for behaviour in their class and not pass it up without taking initial responsibility. Sanctions for everyday misdemeanours should start with the classroom teacher.
- ✔ Support staff by team teaching, lending them status through association by visiting classrooms to ensure good discipline.
- ✔ Send letters home to pupils who regularly make an effort and/or achieve well.

In my school we could:

- ✔ Have a strong discipline policy supported by rewards and sanctions.
- ✔ Ensure the SLG supports colleagues and is involved in taking high-profile detentions.
- ✔ Raise money for rewards.
- ✔ Provide a mentoring system for staff who have problems.
- ✔ Implement mentoring systems for pupils who have behaviour problems through a strong pastoral system.
- ✔ Put behavioural referral mechanisms in place both within school and outside through pastoral teams, senior staff and through the educational psychological service.

✔ Have zero tolerance of pupils who persistently prevent learning.

✔ Have clear hierarchical structures of sanctions that are consistently applied.

✔ Have individual behavioural plans in place for pupils who need them.

✔ Have contract systems/on-report systems/withdrawal systems/internal exclusion systems in place and supported by senior staff.

In my school I could:

✔ Promote an ethos of learning where all lessons are differentiated and where teachers use innovative teaching techniques.

✔ Promote sharing of good practice in behaviour management.

✔ Promote mutual respect within the school for the opinions of pupils and staff.

✔ Have a school council that is funded, meets regularly and is chaired by pupils.

✔ Put in place clear communication structures to disseminate information about pupils who present a challenge.

✔ Promote a 'no blame' culture so that staff who find some pupils and classes challenging feel they can ask for help.

✔ Present staff with behavioural strategies to help them with classroom management.

Time to reflect

✔ Think about when you were in school and the advice you have come across in this chapter.

✔ Think about those teachers who influenced you and whom you rated as good teachers. What was it about them that made them good?

✔ Think about the strategies you have read about and choose the top five that these teachers might have used.

✔ What structures did the school have in place to ensure that pupils behaved and that teachers were supported when they were having difficulties? Were they obvious to pupils of the school?

✔ What aspects of your practice could you improve based on the information in this chapter?

References and further reading

Cowley, S. (2001), *Getting the Buggers to Behave*, Continuum.

Rogers, B. (1997), *Cracking the Hard Class*, Paul Chapman Publishing.

Dix, P. (2007), *Taking Care of Behaviour*, Longman.

Chapter 12

Promoting Inclusion in Our Schools

 What will you find in this chapter?

✔ **What are the main policies?**

✔ **What is an enrichment programme?**

✔ **What is a school council?**

✔ **What is a charity committee?**

✔ **What are buddies?**

✔ **What are peer mentors, student counsellors and mediators?**

✔ **What is an anti-bullying policy?**

✔ **The Children's Commissioners for England and Wales.**

This chapter looks at the concept of inclusion and how schools endeavour to comply with the law to ensure that all pupils within the school, regardless of gender, ethnicity or ability, are given the opportunities and environmental conditions conducive to their achieving their educational potential. We look at Special Educational Needs policies for those less able pupils as well as those identified as being gifted and talented and how schools have established student councils and charity committees in order to ensure that all pupils have a voice and to promote citizenship. An extension of this is seen in the way schools now train buddies and peer mentors to act as a support to those pupils who may need additional help. Finally this chapter looks at a problem that at one time or another all schools will confront, that of bullying.

What are the main policies?

Pupils are all different and therefore the support one child may need to succeed will differ markedly from another.

Equal opportunities policy

All schools by law must have an equal opportunities policy (**EOP**). This is normally based on a policy that the local education authority will have issued as a standard to schools. Schools will then adapt that policy to reflect their own school ethos and the type of children it has to educate. An EOP should be seen as a working document. It should highlight how the school treats its pupils fairly, giving parity to all. These days it ensures that girls and boys have equal access to all areas of the curriculum and all subjects.

An EOP ensures that all minorities in the school are catered for and outlines how the school will do this. For instance, it may refer to children who are in foster homes and are referred to in documentation as 'looked-after children'. Similarly, it may suggest the intervention strategies that are used to aid these pupils. These pupils often need a lot of extra support and help to compensate for the problems they have had to endure in growing up.

All schools should have clear strategies for support. An EOP should also highlight how the school promotes inclusion of all races, religions and creeds within its moral, spiritual and cultural curriculum.

Special educational needs policy

Another policy that should be in place if we want to be fully inclusive is a special educational needs (**SEN**) policy. This policy outlines how all children who are less able and those who are more able will be supported. Most schools now realise that pupils who are very clever also need specialist support and a special programme of study if they are to succeed. These children are often referred to as 'gifted and talented'. Many schools put in place 'enrichment programmes' to cater for their special educational needs. An SEN policy will also outline how a school will support children with specific learning difficulties like Asperger's syndrome, autism, dyslexia and dyspraxia.

Anti-bullying policy

If schools are to be fully inclusive then all pupils must feel safe and protected and this means that schools cannot tolerate bullying of any kind.

By law, all schools must have an anti-bullying policy. All schools will at some time have instances of bullying and it is vital that these are dealt with efficiently and effectively and that schools have clear strategies for dealing with this issue. When a child alleges that they are being bullied the school must ensure that this is logged and all strategies used to overcome the bullying are also recorded. It is also vital that a school investigates allegations rigorously and deals with them. Legally, if a child thinks or perceives that they are being bullied the school has an obligation to treat that child as a victim and to deal with the situation accordingly.

What can we do to ensure that bullying is dealt with effectively?

✔ Record all instances and allegations and investigate this rigorously.

✔ Ensure that pupils understand that bullies and bullying will not be tolerated. Assemblies can be used to overtly show pupils the school's attitude to bullying.

✔ Ensure that when bullying is alleged and it is proven then the bully is punished.

✔ Make sure that the bully realises that if they then involve other pupils and get them to intimidate the victim too they will be punished further, as will the new bullies.

✔ Ensure that parents of bullies and victims are kept fully informed of all investigations and sanctions taken.

✔ If the bullying is persistent then more action will need to be taken.

✔ The victim can keep a small book to record all instances of bullying and all witnesses should be named in the book.

✔ Mediators or outside agencies may need to be called in to help deal with serious bullying, to help the bully and the victim and to put an end to the bullying once and for all. The local education authority may have experts in behaviour support or PSHE teams and these will be able to help. The police can also be involved, particularly if the bullying occurs outside school. In some instances, school mediators and pupil counsellors can get involved and this may help.

What if a pupil or pupils is obviously disrespecting or bullying another pupil in your class?

Action

Do not ignore this at any time. You are the lead adult and professional and you must enable a stop to this behaviour. Explain that in your classroom everyone is entitled to respect. You will not tolerate name calling of any kind. Tell the offenders that you expect them to stay behind at the end of the lesson.

The reasons

It is important that the offenders realise that what they have done is bullying. All schools have an anti-bullying policy and sanctions for bullying should be explicitly stated in it.

The sanctions

You must follow the school sanctions. In addition you may wish to bring the offender and the victim face-to-face. The aim of this is to get the offender to face up to what they have done and be told how this made the victim feel. This is more effective if you can get the victim to explain to the bully how they feel. If you feel that this is beyond you then ask for the help of a more experienced member of staff.

Racial incidents and those of bullying should be logged. Every school has a designated person in charge of dealing with racial incidents and pastoral coordinators or senior staff who will deal with bullying.

Staff inclusion

In a fully inclusive school staff deployment will also reflect this ethos. All teachers in a school, department or team will have an opportunity to teach all abilities irrespective of age but dependent on expertise, experience and qualifications. Where setting or banding is used staff would expect to have a fair range of classes and groups and not just be given lower sets that will not give them a range of experiences. In real terms, inclusion is all about giving pupils *and* staff opportunities to develop within a caring environment that values every individual within that organisation.

How can you tell that a school is fully inclusive and promotes equal opportunities (EO)?

- Boys and girls will have equal access to all courses and subject areas in a secondary school. Boys will be encouraged to take English at A level, as well as food technology, health and social care; girls will be encouraged to take physics, construction and resistant materials classes.

- Schools will monitor the progress of boys and girls and where there is an attainment gap will put in intervention strategies to improve performance.

- All pupils will have access to the resources of the school.

- Pupils of all abilities will take part in school musicals, sport and school trips.

- Pupils of all abilities will have equal access to exam opportunities.

- Able students in primary schools may be advanced a year or enriched in a specific subject. Newspapers report annually on young children taking GCSE examinations early.

- Able secondary students could take GCSE examinations early.

- Able students start AS courses pre-16.

- Looked-after children achieve at a higher level than the national average.

- Children from ethnic minority groups achieve at a higher level than the national average.

- Pupils who are very able are 'enriched'.

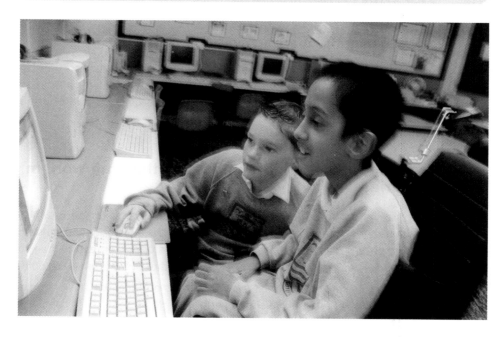

What is an enrichment programme?

Many schools, both primary and secondary, have realised that in the same way that they cater for the less able they must recognise and cater for the most able. Some schools have taken to implementing an enrichment programme. Schools identify pupils who are very able in particular subjects. They then try to develop this ability by providing extra opportunities within that subject area. These opportunities are often negotiated and might vary from subject to subject.

The **National Academy** for Gifted and Talented Youth, based at the University of Warwick, may be a useful resource for very able pupils (**www.nagty.ac.uk**).

How an enrichment programme works in one school

In one secondary school, teachers identify very able students in their subject. Each subject is given a calendared week for enrichment activities to ensure that work is spread across subjects and throughout the year. The enrichment programme runs through years 7, 8 and 9. Pupils who are very able across all the subjects are allowed to choose their favourite three subjects to be 'enriched' in, but it is rare for a child to need to be targeted in every subject.

Case Study

In primary schools, where classes have at most one or two teachers, it might be easier to put in place strategies to enrich able pupils.

What might primary schools do?

In primary schools pupils identified as very able across all subjects can be put up a year or given work to extend their learning. Pupils might study for a GCSE early but if this occurs the department must build in some form of progression for that student or students.

Examples of secondary initiatives that can work in primaries

- A history department gave a group of Year 7 pupils a range of well-known stories from history to read. They then looked at the *Horrible Histories* and chose to write their own horrible history based on one of these stories. These were then published and sold. A copy was sent to Terry Deary, the author of the original *Horrible Histories*.
- A music department took Year 7, 8 and 9 pupils off timetable to work on a composition of their making and to perform it.
- An RS department got Year 7 pupils to produce a PowerPoint presentation for other pupils explaining the different religions that they had studied in year 7.

Case Study

What is a school council?

Many staff and headteachers have realised that schools and pupils have changed over the years. Pupils are now more mature, informed about their rights and have, through their subjects and personal, social and health education (PSHE) lessons, been encouraged to voice their opinions about issues of concern to them.

School councils have 'empowered' pupils, enabling them to have a say in the running of their school. Where a school has a flourishing school council it meets regularly, has democratically elected members, a budget and will in many cases act as a forum for consultation and discussion. Primary and secondary schools alike have set up these councils. In a primary school each junior class usually has a representative on the council; in a secondary school each year group will have a year council and representatives from the year group will sit on the school council. A school council is a really powerful way of promoting inclusion in a school. Pupils regularly discuss issues to do with behaviour, litter, the canteen food, teaching and learning. In many schools the school council plays a part in interviewing short-listed candidates for posts including those of heads and deputies.

School council members might be asked to represent the school at internal and external events. Pupils involved in these events gain valuable social and interpersonal skills.

Although school councils are now well established it has been suggested that they should be made statutory in all schools. They work best when they are well supported by the school SLG and have some autonomy of their own. This might not happen if they are foisted on schools.

However, school councils face problems:

- Finding a focus for meetings and identifying projects that the school council can be involved in.
- Ensuring that in council meetings discussions are fed back to year groups.
- Ensuring that the school council is more than a talking shop and that it maintains a high profile.
- Ensuring that the school council members and their work is known to all.

In order to counteract some of these problems the following initiatives have been tried:

- Having a school council noticeboard that has photos of the representatives on it and highlights projects they are involved in.
- Putting a copy of the agenda up in all classrooms with the minutes of the meeting to follow.
- Having assemblies given by school council members who update pupils on the work.
- Organising and running one 'Big Project' every year that is determined by the school council. This could involve making over one area of the school, organising a merit

trip, etc. These are given a high profile within the school and progress is regularly reported on.

See the website for the Case Study on Langdon School, London.

School councils are helping to make a difference to schools by empowering pupils but they cannot work in isolation. Davies (1998 : 27) states:

What has become clear is that for a school council or other system of pupil representation to work, it must be embedded in a total school ethos of democracy, equity and concern for pupil and teacher welfare and performance.

As part of a whole school approach to inclusion it has been shown that instances of poor behaviour and exclusions have been reduced where school councils exist.

What is a charity committee?

Many schools also have a charity committee whose purpose is to raise funds for good causes. These committees have always been successful as they have a designated purpose and function and their outcomes can be clearly measured. Encouraging pupils to think of others is an important way to promote citizenship in a school and helps pupils to feel good about themselves and the work they are doing. In some schools, each year group identifies a charity that they will raise money and awareness for - this is a good way of encouraging competition between year groups and consolidating a year group identity at the same time.

Pupils in some schools have:

- sponsored the education of a child in a developing country
- raised money for local children's wards
- raised money for local disabled groups
- raised money for Children in Need and Comic Relief
- sponsored a Guide Dog for the Blind
- sponsored animals in danger through national organisations
- raised money for disaster funds
- raised money for Macmillan coffee mornings
- organised visits and fundraising events for children affected by disasters such as Chernobyl and the Tsunami.

In addition, many charity committees have provided meals on wheels to local old age pensioners, delivering them a hot meal and sandwiches two to three times a week.

Students have also helped maintain gardens for those who can no longer manage the work themselves. These initiatives enable a link to be made with the community and encourage the young and old to mix in a way that is mutually beneficial.

In some schools there is an annual commitment to provide parties for the local MIND group or local old age groups at Christmas. Pupils involved in ventures like this are regularly given responsibility for the organisation and fund raising that is expected. This obviously allows pupils to develop good people-skills and problem solve in ways that will be of long-term benefit.

Involving pupils in charity work encourages them to be good citizens and not to be self-centred and selfish. It also encourages pupils to feel good about themselves and their school and can be used to market the school positively. Charity work allows pupils to practise inclusion in a practical way outside school.

What are buddies?

It has long been recognised that starting primary or moving to secondary school can be difficult for some pupils. Schools have trained pupils to be 'buddies' for children entering their school. These buddies are taken from years 5 or 6 in a primary school and, depending on how they are used, from years 7, 8 or 9 in a secondary. (In a secondary school two schemes could operate:

'Being a buddy' - read a personal account on the website.

young pupils act as buddies but older buddies will get more training and will in the latter years in secondary school become mediators, mentors or counsellors.)

Buddies are trained to support and help new pupils to integrate into the life of the school. Trainers may be teachers with a high degree of PSHE experience or advisors from the LEA. Pupils are also trained to identify problems which they are not able to help with and report those to a member of staff for further intervention. The role is a responsible one and pupils who are trained are made very aware of this.

Buddy schemes have proved to be highly successful and have helped pupils who might have found starting or moving school so traumatic that they would have become school refusers. Buddies continue to act as a support mechanism for pupils and offer help on organising work, doing homework, preparing for examinations. They may act as an early warning system for pupils at risk of being bullied. Some primary schools operate a system called the 'Bus Stop'; pupils who need any kind of help turn up at the bus stop and a buddy will be there to help them.

What are peer mentors, student counsellors and mediators?

See website for Case Study on mentoring at Gorseinon College.

Peer mentors act as a support to fellow pupils. They are similar to buddies and are paired with a pupil for a specific reason. In one case mentors have been used to support students moving from secondary education to tertiary education. Pupils identified as needing support were in danger of dropping out of education completely or had specific learning needs that needed supporting. The ethos of a college is very different from that of a school and many past pupils had found this transition difficult. This was for a range of reasons including disability and weak English skills (when a pupil had moved here from abroad). Some pupils mentored had had home tuition in the past and other students had been involved in crime. It is possible to see that pupils being mentored could have a range of problems that needed to be addressed and that support was crucial if they were to succeed. However, using other pupils of similar age was seen to be far preferable to using adult staff and was more likely to be successful.

Mentors have worked well in all school sectors, not just in a transition situation. Mentors support students by acting as role models and support advocates, helping their mentee in a number of ways, for example giving pupils help with their reading and writing, study and IT skills. In nearly all cases there has been a marked positive change in the behaviour and motivation of pupils. Mentors have also benefited as the course that they have undertaken as a preparation for being mentors has in some places been accredited.

Pupils can also act as mediators/counsellors and help solve problems that can occur between pupils in any school. In all cases, pupils will undergo training and there will be a member or members of staff, depending on the size of the mentoring/counselling/buddy programme operating within the school, who will meet regularly with the buddies, etc to oversee their work and check that they are working within set parameters.

An Introduction to Counselling course has been accredited through OCN at level 2. An Introduction to Mentoring Skills is accredited at OCN levels 1 and 2.

Mentoring programmes can also involve teachers within a school who will work with pupils on a one-to-one basis to support their learning. Many pupils who are on the C/D borderline will be targeted in a secondary school for support. However, it has long been recognised that if we are to succeed with pupils who are seriously underachieving then interventions need to occur in the primary school where pupils as young as 8 have been identified as failing and have become disengaged.

The Children's Commissioners for England and Wales

Both England and Wales now have a Children's Commissioner. The aim is that the commissioner speaks up for children's and young people's rights. The commissioner's remit depends on the country but it has children and young people at the heart of the job. Young people as well as adults interviewed the Welsh and English commissioners, playing a part in their appointments. The role of commissioner has at its core a set of values.

To ensure that children:

- are safe from harm and abuse and get the opportunities and services they need and deserve
- are respected and valued
- have a voice in their communities
- know about rights and the UN convention on the rights of children

The commission also undertakes to look into things that affected adults when they were young. Through the work of the commissioner and the teams they employ, young people are being more fully included in the decision making that goes on in England and Wales. The aim is to promote inclusion, not just in schools but within society, so that decisions that affect young people are taken in an informed way and are influenced by those who will be most affected.

The fully inclusive school

To be fully inclusive a good school must have a sound and consistently applied Equal Opportunities Policy in place. This will ensure that boys and girls are treated equally, it will also ensure that all pupils irrespective or race, background or religion are treated with respect and are supported where it is appropriate to do so. This might manifest itself in the case of a school where there is a high percentage of traveller children. When a school is inspected the inspectors check that all minority groups within a school are treated equally and that appropriate support is being given. For instance some schools have groups of traveller children who may attend for short periods of time. The school has to show the care and support the school gives to the children and how it enables the children to 'catch up' on work they may have missed. They might also look at how the school supports those pupils who have a protracted absence due to illness. It is important that schools support all groups in a school equally. For instance if a school was seen to have a large discrepancy between the attainment of boys and girls - inspectors want to see that the school as part of its equal opportunities responsibility is doing something to reduce the gender gap. Where a school has not reduced a gender gap or has failed to even identify the issue, then they are not being inclusive and are actually failing in their duty of care to a significant group. Inspectors will want to look at the many different groups that a school may be catering for and in addition schools are now also expected to be self reviewing. This means that they montior how they are doing and if a school has a rigorous self-evaluation strategy in place, then issues such as these will be identified and targeted for improvements to take place. The Local Education Authority also has a responsibility to promote inclusion and will be analysing statistics for all its schools to try to identify issues that need to be addressed. They may monitor the performance of 'looked-after children' for instance against national norms or the performance of boys versus girls and so on.

An inclusive school will have a strong special educational needs policy that will refer to the more and the less able. Inclusive schools promote citizenship and normally have school councils where pupils are allowed to have a say in the running of the school. In many cases school councils and pupils are now involved in the appointment of staff to the school. Finally, inclusive schools take issues like bullying seriously and realise that if a child perceives that they are being bullied then it is incumbent on the school to investigate and support the child fully. Where a school is fully inclusive then pupils will feel respected and cared for and the ethos tends to be positive and will strongly support learning.

Time to reflect

Is your school or one you are familiar with fully inclusive? Look at the questions below and then make a judgement.

✔ **Does your school have an EOP and a SEN policy?**

✔ **How many strategies to promote inclusion have been used in schools that you are familiar with?**

✔ **How does your school ensure that gifted children are enriched?**

✔ **How does the school support the less able?**

✔ **How does the school support pupils who are lacking in confidence?**

✔ **How does the school promote racial and cultural equality?**

✔ **How does your school prevent bullying or deal with cases as they occur?**

✔ **Does your school have a school council?**

✔ **How effective do you think inclusion strategies have been?**

✔ **How do you know?**

References

Davies, L. (1998), *School Councils and Pupil Exclusions*, School of Education, University of Birmingham.

Part 4

Assessment for Learning

Chapter 13

Assessment for Learning – Marking for Success

🍎 **What will you find in this chapter?**

✔ Why we mark and assess pupils.

✔ What is an assessment policy?

✔ Formative and summative assessment.

✔ Assessment for learning: the research evidence.

✔ Sharing the learning intention and developing self-assessment.

✔ Questioning and formative assessment.

✔ How might a teacher manage the mark load?

✔ What gets in the way of using formative assessment in the classroom?

✔ Putting it into practice.

Preparing a good lesson and delivering it well is important and goes part of the way to ensuring that effective learning has taken place. However, it is not the whole of the story. This chapter is about how you know that learning has occurred through your assessment practices. Recent research has highlighted the need for good diagnostic marking and feedback to pupils. This enables them to progress to the next stage of learning. Marking closely and understanding what has been learnt and what hasn't helps to inform future lesson planning. Read this chapter carefully as it signposts everything that a good teacher needs to ensure that lesson intentions are shared, meaningful targets are set for improvement and that effective learning occurs.

Why we mark and assess pupils

Delivering a good lesson is only 50% of teaching. To be most effective good teachers assess pupils' work on a regular basis. Assessment for most teachers involves the reading of work that is in a written format, for a minority it involves the assessment of practical outcomes such as in a drama/physical education/technology-based context. All subject areas when studied at a higher level will include a significant written element to the course.

Marking, when completed regularly, allows a teacher to form a picture of individual pupils in a class, assessing strengths and weaknesses of the individuals as well as the class as a whole. It is important to remember that whether you teach in the primary or secondary sector, classes that may on paper appear to be similar in ability year on year, can in fact vary markedly in behaviour and attitude and this can significantly influence how you teach them and their responses to the teaching. Marking outcomes should be **recorded and stored carefully** as these will be used to report to parents at parents' evenings, and in interim and end-of-year reports.

> See Chapter 8 for more advice on how to keep detailed records on pupils.

What should marking a piece of work tell you?

- That the work is complete and the pupil up to date. If not, why not? Is it due to absence, poor organisation or disaffection?
- Whether a pupil is underachieving as determined by available data.
- Quality of the work.
- Strengths of a written piece.
- Weaknesses of a written piece.
- What a pupil needs to do to improve.
- The level or grade at which a pupil is working.
- Whether the teaching was effective and significant learning took place.
- What a teacher needs to do to improve the delivery of that lesson.
- What a pupil needs to do to improve their learning outcomes.
- What the next lesson will need to contain to ensure a successful continuation of learning.
- The literacy, numeracy and IT skills a pupil has in written work key skills are now important in all subjects.

Marking pupils' work on a regular basis is the only way to get to know pupils and their capability. Teachers who base their opinions on classroom contribution will fail to recognise able children who are not confident enough to contribute in front of a whole class. Similarly, they are likely to overestimate the ability of some pupils who, though confident orally and who are knowledgeable, may not have completed class written work or homework, and may possibly have less well-developed written skills. Marking work regularly gives a teacher the full picture and ensures that the able are enriched, the less able supported, underachievement is eradicated and lesson planning takes into account the needs of all learners.

It is a firm belief amongst good teachers, as well as inspection teams, that it is the job of the classroom teacher in the first instance to tackle underachievement in any classroom. In every classroom there may be an underachieving pupil who despite a teacher's best efforts will need intervention from a person other than the class teacher. They may need to be referred to a line manager within a secondary school department or to a deputy headteacher or the headteacher in a primary school.

Assessing pupil outcomes is also vitally important as it informs good lesson preparation. When a teacher does not mark/assess they are not aware of how successful or unsuccessful their teaching is. They may repeatedly teach a lesson that leaves the pupils ill-informed about a topic. For this reason alone marking/assessment provides essential feedback to all teachers (see Figure 13.1).

With the emergence of new teaching and learning techniques it is now possible to assess pupils' learning in a classroom through good questioning techniques or through the use of mini whiteboards. Not to be confused with interactive whiteboards these are small, wipe-clean boards similar to the old chalkboards that young children were once given to play with at home. These boards allow all pupils to answer questions and to get involved in the lesson. The teacher asks a question and each pupil writes the answer on their own board, holding it up when asked to do so. The boards can be wiped clean so they can be used over and over again. In this way, assessing the effectiveness of what

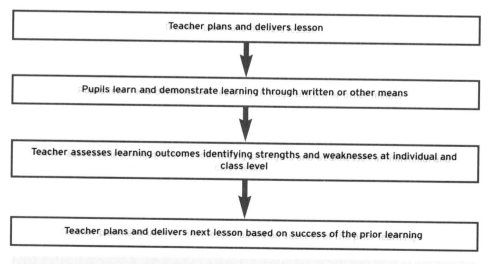

Figure 13.1 The assessment cycle

See the Top
Tips section on
page 178 for
ideas about
how to manage
your mark load.

has been taught occurs quickly. However, although this is a useful assessment tool it cannot be used all the time, assessing as it does recall and content-heavy learning. It has more limited use in assessing understanding where longer, more complicated answers cannot be easily shown in this way.

Having said that it is important to **mark regularly** it is also important to be realistic. Teachers will never have the time to mark rigorously everything pupils do so that compromises will have to be made.

What do we mark?

Marking allows the teacher to determine how successful their teaching has been and how much learning has taken place. Marking can involve looking at or listening to:

- classwork
- homework
- written work
- project work
- oral work
- practical work
- tests
- examinations.

Some teachers and educationalists have suggested that the word 'work' should be replaced by the word 'learning'. Referring to classwork in this way emphasises the purpose of the task not the process of doing. It relates the classroom activity to the process of learning more clearly.

Assessment should always involve the teacher in making a judgement about what learning has occurred. The feedback can be oral or written but it should help a pupil to progress.

What is an assessment policy?

Most schools have assessment policies. These cover all aspects of assessment including marking, setting of examinations and the way they are conducted, reporting procedures, tracking pupil progress, and so on. An assessment policy will outline how a school will mark and record marks and will try to ensure that there is a consistent approach where possible. In a primary or secondary school there may be standard proformas that will need to be filled in with any assessments made on a pupil. These may be used in parents' evenings and aid in reporting progress to parents. It is a statutory obligation of all schools to provide one full report on a pupil's progress in one academic year and it is

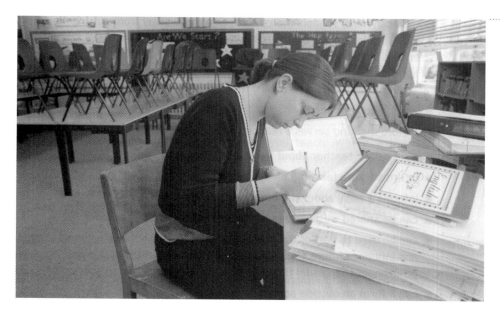

common for interim progress to be reported on in a parents' evening. Most schools also provide parents with a half-year report though this may include grades/levels without full comments. It is also statutory that schools inform parents of pupil levels at the end of each key stage. This external pressure on teachers to present levels or grades for pupils can pose difficulties when trying to use assessment in a formative way.

The assessment policy may suggest how frequently written work will be assessed and whether a mark, grade or level is awarded. In a primary school, assessment may be consistent across year groups, subjects and throughout the school with every teacher marking all work out of 10 or 20, or awarding levels or grades. However, this consistency is not found as often in secondary schools with an assessment policy; individual heads of department determine how work is marked. This is because external assessment by examination boards may be reflected in their individual marking systems. For instance, in English departments it is common to mark out of 20. This is because grading at GCSE is structured this way and many English departments mirror this. In science departments marking of practical work or projects may be out of 8 for similar reasons. Therefore the assessment policy in a secondary school will allow for greater flexibility and although assessment is going on, the awarding of levels/marks/grades may differ from subject to subject.

Many schools, both primary and secondary, insist on departments or class teachers having portfolios of evidence of the work undertaken throughout a key stage or year. These portfolios provide a benchmark against which new teachers can check that their assessment is accurate and that they are awarding the right level, mark or grade for a piece of work. These portfolios of evidence are also used to provide models of learning/exemplars of standards for pupils to learn from.

⬤ Is there evidence that there is room for improvement in assessment procedures?

Black and Wiliam cited a number of sources to suggest that inspection teams in primary schools recognised that groups of subject teachers and teachers from other countries were all dissatisfied with the quality of assessment that was occurring. Due to their work and that of others it is true to say that in many proactive learning institutions the value of formative assessment has been recognised and steps are being taken to improve the quality of assessment. However Black and Wiliam identified three difficulties that are still prevalent today despite the spread in the use of formative assessment throughout the UK.

First, in relation to effective learning:

- Teachers encourage pupils to learn at a superficial level and the emphasis is on learning content and not necessarily developing greater understanding.
- Teachers use questioning techniques that are not discussed within the school and are not critically reviewed to ensure that they are getting the best out of the pupils. (The use of good questioning techniques will be referred to later in this chapter.)
- Primary teachers were found to emphasise quantity and presentation of work over quality.

Secondly, in relation to having a negative impact on a pupil's learning:

- The giving of marks and grades or levels was emphasised *over* the giving of useful advice or on identifying the strengths and weaknesses of a piece of work.
- Assessment became a means for comparing the performance of pupils against one another so that the emphasis was on competing with each other and not on the individual improvement of each pupil's performance. Assessment feedback, in effect, acts as a demotivator for those pupils who consistently achieve at a low level.

Thirdly, in relation to the managerial uses made of assessment:

- Teachers are often able to predict pupils' results on external tests because these tests replicate the type of tests teachers use in school. However, often they know too little about their pupils' learning needs and how they can boost individual performance.
- The collection of marks to fill up markbooks and records is given a much higher priority than the analysis of pupils' work to determine learning needs, and too little use is made of assessment made by prior teachers.

⬤ Can we improve formative assessment?

The above and other research has suggested that merely adding comments to pupils' work and diagnosing strengths and weaknesses is not going to be enough to bring about the significant improvements that are possible. Real improvements will only come about when a range of strategies is used that change the culture of the classroom and the attitude of pupils to their own learning.

Research has also shown that a number of pupils are content to 'get by' and in order for formative assessment to work this classroom habit has to change. Pupils have to want to learn and the ethos of the classroom has to focus on what each pupil has to do as an individual to bring about their own success through learning targets. The ethos has to move away from a culture of competitiveness and comparison with others in the classroom to one where each pupil sees the relevance of the advice on what they can do to improve. It is therefore important to inculcate a culture of success where each pupil succeeds at a level right for them at this point in their learning, and equally a culture where pupils understand the need for them to work appropriately to bring this about.

A number of pupils do not aspire to learn as much as possible, but are content to get by, to get through the period, the day or the year without any major disaster, having made time for activities other than school work. . . formative assessment invariably presupposes a shift in the equilibrium point towards more school work, a more serious attitude to learning. (Perrenoud, 1991)

Sadler (1989: 14) pointed out that two things had to happen for formative assessment to be successful:

'Firstly, pupils had to realise that there was a gap between "the desired goal" and his or her present state (of knowledge and/or understanding and/or skill). The second is the action taken by the learner to close that gap to attain the desired goal.'

Sharing the learning intention and developing self-assessment

Once children have improved self-esteem and know they can achieve they then need to develop self-assessment strategies. Alongside this they also need to develop their ability to assess their peers. Self-assessment has been achieved with children from five years upwards and it has generally been found that pupils are able to assess each other honestly and reliably, and if anything are almost too brutal in their assessment. However, in order to do this well they need to be aware of the learning outcomes that are intended and need to have a clear picture of what they are doing and why. Therefore it is vital that teachers share with their pupils what the learning intention is. Shirley Clarke (2001) in her book *Unlocking Formative Assessment* states that the learning intention needs to be displayed visually for every lesson. She even suggests writing it down for children who are not able to read at that level at that time. She supports this by stating: Imagine you are learning a new language and the teacher is speaking that language throughout the lesson, so most of your understanding is derived from the spoken word. Imagine the teacher writes one of the words she says on a flip chart and points to it, again saying the word. The word stays on display for the whole lesson. What are you most likely to remember about the lesson, even if you could not actually 'read' the word?

Here are some further examples of that strategy at a primary level. Pupils are encouraged to come up with success criteria for their learning, although teachers, in some instances, might think it better to create these themselves when the context is too complex.

Learning intention in teacher's plan: To explore narrative order and identify and map out the main stages of a story.
Shared with children
Learning intention: We are learning how to order our own and other stories.
Success criteria: We will have ordered the story we looked at into our own story plan.
Aside (oral only): Ordering is an important skill in reading, writing and maths.

Learning intention in teacher's plan: To be able to use doubling and halving.
Shared with children
Learning intention: We are learning to use doubling and halving in everyday life.
Success criteria: We can show more than one way of doubling and halving.
Aside (oral only): This will help you in everyday life when shopping for two of the same thing, etc.

Source: Clarke (2001: 27)

It is vital that pupils realise the link between what they are doing and why they are doing it. Learning becomes less a set of exercises that are unrelated seeming to be just work for the sake of it and more a series of lessons that will lead them to fully understanding something. Learning has moved from ritual to something planned and meaningful.

Encouraging self-assessment

Once pupils have understood the learning intention the next step is to ask them how they will know they have achieved it. For young children the teacher may need to guide them by writing down a list of success criteria on the board and asking the pupils to choose the ones that they will most need to achieve. In this way, the pupils play some part in deciding what the success criteria are and become used to deciding these for themselves, albeit with teacher prompting. For older children this may not be necessary as they may be able to deduce their own success criteria.

The next stage in the self-assessment model is to ensure that pupils are able to judge their own learning against the success criteria. This should lead them to be able to fill in a self-assessment sheet like the one shown in Figure 13.2. What do you learn from this self-assessment sheet about the way assessment is being undertaken in this classroom?

SELF-ASSESSMENT SHEET ENGLISH Date 21st May

The learning intention was
We were learning how to order stories and make them make sense to a reader.

What I think I did well
I think my story did make sense and I did remember to use paragraphs which we are supposed to use in all stories. The beginning was good and Miss said it was the best one yet. I used good adjectives to describe the rain and the day and the boy. I know because Miss highlighted this with a blue marker which is good and the comment was good.

What I think I can improve on
My ending was a bit boring because I didn't really think about the ending enough when I was planning it.

My learning target
Plan the story better as the end was boring and I need to think about it more.
Check my work. Luke and me found lots of silly spellings and these are not good for my work.

Figure 13.2 A sample self-assessment sheet

From the self-assessment shown it is clear that:

- The pupil has understood the learning intentions.
- The pupil has understood prior learning about paragraphs.
- The teacher has clearly told the pupil what was good and has used oral feedback while assessing the pupil's work.
- The teacher has clearly shown the pupil what was good via the written assessment.
- The teacher, pupil and the class have agreed what the marking will mean, how the blue highlighter will be used and what it means.
- The pupil has also been involved in peer assessment where another pupil, Luke, has helped her to review her work and checked it for basic spelling and punctuation errors. The pupil has then decided that one of her other targets has to be to improve spell checking.

In the example above the pupil has determined the targets for herself but with classes who are unfamiliar with setting their own targets training is needed. In the same way as a primary teacher might help a class to determine the success criteria by giving them a number to work with, a teacher can do the same with targets. While assessing a piece of work a teacher can easily identify a number of evident strengths and weaknesses. Then the teacher can write a list of strengths on the board and a list of areas for improvement. A class can then be asked to look at the lists and pick out items that they think best suit them as an individual. In time the need to write the lists on the board decreases as the class becomes confident and 'trained' in self-assessment and target-setting techniques.

Questioning and formative assessment

Teachers can learn a lot about the learning outcomes of a lesson by using some very well thought out questions. However, all too often teachers ask questions that are very simple to answer and test superficial knowledge only. In addition, too little time is given for pupils to answer the question, sometimes with a waiting time of 1–2 seconds only. Research (Black *et al.*, 1998) in formative assessment has suggested that this is not long enough. Questioning that could be a rich source of discussion and aid the consolidation of learning for the whole class does not occur. Questioning becomes dominated by closed-type questions that at worst demand a yes/no answer and at best ask for recall of facts.

Research (Black *et al.*, 1998) has shown that for some teachers changing how they ask questions in a class and how long they wait for an answer is very difficult. They have got into a habit, which takes time and resolve to break out of. It is important to leave enough time for pupils to think out an answer and even to allow time for pupils to consult with a partner:

Increasing the wait time can lead to more pupils being involved in question and answer discussions, and to an increase in the length of replies. One particular way to increase participation is to ask pupils to brainstorm ideas, perhaps in pairs, for two to three minutes prior to the teacher asking for contributions. Overall a consequence of such changes has been that teachers learnt more about the pre-knowledge of their pupils, and about any gaps and misconceptions in that knowledge, so that their next moves could address the learners' real needs. To exploit such changes it is necessary to move away from the routine of limited factual questions and to refocus attention on the quality and the different functions of classroom questions. An example is a use of the 'big question': an open question, or a problem-solving task, which can set the scene for a lesson by evoking a broad-ranging discussion, or by prompting small group discussions, so involving many pupils. However, if this is to be productive both the responses that the task may evoke and the ways of following up these responses have to be anticipated. Collaboration between teachers to exchange ideas and experiences about questions is very valuable. The questions then become a significant part of the teaching, with attention focused on how they can be used to explore and then develop pupils' learning.
(Black et al., 1998: 6)

Consolidating learning is one of the most important class activities and is often given too little credence. For new teachers beginning a career, starting with good habits and sound practice seems sensible.

This chapter so far has been about assessment and how teachers can use marking to really inform their own teaching and help pupils to improve. It has also been about the research that has occurred in this area in terms of formative assessment. You should now know:

- why teachers mark
- what they mark
- how an assessment policy will determine your assessment strategy in the classroom
- what formative assessment means and what other strategies need to be in place to ensure maximum benefits for all pupils.

Look at Figure 13.3 to see what should be in place for formative assessment to have its maximum impact.

Formative assessment

Needs the following in place to be fully effective and to allow your pupils to attain their full potential

Shared learning intentions and a positive ethos	+	Self- and peer assessment	+	Good questioning techniques	+	Informed lesson planning	+	Target setting for improvement

Figure 13.3 Achieving the most out of formative assessment

How might a teacher manage the mark load?

This section suggests how to balance the demands of marking against all those other demands made on busy classroom teachers. It will also suggest how to deal with obstacles that prevent teachers from using formative assessment within their own classroom.

Deciding what to mark and how to mark it in a busy teaching day

Many new teachers complain about the workload of preparation and marking and ask how they can best balance the two. These top tips may be of help.

✔ Teachers cannot mark every piece of work rigorously.

✔ You should decide which learning tasks are going to be the most important indicators of learning and ensure that those are the ones rigorously marked.

✔ The teacher does not have to mark every piece. Pupils can be provided with marking guidelines or exemplar. Marking their own work teaches them the criteria that are important for success and is a learning tool in itself. (This is, of course, not possible for very young children).

✔ Take books in regularly to ensure that work is up-to-date and pupils can see that you are keeping an eye on them and checking for continued progress.

✔ **Record marks** in your own markbook or teacher planner.

✔ Ask other more experienced colleagues how often they take books in for marking and seek advice on balancing preparation and marking load.

✔ Identify what you will mark on a daily, weekly or fortnightly basis as being the most important and share this with the pupils.

See Chapter 8 for more on recording data.

How do you choose which tasks to assess rigorously?

To do this you need to think about the SOWs. In a primary classroom teachers will be delivering a number of subjects and therefore this may be more problematic. These teachers may need to choose what to mark on a daily or weekly basis. However, with a mature class in a secondary school where the teacher has contact for much less time the most important tasks may take a few weeks to complete. Therefore, it may be possible to determine what will be marked over a half-term period with all of the classes taught. An example would be an English teacher with a Year 10 class. They may, over the course of a half term, complete:

🍎 an imaginative essay

🍎 a coursework assignment

🍎 a comprehension as examination practice

🍎 a set text with associated tasks

🍎 language assignments intended to improve basic skills as well as additional other smaller assignments

🍎 oral work.

Managing your marking

✔ Peer assessment strategies could be used to assess the imaginative essay or the comprehension. Pupils could be given mark schemes for the comprehension and examples of essays that are very good, average and below average. Pupils could then compare their work against the criteria and models. Marking their own work makes pupils aware of the success criteria needed for specific tasks. These success criteria are transferable, as pupils will need to complete more imaginative essays and comprehensions. In most subject areas there are similar tasks that are repeated and where pupils learn the success criteria needed then this will improve pupil attainment. In terms of formative assessment, once the pupils have assessed the work they could then determine their own targets for the future by comparing their finished work with the mark schemes or exemplar.

✔ The coursework assignment will need to be marked by the teacher at some point and most teachers will want to see how pupils are doing when completing such important work.

✔ Language assignments could be marked by a class with model answers being provided. As a rough guide, it is important to mark books every fortnight and over a half-term three significant assignments are marked rigorously and detailed comments added for upper secondary school classes in a core subject.

✔ New teachers are not alone and it is important to use the expertise around, asking fellow staff how they manage the marking workload and how often they assess pupils' work rigorously.

✔ In a primary school you could assess far more than three assignments per half-term in a core subject as the amount of time spent on producing one assignment could be significantly less.

✔ Other assignments may be read through briefly and a date and initial placed at the end to show it has been looked at. It is important that parents and your line managers can see that you are looking at pupils' books and assessing outcomes.

Assessment is not just about awarding a mark, grade or level. Remember that there are a number of reasons for marking a pupil's book and assessing the quality of learning is only one of them. It is also important to see that pupils are keeping up-to-date and that there are no learning gaps. Some teachers suggest that class teachers mark books on a rota basis, marking all books but only assessing one-third of the books rigorously with diagnostic comments being added. From an organisational point of view this does not seem as easy a system to handle as the former but all teachers are different and ultimately it is for the individual to decide on the best system for them.

What gets in the way of using formative assessment in the classroom?

You may not be able to use formative assessment in a classroom because it is not in line with the school assessment policy or that of the department or line manager. There are still those who are sceptical about putting comments and not marks on a book, who know little about formative assessment or who do not feel it is necessary in their school, possibly because other initiatives are in place that better suit that organisation. In addition, there are those who run large departments or groups of people who feel that marks on a page provide them with a quick way of ensuring that pupils are learning and schemes of work are being covered. This is not the place to comment on whether this a good thing or not.

Formative assessment is not just about the effectiveness of comments versus marks and many of the strategies for its success discussed in this chapter can of course be used. It should also be stressed that because formative assessment may not be used formally in your school as yet, it does not preclude you from using it. Many line managers would welcome someone in their school who is keen, interested and able to offer new ideas. If you want to try out any initiative in your classroom it is worth discussing it with your line manager, who 99% of the time is likely to be fully supportive and interested. It is also worth remembering that if you are going to do something like this then pupil and parent support will be needed and information about the pilot and its reasoning shared. All stakeholders will need to help you evaluate its success at the end of the trial period.

Another reason why formative assessment can be problematic is to do with the nature of schools and the need for summative assessments to be made to inform reports. Summative assessment is used to assess pupils in order to rank them in year groups and for organisational reasons. Teachers using formative assessment often perceive a tension between the use of formative assessment and the organisational emphasis on summative assessment. The reality for teachers is that formative assessment has to work alongside summative assessment. One way of dealing with this is suggested in *Assessment for Learning: Putting it into Practice* (Black et al., 2003). Teachers involved in the project identified in this text tried to work out effective strategies for using formative approaches to summative tests.

What could you do to ensure that pupils use formative assessment to aid their learning for summative testing?

Some teachers found that despite using more active methods of learning in their classrooms pupils, when left to learn for tests, reverted to a passive role of reading over work. The teachers tried to restructure pupils' learning by getting them to identify clearly what they were confident about and what they felt needed more work. They used a traffic light system of red, amber and green to do this. These then formed the basis of a revision plan. Pupils were asked to identify questions on an examination paper that tested their red areas and then work with books and in peer groups to ensure they could answer those questions successfully.

Another innovative idea came out of research studies by King and Foos (cited in Black *et al.*, 2003) This study showed that where pupils are trained to prepare for examinations by generating and then answering their own questions these groups performed better than other groups who had not prepared in this way. Preparation of test questions calls for and develops an overview of the topic being studied.

A third innovative idea was to use the examination or test itself as an opportunity for formative work. This would work particularly well with mock examinations or tests conducted as part of a programme of study leading up to a final external examination of some kind. Teachers and pupils could look at questions that were done poorly and concentrate on improving the pupil response to those questions in particular. Peer marking of test papers can also be used. Pupils can then come up with a set of criteria for future success.

These ideas suggest that formative assessment and summative assessment need not be seen as being poles apart and challenge the view that they are so different that they have to be kept apart. Teachers have always been realistic about the heavy demands made on them to use summative assessment for a number of reasons and these innovative approaches reduce the tension often found between using summative and formative assessments with the same pupils.

Putting it into practice

The final section of this chapter is intended to show how teachers can use the information gleaned from this chapter within the classroom, the department and finally the whole school. To summarise:

In my classroom I could:

✔ Mark work regularly, tracking individual pupil progress and class progress.

✔ Use the assessment information to identify pupils who need enriching, support or who are underachieving.

✔ Keep detailed records in line with school policy to use to inform written reports and oral reports to parents.

▶

✔ Ensure that underachievement is dealt with. First, outline what a pupil has to do to catch up, then the sanctions you will implement if this does not occur, and set a deadline for this to be done. If the deadline is exceeded inform line managers and parents for further intervention to take place. Use the department or school policy to suggest strategies you can use or seek advice. Record all interventions made with dates for reference.

✔ Use assessment information to inform future lesson planning as this is vital to success.

✔ Use questioning techniques as suggested above.

✔ Use the reference list at the end of this chapter to help you become better informed about assessment for learning.

✔ Indicate always the learning intentions of the task.

✔ Encourage pupils to identify success criteria for their learning on the specific learning intentions – 'How will I know I have succeeded?'.

✔ Encourage a positive 'can do' ethos in the classroom.

✔ Use self-assessment and peer assessment strategies.

✔ Encourage pupils to set their own targets for learning improvement but help them initially.

✔ Encourage pupils to take responsibility for their learning.

✔ Use summative tests in a formative way as outlined above.

In my department/school area I could:

✔ Have a clear assessment policy.

✔ Outline how often pupils should be assessed and whether teachers should be using formative assessment techniques.

✔ Ensure that lesson intentions are shared with all classes as standard practice.

✔ Inform parents about how teachers assess in your department/area of the school.

✔ Use self-assessment and peer assessment strategies.

✔ Introduce proformas for pupil self-assessment and target setting.

✔ Introduce proformas for staff to fill in prior to parents' evenings that are standard and show that assessment records are being kept. (Parents are entitled to know what level or grade their child is working at and will probably ask for this information.)

✔ Discuss what constitutes good questioning in the classroom.

✔ Share good practice.

✔ Monitor the pupils' books for evidence of formative assessment strategies being used by all staff and to ensure the assessment policy is being consistently applied.

Although as a newly qualified teacher you will have no control over what happens in the whole school, the following suggests what should or could be in place to ensure consistency of marking and assessment. Formative assessment has been proven to improve standards and the following is something that all schools should be working towards. Many proactive schools are using both formative assessment and proven teaching and learning strategies like the standard sharing of lesson intentions to improve standards.

While on a teaching practice or in your school, you could use the final 'Top Tips' as a checklist.

In my school I could:

✔ Ensure that there is a clear agreed assessment policy that is understood and shared by all.

✔ Ensure that parents are aware of how teachers assess pupils.

✔ Investigate formative assessment strategies and, if necessary, introduce a pilot in the school to see how it would best fit the organisation you are in. Encourage staff to take ownership of the initiative adapting it to the individual needs of pupils, staff and the organisation as a whole.

✔ Ensure that pupils are encouraged and that there is a positive ethos working in all classrooms and that pupils are not disaffected.

✔ Ensure that learning intentions are shared and that self-assessment, peer assessment and target setting strategies are in place as standard practice.

✔ Ensure that monitoring of assessment is ongoing and consistent throughout the school at all levels.

Time to reflect

✔ Think about what you have learnt about marking and your own particular circumstances in your classroom and subject area:

🍎 What will marking tell you about each pupil?

🍎 What will you be marking?

🍎 How do you know how to mark a pupil's work?

✔ Have you seen an assessment policy and do you understand it?

✔ Does your school use formative assessment strategies or are they interested in finding out more?

✔ Do they use any of the strategies identified in this chapter for improving learning outcomes?

✔ What are the three most important things that you can take away from reading this chapter?

References and further reading

Black, P. and Wiliam, D. (1998), *Inside the Black Box: Raising Standards Through Classroom Assessment*, NFER Nelson.

Black, P., Harrison, C., Lee, C., Marshall, B. and Wiliam, D. (1998), *Working Inside the Black Box*, NFER Nelson.

Black, P., Harrison, C., Lee, C., Marshall, B. and Wiliam, D. (2003), *Assessment for Learning – putting it into practice*, Open University Press.

Clarke, S. (2001), *Unlocking Formative Assessment: Practical Strategies for Enhancing Pupils' Learning in the Primary Classroom*, Hodder Murray.

Perrenoud, P. (1991), 'Towards a pragmatic approach to formative evaluation' in P. Weston (ed) *Assessment of Pupils' Achievement: Motivation and School Success*, Swets and Zeitlinger, Amsterdam.

Sadler, D.R. (1989), 'Formative assessment and the design of instructional systems', *Instructional Science*, Vol. 18.

TIMSS-Beaton, A., Madaus, G., O'Leary, M. and Kellaghan, T. (1996), Third International Mathematical and Science Study, 'The consistency of findings across international surveys of mathematics and science achievement'.

Chapter 14

The CAT SAT on the Mat

🍎 **What will you find in this chapter?**

✔ **What data can we gather on children from birth onwards?**

✔ **Why do we use data?**

✔ **How can you use data in your classroom?**

Primary schools and secondary schools are now using extensive data which gives them a lot of information about the children they are teaching. This gathering of information begins on entry to primary school at a very young age and continues throughout a pupil's school life. All teachers are now expected to use this data to help inform their target setting and lesson planning for all pupils in their care. Interviews often ask new teachers what data they would expect to have available on pupils in their class and how they would use it. This chapter is intended to ensure that you know what data may be available and that you use it with confidence and full understanding of its importance.

The example on pages 188–9 is just one profile for gathering data on pupils compiled by one authority but there are other similar ones available. An early years adviser in an authority is the person who should be able to give you guidance as to what is available in your area. As the pupils grow older the emphasis on physical skills and personal development is replaced by information that has more to do with subject/skill-based learning. It is important that information is transferred through the school effectively. An effective transfer is one where all the knowledge about a child and their learning programme is successfully passed on to a new teacher, thus ensuring that the child progresses with their learning without 'slipping' back in any way. This also ensures that the teacher knows the new pupil and they will be able to plan a course of study that will present this pupil with a challenge appropriate to their educational needs.

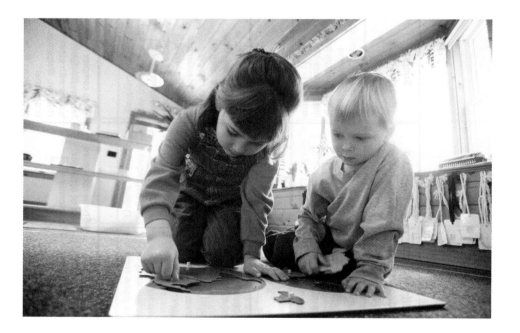

What other data can we expect to come across in primary and secondary schools today?

These are the most common:

- *Standard Assessment Tests (SATs) levels*. On entry to a secondary school the information on pupils that has been gathered in the primary will be trans-

Most people will be familiar with the term SATs or Standard Assessment Tests. However, though it is sometimes suggested that these existed throughout the United Kingdom this was never the case. For instance they were never used in Scotland. Look at your curriculum authority website to see how pupils are assessed at the end of key stages in your nation. Most nations still insist on some form of end of key stage teacher assessment even if standard national tests are no longer in existence.

ferred. This will include assessment of the pupils in English, maths and science, and a level has to be awarded. This has until recently been assessed by a SAT conducted nationally. However, although some parts of the UK no longer have tests or did not have them in the first place, LEAs will still want teachers to award a level to pupils to identify how they have done over the course of the two key stages or will want to see some form of summative assessment of their primary experience. This data will be used by the LEA and the secondary school to set targets for teaching and learning outcomes.

🍎 *Reading and spelling test scores*. These can be reading and spelling tests similar to those produced by the National Federation for Educational Research. Many primary schools and some secondary schools conduct reading tests on each year group annually. If a school compares these results year on year it can make judgements about its intake based on prior performance of years with similar/stronger/weaker results.

🍎 *Predicted grades or levels* based on prior attainment.

🍎 *Target grades/levels* set by teachers.

🍎 *Internal assessments*. These can be tests or examinations and will be reported on to parents once a year.

🍎 *Pupil self-assessment*. If pupils are to take greater control over their learning they have to learn to assess where they are at present and how they might improve in future.

🍎 *Tracking grade sheets* allow teachers to see how pupils are doing across a range of subjects and provide a 'snapshot' of total performance at different times of the year.

🍎 *Cognitive Abilities Tests (**CATs**)* provide information on a child's verbal ability (verbal reasoning – **VR**) and quantitative ability (quantitative reasoning – **QR**). These tests require the pupils to have a basic store of verbal and quantitative concepts and are more closely linked to what they already know. Finally, it assesses a pupil's non-verbal reasoning (**NVR**). This battery of tests assesses ability that is not bound by what pupils have learnt in school. It is best described as measuring potential.

🍎 *Attendance*. It is important to look at trends in attendance and if it is poor to intervene quickly to find out why.

🍎 *Behaviour*. Negative behaviour is recorded and in some case pupils will have education plans. These are plans specifically relating to behaviour and indicate how all teachers who have contact with a pupil should manage them.

🍎 *Health plans*. Some pupils have health problems that are above what is normally expected. In serious cases schools must put in place a health strategy explaining how they will manage this pupil's health problems during the school day.

Table 14.1 A quick guide to CATs and what the scores mean

Pupil	VSAS	QSAS	NVSAS
A	88	94	110
B	101	110	78
C	112	96	99
D	82	105	107
E	94	107	108
F	112	96	103

VSAS = Verbal standardised age score
QSAS = Quantitative standardised age score
NVSAS = Non-verbal standardised age score

Look at the scores shown in Table 14.1:

- two-thirds of pupils score between 85 and 115 (pupils with a triple score of 100 should access five A*–C grades),

- 12 points or more difference between VSAS, QSAS and NVSAS is significant: for two-thirds of pupils there is no significant difference.

What do the scores tell us about the pupils?

See Chapter 6 on learning styles.

- Pupils like A with low VSAS and QSAS but high NVSAS take off rapidly with early intervention to improve their literacy and numeracy skills. The NVSAS tells us that they have good innate ability. Pupils like A prefer pictorial representation and might be visual learners.

- Pupils like B with low NVSAS but high VSAS and QSAS have poorly developed non-verbal skills. They need support in the higher-order skills (eg problem solving, algebra). Perhaps girls are more likely to suffer here.

- Pupils like C with very high VSAS but lower QSAS and NVSAS may need support in maths, science and technology. Schools need to play to their verbal strengths here.

- Pupils like D may have specific language difficulties (eg dyslexia or have English as an additional language). These pupils would benefit from language support/reading programmes, etc.

- Pupils like E would benefit from language support.

- Pupils like F would benefit from numeracy support.

CAT scores can predict the following (Birchgrove School, 2000):

- The outcomes in key stage 3 tests in the core subjects of English, maths and science.

- GCSE grades for English, maths, science, history, geography and French.

- A score of 100 usually leads to five or more A*–C grades.

How can subject team leaders use data to improve pupils' learning?

Many new teachers find themselves in charge of a subject area. This is especially true of primary teachers. Here we consider how subject leaders use data to improve pupils' learning.

The role of the head of department is crucial as they have an overview of progress within a subject and within the school. They will be able to compare progress in English, for instance, with that in science or maths.

Heads of department or subject team leaders should:

🍎 Keep data in a specific file.

🍎 Distribute a second copy of all data they hold to those in their department or team.

> **Enrichment:** Some pupils are very able and they need special educational support in the way that we would support the less able.

🍎 Use data on a regular basis to show how the subject area is performing in relation to other subjects or how pupils are achieving in the subject.

🍎 Compare the performance of the same pupil in different subjects.

🍎 Give guidance on how to use data and what data are relevant.

🍎 Use data to highlight those pupils who need **enriching** and those who need supporting. It will also help to show those who are not working to their potential (ie are underachieving) and strategies can be put in place to remedy this. Those pupils' progress will need to be monitored and they will need mentoring.

🍎 Use data to decide where to place pupils in groups if setting is applicable.

🍎 Use data to decide what courses are appropriate for pupils. Sometimes subject leaders will change examination boards based on what the data tells them about the cohort and how it is performing.

🍎 Set realistic targets for the subject in national examinations/tests.

🍎 Agree targets (with the subject teacher) for the class, set or group and then check progress against the targets.

🍎 Compare the results achieved in the subject with national statistics or benchmarking data.

Most schools use data to improve their teaching and compare themselves with other schools. This chapter highlights some of the information that might be available to help you better understand the type of pupils you teach. Your school could well be using other assessment tests to determine how well pupils are doing and to predict their likely final success.

Time to reflect

Consider the following questions.

✔ Think about what data you have already come across in your school.
- Where is the information kept and how is it used?
- Is there someone who is seen as the assessment manager or expert?

✔ Think about the type of data that you would have to use as a statutory obligation. Behaviour plans and individual learning programmes must be followed and a review completed.
- What data would be most helpful in your classroom?
- How would you use these data to plan your lessons more effectively?
- Would you use the data to group pupils in your class so that more learning takes place?

✔ In interviews, teachers are asked about what data they might use to inform their teaching. You may also be asked why it is important to track a pupil's progress and ensure effective movement from one stage of learning to another. What would your answers be?

References and further reading

The Association for Achievement and Improvement Through Assessment, 'Baseline assessment', **http://atschool.eduweb.co.uk/aaia/index.html**

Birchgrove School (2000), 'Making performance data work', Birchgrove Comprehensive School, Swansea.

Birmingham Profile, Birmingham Local Education Authority.

Chapter 15

How Schools Use Data to Improve Achievement

🍎 **What will you find in this chapter?**

✔ How to use data to inform intervention strategies.

✔ How to use data to improve attendance and behaviour.

✔ How to use data to identify pupils who need mentoring and support.

✔ How to use data to identify pupils who need enrichment and support.

✔ Using data to determine the success of the school at all levels.

✔ Looking at value added in detail.

Schools are now data-rich and this should mean that they are knowledge-rich about the pupils who form the cohort of the school. Data is power; proactive schools can use this information to put the best strategies in place for their pupils. This chapter leads on from Chapter 14 to show you how schools can use the data they collect to inform best practice. It sets out to show how specific information on individual pupils can be used to bring about school improvement.

Storing data electronically

Good behaviour is vital to the success of any school. Many schools use information technology to store data electronically. These systems enable a school to store a variety of information on individual pupils and this can include negative behaviours and the sanctions that have been used in response to them. These data are important, enabling schools to track behaviour generally and identify the most common forms of negative behaviours. Schools can also track the success of various strategies that might have been put in place and can then review their effectiveness. Schools can identify particular year groups that may cause problems and track the behaviour patterns of individual pupils. Where pupils are involved in repeated negative behaviours schools will use data to support their use of external agencies to intervene and support pupils. These might include any behaviour support units that exist within the local education authority, EPs and those trained in behaviour management techniques. Extreme sanctions include: internal exclusions where pupils are kept in school but apart from their fellow pupils; excluding pupils for a set number of days; or, in extreme cases, permanently excluding pupils.

When a school is trying to improve behaviour, comparing the records of these types of exclusions prior to strategies being put in place and post-strategy are vital. This is one powerful way that data can be used to track the success of intervention strategies being used for behaviour management within a school. If they are succeeding then the amount of negative behaviour and the figures for exclusions of all kinds should be reducing. Similarly at an individual level, data on a pupil who is having help with behaviour should show that the number of negative behaviours is lessening and the intervention is working.

How to use data to identify pupils who need mentoring and support

Mentoring is a term that refers to the way certain pupils are identified and targeted for extra help with organisation of work, etc. Mentoring can be useful with pupils who are not achieving what the data suggest they are capable of.

In many schools a variety of staff use data to track and measure the progress of pupils against their potential. Where a pupil is seen to be underachieving and thus failing to achieve their potential, then intervention strategies such as monitoring and **mentoring** are used. Teachers normally identify two or three pupils who need support and keep records on their progress. Sometimes it is enough for a pupil to know that they have someone they can talk to about their work and who is prepared to give them some individual time. In some cases this monitoring/mentoring will only go on for a short time (eg half a term), but in certain circumstances this may need to be extended. Data are stored on the monitoring files and copies of the records will be passed on to a member of staff who may have responsibility for pupil monitoring/mentoring in the school.

This type of intervention can make a huge difference when it is undertaken as part of a whole school strategy to improve achievement. It ensures that a large number of pupils have some form of strategic support put in place for them and over time most children at risk of under-achieving will have some form of support. For instance, if every subject teacher identifies three pupils that they teach in each class and closely monitors them, and this model is replicated throughout the school, then a large number of pupils are being supported.

Improving borderline cases

In some schools the monitoring and mentoring is even more strategically defined. In a school where they are trying to improve the number of pupils who get five A*–C grades at GCSE it might be used to identify those who are on the C/D borderline. Their subject teachers will have identified these pupils by indicating they had the potential to get a C+ grade but were currently working at a D grade or even below. These pupils can be supported in a number of ways:

- They may be sent on intense revision courses that are organised within schools or in neighbouring Further Education (**FE**) colleges.

- They may be mentored and supported by pastoral teams who help identify individual problems and put in place strategies to help pupils organise themselves, complete outstanding coursework and provide them with revision strategies and techniques to ensure they attain their potential. In serious cases it may be necessary to reduce their GCSE entry by allowing the pupil to withdraw from a subject that they are not going to achieve a positive outcome in and use that gained time to catch up on the others. This is usually a strategy of last resort.

- Parents and pupils will be invited to meet with the pastoral teams to discuss individual progress and ensure that every party involved realises what needs to be done to ensure a successful outcome with the pupil attaining at or above their potential.

> **The CSI is an** important indicator of how well a school is doing in preparing pupils in the three important subjects of maths, science and English. It is the figure arrived at when the numbers of pupils gaining a level 3 at key stage 1 (English/Maths/Science), a level 4 at key stage 2 or a level 5 at key stage 3 is calculated as a percentage of the total cohort.

This type of mentoring is now more common in primary schools where underachievement has been recognised in pupils as young as 7 years of age.

Another use of data is to identify those pupils who schools want to achieve level 3 in science, maths and English at the end of key stage 1, or level 4 at the end of key stage 2, or level 5 at the end of key stage 3. When pupils achieve these levels across the three subjects the pupil is said to have achieved the **core subject indicator (CSI).**

In some schools a lot of work is done to identify pupils who should get the CSI but who may need extra help in one of the subject areas. Where this occurs schools put in place subject-specific support to try to get pupils to attain this target. This is a good example of a very specific use of data to track progress and a customised intervention targeted at an individual for a clearly defined and measurable reason.

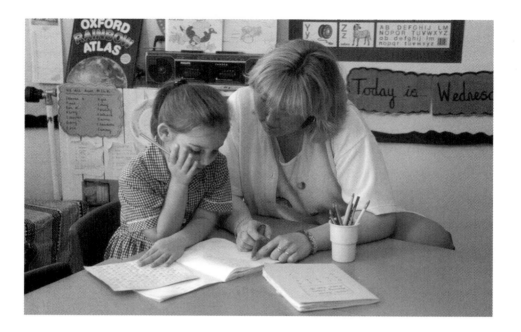

How to use data to identify pupils who need enrichment and support

Data is now routinely used to determine those pupils who are succeeding well above expectations and who would benefit from support and enrichment. Some pupils will succeed significantly above the norm in all subjects and for such pupils it may be necessary to move them up a year group from their chronological age. In other cases it is possible to enrich them in curriculum areas that they excel in. Some pupils may be encouraged to develop their skills in certain subjects early. A primary school pupil taking a GCSE in IT would be one example. Likewise, talented pupils being encouraged to begin AS course modules pre-entry to sixth form. The problem is that to be truly successful there has to be some form of progression built in for that pupil.

More schools realise that they need to be flexible and cater for the individual needs of certain pupils. This does mean a willingness on the part of the school to adapt the curriculum and put in place teaching resources to enable this to occur. Schools have teachers who manage the education of the gifted and talented and very often this is the remit of the SENCO. Identified able pupils are set projects and work that develops their skills and fulfils their individual needs. More primary and secondary schools are building in strategies to identify the gifted and talented and then to support them. This talent may be sporting or musical and again schools are ensuring that pupils talented in these areas are allowed time and resources, where possible, to develop these skills. In some cases pupils have good 'people skills' and these can be developed through involvement in buddy schemes and through the work of the school council and charity committees.

Finally, bear in mind that where pupils may not be as advanced and where early entry is not right for them it is still possible to enrich their subject education.

Using data to determine the success of the school at all levels

It is possible to use information on the results of a school to determine how well that school is doing. At a simple level the league tables enable the public to judge one school against another using raw statistics such as the percentage of pupils who gained five A*–C grades at GCSE, or the numbers of pupils who gained level 5 in maths, English and science in SATs. This raw data is meaningless unless you know the quality of the pupil intake that the school is working with. For instance, consider the two schools in the Case Study.

Data comparison of two schools – a lesson in not jumping to conclusions

School A

This school is sited in an impoverished inner-city area. There is high social deprivation and unemployment. Pupils come from a high proportion of single-parent families and the numbers of pupils on free school meals is above the UK average at 40%. Parents are mainly employed in the manual sector and few have had further education. This school achieved 48% of five A*–C grades in the GCSE examinations of 2005. There is a high number of pupils with statements of educational need and 25% of the pupils have English as a second language.

School B

This school is sited in a suburban area only a few miles from School A. There is high employment and many parents are employed in the two universities in the city centre and in the two hospitals located within a five-mile radius. Over 70% of parents have had experience of further education and most of them work in white-collar occupations. The school has only about 10% of pupils on free school meals. This school achieved 55% of five A*–C grades at GCSE in the 2005 examinations. The number of pupils with state-ments of educational need is well below the UK average and only 5% of the pupils have English as a second language.

Case Study

The bald statistics

Bald statistics suggest that school B is outperforming school A, which it is. However, the question should be: Are they adding significant value to their intake? With an intake like that of school B it is likely that these pupils have the potential, due to their background and supportive parents, to achieve at a much higher level than they are currently. In this case school B is significantly *underperforming*. In comparison, school A is overperforming as it has added considerable value to its intake in order to get the percentage of passes at GCSE.

When inspection teams visit schools they look at the raw statistics as a starting point only. This could be the number of pupils achieving level 3 at age 7, etc. However, inspection teams (and in fact schools) are able to get more information than this in the form of benchmarking data. It is benchmarking data that really provide information about a school's progress. They tell a school how it is doing in relation not just to the school next door, which is often a meaningless comparison (take schools A and B in the Case Study for instance), but allows it to compare progress with schools all over the country that are similar in size, ethnic mix, numbers on free school meals, and so on. This benchmarking allows schools to compare how they are doing in very specific ways.

Data comparisons at secondary level

At secondary level you can compare:

- the numbers of pupils who enter examinations at age 16
- the numbers who gain five A*–C grades
- the numbers who gain one A*–G grade
- the numbers who gain the CSI
- the average number of points each pupil gains
- the average number of GCSE subjects pupils take
- attendance levels
- the percentage of pupils with statements of special educational need
- authorised and unauthorised absence figures
- the attainment gaps that may occur between boys and girls in all subjects.

It is likely in the case of school B in the Case Study that if benchmarking data were to be used then this school would in fact fare badly. It would probably be in the bottom quartiles for many of the comparisons cited above.

Data comparisons at primary level

At primary level you can compare:

- baseline data on entry
- progress rates up to key stage 1 and attainment in core and foundation subjects
- reading and spelling levels
- CAT test results if they are available
- CSI percentages at the end of both key stages
- attendance figures
- progress rates up to key stage 2 and attainment in core and foundation subjects
- numbers of pupils with statements of educational need.

Other comparisons

Benchmarking data can be used further to compare the efficiency of one school against another in terms of resource management. For instance, data can compare:

- the staffing levels in equivalent schools
- the amount of money spent on capitation
- the number of pupils who continue into the sixth form
- the amount of non-contact time staff have.

Schools can also measure their success against other schools within their local education authority as well as the targets that they have set. Schools will determine targets for their pupils at the end of each key stage. Where schools are under LEA control, the authority will also be tracking the progress of the school against agreed targets. Where these targets are not met then valid reasons have to be put forward to explain why there has been a failure to achieve them. In addition schools can measure their performance at a national level. This is only really possible with examinations that occur at age 16 and after because of differences between the nations regarding SATs, etc. With examinations that occur at ages 16, 17 and 18 national data are available that suggest how the full cohort for a subject has achieved and it is possible to see how pupils have achieved comparatively across the four nations.

Schools like to see subject areas attaining above the LEA average and the UK average. Where this occurs schools are probably adding value to their pupils. Schools can also determine whether they are getting enough pupils achieving A* grades and passing extension papers at A2 and therefore enriching the most able in their entry cohort. It is also possible to identify how each subject teacher has performed with their class in relation to others in a department.

Table 15.1 Data set for five teachers

Teacher	Student numbers	A*	B	C	D	E	F	G	U	Average	All average	Residual
1	27	4	15	4	4	0	0	0	0	50.22	47.45	+2.77
2	27	0	0	7	18	2	0	0	0	41.11	38.79	+2.32
3	27	1	1	14	10	0	0	0	0	42.74	42.99	−0.25
4	27	0	0	5	5	16	1	0	0	37.11	35.62	+1.49
5	18	0	0	0	4	10	2	2	0	33.33	29.53	+3.80

Look at value added in detail

Look at Table 15.1. It shows five teachers in a department, the numbers of pupils in their Year 11 class and the numbers of those pupils who got various grades. The **average** column indicates the numbers of points gained by the combined named pupils in that class. This is compared to the points that the same pupils gained in all their other subjects together when those data have been averaged (shown in the **all average** column). If they have done better in this subject a positive residual is shown. So teacher 1 has added value to her class by gaining 2.77 points on average more than they achieved in other subjects. This is a significant improvement and is the equivalent of more than one level. The department uses setting to group pupils and you can see this from the difference in the average for each class, with set 1 (taught by teacher 1) gaining the highest average compared to the lowest set which gained an average of 33.33.

The data above show which teachers have added value and the one teacher who has not in this case, although −0.25 is statistically insignificant and only +/−0.50 is usually regarded as having statistical significance. This type of information is important and curriculum managers in primary and secondary schools are now expected to be able to interpret such data. In many cases such data is produced by the LEA for schools. Schools are also expected to be able to gather information of this kind themselves and interpret it in order to monitor, evaluate and review their progress.

It is also possible to compare how subjects have done in relation to one another. Table 15.2 shows the type of data that any UK secondary school can be given. It tables the achievement by pupils in one school in a few of the subjects offered at GCSE. Such data is compiled by education authorities in the four nations and refers to the respective examinations taken within their nation.

How do we judge which department is doing the best for its pupils? Do you judge the department against the LEA and national outcomes for all pupils in the subject? For instance the national figure for the percentage of pupils who gained an A*-C grade in single science was only 20%. Therefore should we assume that this science department did well to get 37.9% of its pupils an A*-C grade? There are two departments which

Table 15.2 Data by subject

Subject	Entries	A*	A	B	C	D	E	F	G	U	X	A*-C	A*-G
Art and design	53	1.9	15.1	20.8	41.5	17.0	3.8	0.0	0.0	0.0	0.0	79.3	100.0
Business studies	58	7.4	22.2	55.6	7.4	3.7	3.7	0.0	0.0	0.0	0.0	92.6	100.0
English language	223	2.2	7.2	17.0	34.5	22.0	10.3	3.6	0.4	2.7	0.0	60.9	97.3
Maths	198	0.5	7.1	18.2	15.7	23.7	12.1	0.5	3.5	0.5	0.0	43.9	99.5
Biology	16	18.8	31.3	18.8	31.3	0.0	0.0	0.0	0.0	0.0	0.0	100.0	100.0
Single science	29	0.0	0.0	13.8	24.1	20.7	13.8	20.7	3.4	3.4	0.0	37.9	96.6
Drama	33	6.1	27.3	42.4	24.2	0.0	0.0	0.0	0.0	0.0	0.0	100.0	100.0

achieved 100% A*-C grades. How then can you compare these departments with others? The numbers of pupils taught? The numbers of A* grades achieved?

Here are the value added figures for the various subjects:

- Art and design +3.81
- Business studies +0.94
- English +1.32
- Mathematics −0.88
- Biology +2.83
- Single award science −6.69
- Drama +7.78

Remember that value added is achieved by analysing the individual results for named pupils who took your subject and comparing this result with the average grade achieved in all their other subjects.

Value added figures really provide a school with the best indicator of success. Though on the face of it the single science result was good compared to the national figure, the value added tells a different picture. These data may seem irrelevant to those readers who are primary teachers but it is possible to make a detailed analysis of how pupils are doing in a primary school. LEAs can take baseline information on the ability profile of a primary school and can extrapolate and predict how those individual pupils should do at the end of each key stage. Further data once pupils have reached that outcome age can then be gathered and this compared with the original target to arrive at a decision as to whether the school has attained the optimum target, exceeded it or failed to reach it.

Time to reflect

Think about what data has been referred to in this chapter and then find out what data are used on a regular basis in your own school.

✔ What data is available to the ordinary class teacher?

✔ Who manages the data in the school and who analyses it?

✔ Is the school data-rich and knowledge-rich or has it got access to a lot of data which is not being analysed?

✔ How are ordinary teachers expected to use data and add to it?

✔ Does the school receive statistical data from the LEA?

✔ Has LEA data been analysed for the school for a specific purpose? If so, what purpose?

References and further reading

New Community Schools @ the informal education homepage, **www.infed.org/schooling**

Chapter 16

Reporting to Parents – Best Practice

🍎 **What will you find in this chapter?**

✔ Reporting on progress.

✔ What makes a good report?

✔ Meeting parents face to face.

✔ Making contact with home.

✔ Reporting difficulties.

Good teachers know their pupils well and are able to report at length on an individual's potential and progress in their subject area. This chapter is about how teachers gather the information on a pupil, store it for reference and then use it to report either orally or in a written format to a parent or guardian. It is intended to provide you with good diagnostic reports from the primary and secondary sectors in a variety of subject areas that will provide a benchmark for your own good practice.

Making contact with home

Many schools use pupil planners. These are similar to a pupil diary and allow pupils to record homework and other important information. They are also used as a means of communicating between home and school and vice versa. Teachers can record merits and sanctions in them and the reasons for either. There is usually room for parents to enter any absences with reasons and this helps reduce the pressure on busy parents. Ensure that where possible absences are authorised and that schools are kept informed about illness, medical appointments, etc.

However, it may be necessary or useful for teachers to make direct contact with parents and the only way to do this may be by phone or letter. Schools usually have set policies and procedures in place for this and it may be inappropriate for class teachers or subject teachers to do this without it being discussed first with the line manager. When writing a letter certain formalities might need to be followed. Ensure that a copy is made and that the letter's contents have been agreed with a senior member of staff. If it is appropriate for a new teacher to ring home then make a note of the important and salient points they wish to make. Make a note of the discussion held by logging it in a diary or teacher planner. Some parents have a reputation for being difficult and therefore it is useful to make sure that your intended phone call is not to a parent like this. If it is then make sure that there is a witness to the conversation by your side.

Reporting difficulties

Some children come from families where parents are separated or divorced and in some cases both parents will request a copy of a progress report on a child. Normally it is appropriate to accede to this demand and simply provide two reports. However, in some cases there can be injunctions in place against one parent or another. It is important that where there is a legal restriction the school complies with the wishes of the court. In some cases pupils may be in foster care but it may be appropriate for the real parent to be given a copy of any reports provided on the progress of the pupil. Pupils can be in care for a number of reasons, including the illness of a single parent. It may be the case that the parent is still very involved in the life of their child but unable to physically look after them. This is why it is normal for a school to have someone in charge of the reporting procedures for the school. They will be aware of any specific arrangements involving individual pupils that need to be dealt with. In large secondary schools the pastoral team will have information of this kind and the team will arrange for the extra duplication of reports. These will be passed on to the form tutor for distribution. Dealing with issues like these needs sensitivity. Form tutors and pastoral teams encourage pupils to get parents to write in if they want an extra report.

In some cases parents do not speak English. Though it is not possible to translate a whole report, it may be possible for a summary of the report to be passed on verbally through ethnic minority language staff or community workers.

Time to reflect

Consider the following questions.

✔ How do the teachers you have worked with store data and record pupil progress?

✔ How do they determine how well a child is doing both against criteria for each subject and other pupils?

✔ Are there standard recording sheets used within the school or department?

✔ Do the reports include information about the strengths and weaknesses of the pupil in the subject?

✔ Do the reports include targets for improvement?

✔ How are parents' evenings arranged?

✔ Do teachers show marked pupils' work to parents?

✔ Do the teachers prepare some comments beforehand that they will share with parents?

✔ Who is in charge of reporting arrangements in the school?

✔ Who arranges for duplicate reports to be made and distributed?

Part 5

The Pastoral Programme and Curriculum

Chapter 17

The Role of the Form Tutor and Pastoral Team

🍎 **What will you find in this chapter?**

✔ **The pastoral system.**

✔ **What does a good form tutor do?**

✔ **What is the role of the pastoral line manager?**

✔ **The role of the key stage coordinator.**

✔ **Teaching and learning responsibility allowances.**

As well as being employed as a classroom teacher all teachers are also involved in looking after the pastoral welfare of the pupils in a school. This chapter is about what that role entails and how staff are generally involved in the pastoral welfare of pupils. Good schools have strong pastoral systems and teams. This chapter sets out how these work and who does what within the pastoral framework.

The formal pastoral curriculum of any school is determined by guidelines that outline what a child should be aware of and achieve by the end of each key stage. However, the way schools look after pupils on a day-to-day basis and cater for their individual welfare and well-being is referred to as the *pastoral system* of a school. Schools that achieve well and are successful usually have a very strong pastoral system that supports other systems at work in the school and cares for the well-being of all pupils.

The pastoral system

The pastoral system has a structure that varies between the primary and secondary school but in both the class teacher or the form tutor is the most important person in the system. This is because they are the equivalent of front-line personnel and will know the individual children in their class well. These class teachers/form tutors will have first-hand knowledge of the home circumstances of the pupil and will be aware of any changes that occur that can affect a pupil and their ability to work in school. In addition they are also able to monitor subtle changes in behaviour, presentation (here referring to the way a child is dressed and comes prepared for school) and attitude that could indicate causes for concern. The role that a form tutor/class teacher holds is a crucial one and enables them to build up a close and trusting relationship with many pupils. For this reason they may be the person to whom a pupil will divulge serious or confidential information that may need to be passed on to the **child protection officer** of the school.

See Chapter 20 for more on the role of child protection officers.

In a primary school the class teacher will have the benefit of teaching the pupil for all or most subjects. This has advantages as the academic performance of the child is known at first hand. In a primary school the next person involved in the pastoral system may be a key stage manager (**KSM**) who is in overall charge of key stage 1 or 2. However, in smaller primary schools the deputy headteacher or another member of staff with considerable middle-management responsibility performs this role.

In a secondary school this is not always the case and a form tutor who may be with a pupil for the first five years may never actually get to teach them in a formal context. At this level the system may be more complex with a pastoral coordinator/head of year in charge of a year group. It is often the case that year teams will move up the school with their year group so a pupil in year 7 may have the same form tutor and pastoral coordinator for five years. However, this is not the only model and in some schools a year 7 team may stay in year 7, building up links with partner primary schools and working as the expert team on primary–secondary transition. Some schools do the same with a year 9 team where they are the experts on delivering options and careers information to this age group. In a school where this occurs the year 7 and 8 teams will rotate but year 9 will stay in place. When this happens information about pupils will need to be carefully passed on to new form tutors and pastoral coordinators.

> **PSHE** (also known as PSE) is personal, social and health education – see Chapter 18

There are advantages and disadvantages to both systems. One advantage is the way that a team can build up expertise and build on that year on year when they stay in a particular place in the school. The delivery of the formal **PSHE** programme may also be better. However, the disadvantage is that knowledge of pupils that takes time to build up can be lost if proper transition arrangements for the passing on of data are not secure. In a primary school the class teacher may have a form class for one or two years and then the class will move on to another teacher. When this happens pupil information must be carefully transferred. The more efficient the mechanism for this data transfer the more effective the pastoral system.

In most schools, whether primary or secondary, data transfer is being formalised through the use of advanced IT packages. Baseline information gathered at the beginning of a pupil's life in school is passed on to relevant teachers along with key stage levels. In addition, other information about pupil attainment and potential as well as attendance, attitude and home circumstances is also forwarded.

The form or class tutor, plays a vital role in monitoring the progress of pupils in their class as they have an overview of how the pupil is doing in all subjects. However, the academic progress of a pupil is just one aspect that is monitored. The form or class tutor also gets to know the pupil on a personal level learning about their family background as they collect contact information. They will know who lives with two parents, one parent or a legal guardian and will be the first to know if there are problems at home that the school needs to be aware of. In a primary school where the class teacher is also the subject teacher this information may not need to be passed on, but in a secondary school ensuring that subject teachers are aware of issues that can affect a child's progress is vital. For instance pupils can react badly when any of the following occur:

- divorce or separation
- serious family illness of a close relative or friend
- bereavement of a parent, sibling or close family member
- criminal incidents involving the family as victims or perpetrators
- loss of a family home (eg through fire or bankruptcy)
- prosecution of a parent for child abuse
- being taken into care or being on the 'at risk' register.

All these are real situations that can and do arise and supporting a child through times like these by making allowances for them and ensuring that all subject teachers are aware of issues is important. This is where a strong pastoral system is useful. It enables a school to support a child when they most need it. It also places a responsibility on the school in that it has to work closely with other agencies involved, such as social services health professionals and the police.

For more on workforce remodelling see the website.

The role of the form tutor is changing and the **workforce remodelling** that is ongoing has taken the majority of administrative tasks away from teachers. In a lot of schools this has meant that teachers will not give out letters for parents, collect money for trips, and so on, but this administrative aspect is a minor part of what makes a good tutor.

What does a good form tutor do?

A good form tutor does most of the following:

- Ensures that pupils are attending on a regular basis and that they arrive in school on time.
- Plays a large part in promoting the values of the school and a positive ethos. Each school is unique and has an individual identity determined by the way it operates and interacts with pupils, one determined by the vision propounded by the senior team and the staff. The form tutor is a key part of that framework.
- Ensures that parents come to parents' evenings where possible and remain informed about their child's school and any relevant activities.
- Monitors the well-being of pupils, noticing differences in their health and happiness or a change in their circumstances. There is a reason pupils come to school hungry or upset or in a dishevelled state with clothes that are not clean.
- Counsels pupils about behaviour and if necessary uses the school's systems of sanctions and rewards to keep them on track.
- Knows about the hobbies and interests of the pupils in their form as well as any successes they have had outside school in sports or extra-curricular activities. Recognising and celebrating achievement, however small, is a good way of promoting inclusion and mutual respect in any school.
- Ensures that pupils in their class are keeping up to date with homework, and in other classes if they are in a secondary school.
- Is a good listener and mentors individual pupils who need help and support with organisation and motivation.
- Works closely, where necessary, with the head of year/pastoral coordinator or the next person in line within the pastoral system to support pupils whose behaviour or schoolwork gives cause for concern.
- Keeps the class informed about what is happening in school.
- Is a problem solver for some pupils who will go to them for support.
- Encourages children and develops their confidence and self-esteem.

- Monitors the social development of pupils, seeing how they interact and communicate with their peers. Where there are issues with this they will be able to get support for pupils who may need external help with anger or behaviour management, or support from the educational psychology service through an EP referral.

- Is a team builder to bring a disparate group of pupils together to form a cohesive group, ensuring that all pupils are valued and protected.

- Understands the school data held on pupils in their form and monitors their academic progress, thus ensuring that each child is performing to their full potential.

- Checks that pupils are being awarded merits or are receiving sanctions.

- Provides parents with an overview of how their child is developing academically and personally throughout the current academic year and through the formal reporting system.

> **See the websites** at the end of Chapter 3 in order to find out exactly what is expected of pupils in your nation and in the key stage that you are **responsible** for.

The form tutor will have a line manager who is responsible for the delivery of the pastoral curriculum in that area of the school. In a secondary school this could be the head of year/pastoral coordinator, but this may not be the case in a primary school. Whoever the person is will determine what the pastoral curriculum should be for that area of the school and this is based on national curriculum guidelines. Like curriculum coordinators or heads of department, the pastoral team has the same **responsibility** to write a scheme of work that interprets the statutory guidelines.

CHAPTER 17 THE ROLE OF THE FORM TUTOR AND PASTORAL TEAM

The role of the form tutor as mentor

In many secondary schools the form tutor is expected to monitor the work of pupils on a regular basis and act as a mentor. Form tutors identify pupils within the class who may need extra support and will, over a period of time, monitor their books/files/projects/coursework. Their role is not to comment on the work set by other subject teachers but to look at the work of the pupil and ensure that they are keeping up. Where the tutor is a mentor they will monitor the whole form at some point in the year but may give more time to some pupils than others depending on the degree of need. Figure 17.1 is an example of a monitoring sheet that you may be expected to fill in. Where this system occurs in a school, tutors will have monitoring files with data on their pupils. This will include key stage results, CAT data, etc. This tells a form tutor what a pupil is capable of achieving and their likely potential.

Visit the website for an account of the personal experience of a form tutor.

Tutors will be expected to monitor a number of pupils each half term. In order to find time to do this they may not be expected to attend school assemblies and will use this time to meet pupils and discuss their progress. The role of monitoring cannot be underestimated and provides tutors with an insight into the progress of their tutor group. As the workforce remodelling takes place it may be that this role will be lost to teachers and will be undertaken by LSAs or other non-teaching staff who form part of a school's 'counselling' team. In fact in some schools this has already occurred. In future, in order for the form tutor to remain in contact with their form's progress they may have to liaise more with LSAs who also work with the class. Monitoring sheets like

Name of pupil	Form	Date	Subjects monitored	Homework completed	Classwork completed	Literacy / numeracy	Comments/ action
Lisa Rowe	7Y	March 06	History Science English Technology	In Hi/En etc not in science	✓	Lisa finds science and maths work difficult	See science teacher for support
Shafi Begum	7Y	March 06	All books seen	No	No	Basic skills are good and EAL support in place	Shafi needs more support to complete all his work in class and at home. Passed onto PC meeting arranged with parents
Seven Morris	7Y	March 06	All books seen	✓	✓	Excellent	On target

Figure 17.1 Example of a monitoring sheet

those shown in Figure 17.1 will be even more important as they will provide a way of sharing information on pupils with the team responsible for their progress.

What is the role of the pastoral line manager?

The pastoral line manager plays a vital role in interpreting the curriculum guidelines for pastoral work in the school. They will write the pastoral programme, put together the materials and the scheme of work and ensure that it is taught effectively and appropriately. They will also monitor delivery and ensure consistency of standards and practice. Finally, they will review the process and evaluate its success as part of a school's *self-evaluation* process.

In most schools the role of the pastoral line manager is now treated equally with that of the subject or curriculum manager. They are both middle managers with a curriculum responsibility – one academic, the other pastoral. The pastoral manager is in charge of a number of staff and will meet with them to determine progress and a vision for the future, taking account of any changes in syllabus determined by changes in national curriculum guidelines for PSHE. The effectiveness of the pastoral system is judged by inspection teams who visit the school, as is coverage of the pastoral programme. Inspection teams will also judge the impact that the system is having on standards. The effectiveness of the pastoral programme, the system, teams and managers can be judged equally alongside the effectiveness of subject team delivery.

> **All schools are** now expected to complete a self-evaluation report for an inspection team before it comes into the school. However, many schools have done this for a long time to enable them to have an overview of what is and is not successful. All middle managers review their area of responsibility and contribute to the whole school report on an annual basis. See Chapter 21 for more details.

The pastoral line manager has the following responsibilities:

- Ensures that the pastoral team works well to deliver the programme of study that it has written and, like a curriculum manager/head of department, ensures that this is done consistently.
- Ensures, along with form tutors, that the school's vision and ethos is disseminated.
- Promotes high levels of good attendance, behaviour and achievement.
- Ensures that their year group or area of the school is achieving in line with data that they have and uses data to monitor progress and set numerical targets.
- Writes pastoral development plans for their area of the school sharing the role of visioning for the future with the senior team.
- Contributes to the school vision for developing the effectiveness of the pastoral system within the school.
- Monitors individually targeted pupils' work in the same way a form tutor does and acts as a mentor.

- Liaises with outside agencies involved with any pupils with special educational needs within their area. This does not only mean less-able or more-able pupils but also those involved with the police or Social Services, or looked-after children (ie those who are not living with their parents but are in foster placements, etc).
- Meets with parents to discuss the progress of individual pupils who may need support.
- Puts in place behaviour support plans for pupils at risk of permanent exclusion.
- Sets targets for attendance, exclusion figures, achievement for their year/area, in negotiation with subject leaders and senior staff.
- Becomes involved in performance management of staff within the pastoral system.
- Contributes to the reporting system of the school and writes individual reports, providing an overview of the academic and personal development of pupils.

How do we judge whether a pastoral system is effective?

> **Authorised absences** are those that a pupil, parents and the school have accounted for (eg illness, family holidays, hospital visits, school visits, field trips, extra-curricular activities). Unauthorised absences are those for which no reason is given.

For a system to be effective the staff involved will ensure that attendance figures are high or improving and this will apply to **authorised and *unauthorised* absence** figures.

In any school the attendance figures should be over 90% and unauthorised absence figures should be as low as possible. The pastoral system should also contribute to a reduction in fixed-term and permanent exclusions and issues resulting from poor behaviour. The pastoral team will ensure that all pupils are adequately supported and that subject teachers are aware of and take account of any issues relating to individual pupils. The pastoral team ensures that pupils integrate into school life and where transfers occur between key stages or from one school to another that these are successful. When pupils who transfer feel safe and assured about what the next step is going to be for them, the pastoral system can be said to have succeeded. It is also successful when pupil information that has been gathered is passed on and used as part of the normal practice of the school. In addition, the system is successful when pupils within the year group or area perform in external assessment and achieve their potential. This will result from careful pupil tracking and pupils who are not on target being focused accordingly.

The pastoral system of a school contributes significantly to how the school feels as you walk through the door. Schools that are orderly environments - where pupils feel safe, secure and confident, where staff and pupils work together in a spirit of mutual respect and where the main focus is on teaching and learning - usually have an effective pastoral system in place.

The role of the key stage manager

The KSM is a role common in secondary schools and is increasingly being found in large primary schools. The KSM is responsible for pupils across a range of year groups and for the staff involved in the pastoral system within those years. In some schools this involves as many as 30–40 staff. The KSM provides an overview of a significant area of the school and very often is responsible for transition from one key stage to another. The actual process of transition between primary and secondary schools and within the secondary and primary schools will be looked at in Chapter 19. The KSM will oversee the process and has a vision for how it can be improved. In addition they will monitor, evaluate and review the process and its effectiveness. Like all staff involved in the pastoral system they will be looking across subject boundaries at general trends in achievement, attitude, attendance and behaviour, and a significant responsibility for school performance lies with them and their teams.

The KSM will work with many agencies outside the school such as youth offending teams, educational psychologists, Social Services and family group conferencing groups. They will also be responsible for many of the referrals that occur in schools in order to support vulnerable groups of pupils. In some circumstances their specific knowledge of the academic ability of a year group might suggest that in the future the curriculum plans for the school will need to be adapted to take account of specific needs. For instance if a KSM working with primary partners identifies that a future secondary school intake will be weaker than usual they may suggest that more English and maths classes will be needed with smaller numbers to cater for more pupils with specific learning difficulties. This could also work the other way – a potential intake group could be stronger and more enrichment of the cohort will be necessary. In another case they may suggest that a year 9 group is strong and may not need any special places on college-based courses available to those who do not access GCSE courses in year 10.

It is impossible for a headteacher to know every pupil. The benefit of a highly developed pastoral system is that it ensures that the pupils are well known by someone within the school. This information, combined with what is known about a pupil's academic performance, gives a rounded picture of the whole pupil. The academic performance of the pupil is only one area that a school has to be involved in. The personal and social development of the pupil including how they relate to others in the class and those around them is also of vital importance if they are to leave school ready for the world they will become a part of. In large schools the pastoral system allows a school to be broken up into manageably-sized units so that this information can be collected and all pupils' needs can be taken account of.

The higher up the pastoral system a member of staff is then the more contact with outside agencies they are likely to have and the more staff they will be working with. In addition they will deal with the more serious issues to do with behaviour, achievement and attendance. Like pastoral coordinators they will be involved in writing programmes of study for the pastoral curriculum and will have a greater responsibility to ensure its consistent delivery. They will monitor both staff and pupils and will play a key role in performance management of staff. In addition they will monitor parents' evenings and, with subject coordinators and pastoral coordinators, will ensure that reporting to parents is effectively managed.

Teaching and learning responsibility allowances

Schools are in the process of remodelling their workforces for a number of reasons. Teachers who are paid responsibility allowances for duties that they undertake will now only be paid those allowances for managing areas that are directly linked to the teaching and learning of pupils. In the past a member of staff may have been given a responsibility for health and safety within a school or for looking after the school mini-bus. These tasks are now seen as administrative and, as such, outside the remit of teaching staff. With this in mind many schools have taken this opportunity to rethink the staffing structure of a school. In some cases they have appointed new non-teaching members of staff to support positions. One of these posts is that of the pastoral support assistant (PSA). PSAs work closely with the pastoral team of teaching staff to support its work. They may undertake administrative tasks that teachers no longer do, give out letters, chase up absent pupils and organise meetings with parents. They may also work on a one-to-one basis with pupils in the same way that LSAs do. PSAs may help pupils to organise their work, ensure that they are in class when they should be and know where they should be. They may work with a small group of pupils on behaviour management. The role of the PSA is flexible and determined by the school. There is no doubt that over the next few years there will be more **non-teaching staff** in supportive roles like this who may act as mentors, counsellors and learning coaches to pupils. The advantages of such staff is that they are

For more on the role of non-teaching staff see the website.

non-teaching and have a more flexible day as they do not have to be in a classroom to deliver a lesson to 30-plus waiting pupils at a specific time. They may also have been recruited because they have experience as counsellors, support workers, project workers, etc and therefore bring to the school a wider range of expertise.

Time to reflect

Consider the following questions.

✔ Have a look at the pastoral system working in your own school.
  - Who writes the pastoral programme and how is it delivered?
  - Who has responsibility for pupil welfare in your school?
  - Are they regarded as having equal status with those who have academic responsibilities?

✔ Find out which outside agencies your school deals with on a regular basis.
  - Is there a clear hierarchical structure in place for dealing with pastoral issues?
  - Find out how it works.

Chapter 18

The PSHE Curriculum in Our Schools

What will you find in this chapter?

✔ The PSHE framework.

✔ Social and emotional aspects of learning (SEAL).

✔ What constitutes good practice in delivering PSHE?

✔ What is circle time?

Schools play a huge role in developing the whole child. This means providing pupils not just with academic knowledge and subject-based skills but also providing for their social and personal development. Schools endeavour to prepare pupils for the world they are a part of outside school. The teaching of personal, social and health education **(PSHE)** forms an important element in a balanced and all-round education. A successful programme of PSHE should ensure that pupils will leave school emotionally mature, articulate and confident, with positive attitudes to society and able to play a greater part in the community and the democratic process.

Although the term is referred to as PSHE and includes the health element, some schools, documentation and websites refer to it simply as PSE.

The PSHE framework

The Education Act of 1996 (in section 351) states that each pupil should receive a broad and balanced curriculum which:

Promotes the spiritual, moral, cultural, mental and physical development of pupils at the school and of society and prepares pupils for the opportunities, responsibilities and experiences of adult life.

> **See the curriculum authorities** websites at the end of this chapter for detailed guidance on **PSHE** in your school's nation

The term PSHE relates to everything the school does to promote the personal, social and emotional development of pupils. Though there are differences between the four nations – for instance citizenship is a foundation subject in the secondary schools of England but this is not the case in the other three nations – there are also many similarities.

Most primary and secondary schools have a written policy for PSHE and a scheme of work that is delivered by:

- class teachers/form tutors

  and/or

- a specialist team of trained PSHE staff who deliver the programme of study
- outside deliverers such as nurses, doctors, the police, business people, etc
- subject teachers where their expertise can be used to deliver certain aspects of the PSHE programme.

In most schools the PSHE programme is delivered in a number of different ways, all of which make up a cohesive approach to the teaching of the subject. It can be delivered through:

- themed assemblies
- discrete lessons
- subject lessons that via their SOW cover aspects of the PSHE course (eg science lessons that deal with puberty and pregnancy, the effects of the sun, etc; geography lessons that deal with environmental issues such as global warming; religious education lessons that deal with different cultures, religions, beliefs and raise issues such as tolerance; English lessons where literature stimuli focus on growing up, health issues for young people, bullying, abortion, suicide; and so on)
- PSHE days that are devoted to careers guidance, health education, industrial and economic awareness, etc.
- **inclusion arrangements** in the school such as class representatives on year and school councils.

> **Visit the website** for a case study outlining how Grange Primary School delivered a comprehensive PSHE programme.

> **See Chapter 12** for more on promoting inclusion.

At present the delivery of good PSHE programmes in schools is inconsistent, with some delivering excellent provision and others not delivering any at all (Ofsted, 2005). However, in the best schools there is a detailed working policy with an SOW that clearly states what will be taught, when and how, and identifying resources that staff can use to deliver the SOW. In many cases schools use outside agencies to help them and form effective links with community police and health agencies, social workers, careers guidance staff, members of local businesses and industries. The **PSHE programmes** in all nations stress similar aspects that schools need to address.

What have the PSHE programmes got in common?

Most programmes have the following factors in common:

- All the PSHE programmes stress the need for pupils to be encouraged to value good *interpersonal relationships*: the importance of family, friendship and the need to respect similarities and differences that people might have. In addition, as the pupil grows older the need for recognition of what makes a good parent is also a part of the programme of study.
- Pupils are encouraged to see themselves as *part of a community* that begins with their own community but then moves outwards from the local to the national and global. It is also important that within the PSHE programme pupils are encouraged to see the value of good citizenship and to understand how important it is for citizens to understand the political and legal structure of the nation and country they are a part of.

- PSHE programmes stress the need for a *healthy lifestyle* and cover aspects like nutrition, physical exercise, hygiene and health and safety. It is important that pupils are encouraged from an early age to take responsibility for their actions and understand the effects these can have on their well-being. Pupils are given knowledge in order to help them do this. From an early age they are given information about road safety, the danger of certain substances in the home, the threat from certain adults, the danger of overexposure to the sun, etc.

- PSHE programmes help pupils to understand how they develop sexually. *Sex education* forms a part of the statutory programme of study. Pupils are given information about how they grow and develop, puberty, sex and sexuality, sexually transmitted diseases, contraception and abortion as well as relationships. Pupils are encouraged to think about being morally responsible, about being aware of their own feelings and about how to behave in a relationship. They are also encouraged to keep themselves safe.

- Through the PSHE programme pupils are encouraged to consider their own *emotional development*. Pupils are encouraged to think about how they feel and how they respond in different situations. Programmes stress the need for pupils to be encouraged to build up their self-confidence and self-esteem and to learn coping strategies for dealing with stressful situations. Increasingly, there is further emphasis in this aspect to encourage pupils to cope with conflict, anger and to manage their own behaviour. Pupils are also encouraged to cope with the changes that will occur both at a personal level and in their progression through school. Coping with moving from one school to another, with divorce or bereavement are all likely events for children to have to deal with at an emotional level.

> **When aspects of the PSHE programme are delivered in different ways – ie through a subject area and through other methods such as assemblies – the PSHE coordinator will have this recorded in the scheme of work and this delivery needs to be monitored.**

- Schools are expected to play a part in the *spiritual development* of pupils. Individually, pupils are encouraged to develop an understanding of values and through discussion to come to some sense of where these values come from and how society works to uphold them and why. They are also encouraged to think about their own beliefs, spiritual and otherwise. They should have knowledge of the different religions of the world and schools are expected to promote tolerance and respect among pupils for those whose religions and beliefs are different. Specialist teachers of religious studies provide a focus for this work within the subject scheme of work but this aspect should be evident across the whole school within the assembly structure and in discussions that may occur in other subject areas. Schools are expected to hold a corporate act of worship every day and this should have a Christian dimension to it.

- Schools also have a responsibility to instil *moral values* and departments in schools are often asked by inspectors how they contribute to the spiritual, cultural, moral and social aspect of the school. Every area of the school should be promoting values such as respect, honesty and integrity. Recently it was suggested that schools in England would be given a sum of money to encourage pupils to get into the habit of giving. This care and concern for others forms part of the moral aspect of the PSHE programme. Pupils are also encouraged to think about the purpose of having school rules and regulations, and the importance of working in a safe and secure environment where these core values are promoted. Pupils are encouraged to develop their own code of conduct and to make decisions based on sound moral judgement.

- Throughout school, pupils will be given support in *study skills*. The PSHE programme supports pupils by teaching them how to be effective learners and how to manage their own learning. It encourages pupils to identify their preferred learning styles and shows them ways to use this knowledge to improve their performance. Improving learning and performance is one of the key skills and as such pupils can also gain accreditation for this. Self-assessment and self-review are also important parts of this aspect and increasingly pupils are expected to set targets for their own improvement. Schools also stress that pupils are going to be learning after they leave school and the emphasis is on seeing school as part of a life-long learning process.

- *Environmental awareness* is another aspect of the PSHE programme and is covered in some cases through subject areas like science and geography. However, when pupils get to key stage 4 not every child will follow the same courses in science and some may not take geography at all. Therefore in order to ensure consistency and that every pupil's entitlement to this aspect is met, education about the environment also needs to be delivered as part of the overall PSHE programme. It is important that pupils are taught to respect the environment and understand the part that responsible consumers play in protecting the world and its resources for future generations. This aspect begins in the primary school where schools might look at a local level at the environment and develops into pupils having a global perspective on environmental issues. Many schools are also involved in sustainability projects of their own, which provides hands-on knowledge of how important it is to protect the environment and to consider ourselves as temporary custodians of the planet.

- Pupils are encouraged from an early age to think about the *world of work* - industrial and economic awareness, careers guidance and work-related experience (**WRE**) are important aspects of any effective PSHE programme. In primary schools this aspect may focus on local businesses and pupils may visit local shops and factories to give them some insight into the world of work. Schools may also encourage outside speakers to talk about their jobs and national schemes where parents are encouraged to take a child to work support this aspect. As pupils progress through the school the PSHE programme is underpinned by good careers guidance from outside providers as well as detailed transition programmes. Pupils are given detailed information about the changing workplace.

Work experience

At present pupils are expected to undertake some form of work experience organised by the school and much PSHE time is spent on preparing pupils for this WRE. However, as pupils have become more reliant on the money they can earn from Saturday jobs and more than ever are gaining experience of the world of work prior to formal work experience, concerns have been raised about whether schools need to provide this WRE. Increased concern about pupil safety has also called into question the need for criminal checks to be put in place for work placements. There are two questions that are now being asked in relation to WRE:

- How much longer will this type of organised school placement be necessary for today's pupil who is often already involved in the world of work?
- How viable is it to organise WRE for large numbers of pupils if police checks become necessary?

Schools try to prepare pupils for the world of work, employment and adulthood by providing advice on how to manage their finances and those of a household. The aim is to ensure that pupils will arrive at the point of employment having made meaningful and correct decisions about their chosen career. They will also be prepared for the changes that occur in employment nowadays and will be able to make sound financial decisions in relation to managing their own affairs.

Social and emotional aspects of learning (SEAL)

In May 2005 the Primary National Strategy for Social and Emotional Aspects of Learning was launched in England. It is a programme of study that provides guidance, a framework and resources for the explicit development of social, emotional and behavioural skills. The study pack was developed over two years with the help of over 500 schools. It is intended to be used by schools who have identified that some of their pupils have problems dealing in understanding and managing their feelings and emotions. SEAL is intended to help schools address some of the issues that prevent pupils from engaging with learning. However it is also recognised that much of what is dealt with in the SEAL packs will be relevant to all schools. The materials are intended to promote positive behaviour and to encourage pupils to learn effectively. The pack focuses on five social and emotional aspects of learning: self-awareness; managing feelings; motivation; empathy; and social skills.

The materials include:

- a guidance booklet
- a getting started poster
- a whole school resource with photocards.

It also contains seven sets of thematic materials that are colour coded, each containing:

- an assembly and overview
- a red set for foundation stage
- a blue set for years 1 and 2
- a yellow set for years 3 and 4
- a green set for years 5 and 6.

The booklets in each set cover seven recurring themes:

1 New beginnings
2 Getting on and falling out
3 Say no to bullying
4 Going for goals
5 Good to be me
6 Relationships
7 Changes.

Each theme is designed for a whole school approach and includes a whole assembly and suggested follow-up activities in all areas of the curriculum.

The whole aim of the packs is to build on the already effective work that goes on in schools by encouraging pupils to work cooperatively as part of a group, to keep trying despite suffering setbacks, and to cope with conflict and emotional stress. The aim is that these materials will support the whole school ethos that many schools have sought to develop through their use of inclusion policies such as school councils, buddy schemes and the increasing use of circle time.

What constitutes good practice in delivering PSHE?

In January 2005, Ofsted published the most recent report to date on the quality of PSHE delivery in secondary schools. The report found that personal, social and health education was delivered through discrete lessons as well as through the delivery of the national curriculum, tutorial programmes and assemblies. The report also cited work experience, mini-enterprise schemes and other initiatives that enrich the lives of pupils in school and develop them as individuals as playing a part in delivering the PSHE programme. The report was based on inspections in 60 schools and by referring to over 100 inspection reports.

● What did the report find?

● The findings suggested that the delivery of PSHE was inconsistent across schools with some schools ignoring its delivery in any form.

● There was a narrow focus in some schools with a failure to deliver information on financial management, coping with stress, maintaining good mental health and good parenting.

● The need to deliver citizenship as a foundation subject had in some cases eaten into time for other important aspects of the PSHE programme.

● There was undue emphasis on giving pupils knowledge and delivering content, and too little time spent on allowing pupils to explore issues and develop their own ideas, understanding and beliefs.

● There was a tension between the role of the form tutor and the need to deliver the programme; on occasions too much time was spent on monitoring and target setting at the expense of the PSHE programme.

● Few form tutors had any training in delivering PSHE and this adversely affected the quality of the delivery.

● The most significant finding was that pupil achievement and contribution in this area was not being assessed and no account was being taken of what they had learnt and the progress that had been made.

● The quality of lessons in PSHE was not monitored as rigorously as the delivery of subject-based lessons; in many cases they were not monitored at all.

● Few schools consulted pupils about what was provided on the course.

● The majority of staff who are PSHE coordinators provided good guidance and leadership.

(Ofsted, 2005)

Although this report deals with the secondary sector it is likely that some findings would also apply to the primary sector: the delivery of PSHE in primary schools is inconsistent. Some schools have very detailed PSHE programmes that form a part of a whole school approach to developing the pupil. All staff deliver the PSHE programme consistently and the quality of the delivery is monitored and the effectiveness of the programme is regularly reviewed. In some primary schools pupils' views are sought and taken account of. However this is not always the case and in some primary schools PSHE delivery is poor with only those aspects found in the subject orders of the national curriculum are being delivered.

PSHE advisors would support the report's findings that specialist trained staff are the best quality providers for any PSHE programme. They might also suggest that where a primary school has an established PSHE programme then the quality of delivery in the primary school might benefit from the fact that most primary teachers work with only a small, stable number of pupils. Primary teachers are also well versed in using techniques such as circle time that work well when pupils need time to explore an issue openly and need to listen to others' view points.

What constitutes best practice?

Bear in mind the following points:

- Like a national curriculum subject there is a programme of study for PSHE that schools need to take account of when developing the SOW that will be delivered to each year group.

- Schools need to identify what can be covered in assemblies, subject lessons and discrete PSHE lessons.

- Schools need to identify who can deliver what and where the expertise lies in the school. Where parts of the PSHE programme are delivered by subject specialists this must be highlighted in the SOW for PSHE and in the subject SOW. Cross-referencing between the two is essential to ensure consistency.

- A detailed SOW identifying the aims and objectives of the course for each year group needs to be written.

- A coordinator needs to have responsibility for this SOW and a senior member of staff should have an overview of the whole PSHE programme.

- Resources for the delivery of the course and the use of outside links and agencies should be identified and written into the SOW. These should be regularly reviewed and updated as well as measured against any new additions to the PSHE framework.

- Teachers need to be trained to deliver the PSHE programme although best practice suggests that some teachers who have an interest or are specialised in certain aspects of PSHE are better able to deliver high-quality lessons.

- Pupils should be encouraged to evaluate what they have learnt and their views should be taken into account when planning, monitoring and reviewing.

- Monitoring the delivery of PSHE is as important as monitoring the quality of subject delivery.

- Pupil's knowledge and understanding of the issues being discussed and the progress they are making should be assessed somehow.

- Teachers in both secondary and primary schools need to have continuing professional development and training to ensure the effective delivery of the PSHE programme.

What is circle time?

Circle time refers to a method of working with children that improves their ability to talk confidently in front of others and to listen with appreciation to others' points of view. It has the benefit of being suitable for all ages and can be used very easily in PSHE programmes because, at a fundamental level, it can be used for classes to get to know each other and for bonding purposes. As time progresses and the group becomes cohesive and less self-conscious it can be used to discuss spiritual, moral and cultural issues.

Primary teachers use this method of working as and when the need arises. Although they follow a timetable it is sometimes possible to suspend this routine to deal with a more pressing issue. Circle time can be used to raise issues that are causing concern. In one school, where staff felt behaviour was an issue, it was used to initiate a discussion about feelings. This then led to a discussion about respect and behaviour in later circle time sessions. This flexibility is not as easy to achieve in secondary schools but circle time is still a valuable way of opening up discussions and allowing all to feel that they can have a valued opinion.

● How to manage circle time?

However old the pupils are it is important to follow a few simple rules. For any class it is important that they are encouraged to get to know each other. Therefore there are stages of circle time that need to be worked through before any teacher can use it effectively to tackle big issues.

The introduction

Like any teaching and learning that goes on in a school, it is vital that circle time is introduced and the learning intention stated. Explain that circle time will give everyone an opportunity to get to know each other, have a say about an issue and allow them to practise the skills of talking and listening. This will need to be restated regularly at the start of circle time until it becomes a type of mantra.

Getting to know each other

Arrange everyone in a circle so that everybody is visible to everybody else. Many teachers who use circle time like to give the speaker an object to hold, like a soft toy. Only the person with the object can speak although others can indicate that they wish to (or can say 'pass'). In early sessions it is useful to get people to move around first, by saying things like 'All those with shoelaces in their shoes move now', 'All those with pierced ears move now', 'All those who have watched the latest Harry Potter film move now'. Other examples include, 'Change places now if you hate ...', 'Change places now if you love ...', 'Change places if your birthday is ...'. This acts as a warming up activity and also encourages pupils to move out of friendship groups and to sit next to a person they may not know very well.

> Circle time needs to be planned and it is useful to write down a list of questions that you can ask. Trying to ad lib this type of activity is not a good idea. This is a lesson and as such needs the same careful planning that is given to one with a subject base. Ten minutes is enough for young children as a start; for older ones 30 minutes is a good cut-off point.

Beginning to speak

The aim of circle time is to develop the speaking and listening skills pupils will need as they grow. Once established it is also a way of getting pupils to articulate a point of view and to get to know how others feel emotionally about certain things. Pupils will move to an understanding of what constitutes a 'norm' in our society and circle time should reinforce those values and standards that are important. No matter what the age of the pupils, encouraging them to speak aloud means the teacher being resourceful enough to break down inhibitions and develop the confidence of the group.

In early sessions pupils will be asked to end a sentence:

- My name is ...
- I live with ...
- My best friend is ... because ...
- My favourite book/film is ...
- My favourite food is ...
- I hate ... because ...
- I love ... because ...

Talking from the heart

The real aim of circle time is to get to a point where pupils feel able to talk about issues of real concern to them. When circle time is done well, pupils are not only speaking and listening but are actively involved in putting forward a reasoned and rational point of view on an issue of importance to them. This skill is highly important and is one that will improve their ability to structure a written argument as well. Circle time also develops self-confidence and respect for others. It ensures that those who can sometimes dominate and take over discussions have to give way to those who are more reluctant to speak.

Establishing rules

The group or class can establish circle time rules but one of the most important rules is to ensure that no one uses circle time to get at another person in the group. There should be zero tolerance of this type of behaviour. It is also useful to use a focus sheet that pupils can fill in at the end of the session. This is not always possible with very young children but for those who can write they can be adapted to their age and ability.

In many schools circle time forms a part of a whole school model for delivering parts of the PSHE programme. Where this happens it is often possible to see a very visible 'moral values system' operating around the school. These come from the pupils themselves and are generated initially in the classroom (as in the circle time sheet exemplified in Figure 18.1) and are then passed up to the school council, where they become embedded in the school ethos.

Circle time sheet

Date . . .

Circle time today was about FEELINGS

These are our ideas about feelings.
We thought about how we feel when good things happen like having presents or going somewhere nice.
We thought about how we feel when bad things happen like having a row with a best friend or doing something wrong.

This week we are working on why it is important to have rules and how people feel if they are broken. We talked about how we feel when it is not good in the lesson because people are bad and then we can't do what the teacher has promised.

These are our ideas.
We should have rules that we all listen to.
If we don't listen then the teacher feels bad and we don't have a good lesson and we feel bad.
In our school council we should talk about rules and put them up around the school and maybe words like respect to remind people.

Figure 18.1 Sample circle time sheet

Time to reflect

✔ Access the appropriate website for the nation in which you are currently teaching:

  - www.qca.org.uk for England
  - www.accac.org.uk for Wales
  - www.scotland.gov.uk for Scotland
  - www.ccea.org.uk for Northern Ireland

Look at the PSHE framework for the age group relevant to your work. What are the attitudes, values and skills listed? Make a note of these.

✔ Who is in charge of the PHSE curriculum in your school?

✔ Have you seen the policy and the scheme of work?

✔ Have you seen any lessons of PHSE delivered?

✔ Is this part of a whole school programme that includes assemblies, tutorials, subject lessons as well as discrete PHSE lessons?

✔ Does the school have links with outside agencies that help deliver the programme?

✔ Does the school monitor, evaluate and review the programme of study and its delivery?

✔ Does the school use circle time?

✔ Have you seen any teachers using circle time?

✔ How could you use circle time in your subject to discuss an important issue?

References and further reading

Bliss, T. and Tetley, J. (1993), *Circle Time: A Resource Book for Infant, Junior and Secondary Schools*, Lucky Duck.

HMSO, 'The Education Act 1996', **www.opsi.gov.uk**

Ofsted (2005), 'Personal, social and health education in secondary schools', HMI 2311.

Social and Emotional Aspects of Learning (SEAL) @ **www.standards.dfes.gov.uk**, *Circletime* @, **www.circletime.co.uk**

Chapter 19

Pupil Induction and Transition from Key Stage to Key Stage

🍎 **What will you find in this chapter?**

✔ **Ensuring a smooth transition.**

✔ **Induction and transition: good practice guidelines.**

✔ **Supporting pupils making choices.**

This chapter shows how primary and secondary schools induct new pupils. All new students will have experienced a period of induction and where possible will be made as familiar as possible with the day-to-day routine and the teachers they are likely to come into contact with. Transition is also discussed in this chapter. Schools now gather a lot of information about pupils and in order for them to move between classes, key stages or even schools it needs to be collated and passed on. This information provides schools and teachers with valuable data about, eg a pupil's attendance, aptitude and extra curricular activities. Many schools have strategies in place to ensure that teachers gather and transfer this data and in most there will be individuals with responsibility for this task. This chapter is also about how pupils are prepared for the next stage of their learning – which may mean making them ready to move from primary to secondary school or from secondary school to tertiary institutions.

Ensuring a smooth transition

The aim of transition at all stages is to build bridges between pupils, schools and parents. There are three types:

- the pastoral bridge
- the curriculum bridge
- the loyalty bridge.

First, schools want to ensure that pupils transfer feeling safe and secure, confidently knowing where they are going to and who will be there for them, as well as what they will be doing. Secondly, the transfer is intended to build a bridge between what has gone before and what is going to happen in the future. When learning has already taken place, as in the primary pupil moving to a secondary setting, the aim is to build a curriculum bridge so that learning that has occurred is built upon. Finally, schools want to ensure that there is a built-in loyalty between the parents and their chosen school. Along with this is the need for a secondary school to build up the confidence of a partner primary school so that the primary believes that this secondary school will provide a vital next step for their primary leavers.

Many primary schools run their own nursery facilities and many potential pupils will join the school nursery and then progress on to the reception class. Even the move to nursery school is carefully managed and pupils may visit for a morning or afternoon until they gradually build up the amount of time they spend there. The aim of this period of their education is a social one. Staff will ensure that a pupil feels safe and secure in the school and much of the time there is devoted to structured play where pupils learn to socialise, share and work together. For some children this may be the first time that they have been with a large number of other children. In some areas the numbers of children being born is reducing and this is resulting in falling rolls. In these cases some schools, eager to capitalise on pupils in the area, are even beginning their own pre-nursery groups that take pupils from as early as two and a half years of age. At age three they transfer to the school nursery having been gradually inducted from pre-nursery to nursery. Structured play then forms an important element of their learning.

What is structured play?

Structured play enables staff to ensure that pupils know colours, numbers and letters of the alphabet. Pupils will learn to recognise their name written in lower case and learn to be more self-sufficient than they were before. Staff will read them stories, help them make things, paint, crayon, encourage them to hold pencils and paintbrushes, use plastic scissors, glue, etc. They will talk with them and encourage them to talk to other pupils. They will play games with them that allow them to practise physical skills like standing on one leg, hopping, catching and throwing a soft ball. The varied activities are intended to build up knowledge, as well as physical, mental, verbal skills and agility. There is a large difference in the way certain pupils come to school ready to learn. Nursery classes of this kind allow some pupils to catch up on some activities that they may have missed due to their home circumstances.

Nursery classes also provide refreshments – fruit and milk at breaktime – aimed at making the pupils feel at home and introducing them to a healthy lifestyle. **Health** is an important part of the pastoral programme in all schools. This is a good example of how a school instils good health habits early and how the pastoral programme is reinforced through such action. As pupils settle into school, teaching and non-teaching staff are able to begin to make assessments and determine where pupils are on a learning continuum. This is the beginning of a baseline assessment and enables the teachers to differentiate learning for the pupils being inducted. A child who comes in knowing numbers, letters and colours (and there will be some like this) needs to be challenged and allowed to progress or they are likely to become bored and disaffected even at an early age.

See Chapter 18 for information on health in the curriculum.

The role of the nursery teacher is to ensure that all pupils feel safe, secure and confident in their new school and that pupils want to come to school. In addition, there is a responsibility to differentiate the structured play so that those who are advanced on entry are able to build on this at a rate commensurate with their own ability. The structured play devised by the school will have a basis in the foundation stage of learning found in the national curriculum guidelines for the nation where the school is based. Remember that the national curriculum guidelines are different for the four nations, and when using the word 'national' it is a reference to one of England, Wales, Scotland or Northern Ireland.

Schools have different induction periods based on their own capacity and staffing. In most schools the nursery class day is shorter than that of other pupils in other parts of the school and as pupils progress through a primary school the time spent in school increases. A nursery pupil may start at 9.30 a.m. and finish at 3.00 p.m. because young children find a school day very tiring and shortening the day is beneficial to them and their well-being. Some schools even allow very young pupils to have 'rest' time or 'quiet' in the afternoon thus making allowances for their age and needs.

However, no matter how well primary schools induct pupils there will always be those who find it difficult to settle. Many primary schools are now very flexible and will make specific arrangements for a pupil. This may include allowing the parent to come to school with the pupil for a fixed amount of time or shortening the amount of time that the pupil spends daily in school. Gradually the amount of time spent in school is increased. In very rare cases some pupils will need to be referred to an educational psychologist who will be able to support the pupil, parents and staff in successfully getting the pupil into school.

Induction and transition: good practice guidelines

Moving from primary to secondary school will affect nearly every child who goes to school in this country. Some find the move traumatic and it often involves some level of anxiety, no matter how well the transition is handled. Remember that there are three bridges that need to be built in any transition and the most important one is to ensure that pupils feel safe, happy and excited about the move to secondary school. This is the pastoral bridge and the transition pastoral team will be working to ensure that pupils do feel safe and secure.

Some secondary schools have recognised partner primary schools and pupils may be expected to progress to that secondary school. However, pressure on certain schools for places and parental choice do not always mean this will happen. Wherever a child is moving to there will be some established form of contact between the two schools. Etiquette is such that secondary schools are encouraged to formalise contacts with primary schools that are designated partner schools. The following strategies, if all in place, present an ideal model of transition encompassing all relevant good practice:

- Primary headteachers, the secondary headteacher and those with responsibility for transition will meet regularly in calendared meetings.
- There will be regular visits between key personnel including SENCOs. A key stage 2 manager and key stage 3 manager meet on a regular basis to transfer information about pupils and discuss issues as they arise. Information about the level of attainment of the new intake is vital as this can affect the way the curriculum is managed in the secondary school. The secondary deputy headteacher in charge of the curriculum can take account of a weak intake with more support classes, or for a strong intake by moving resources away from support and towards enrichment.
- Noticeboards in the primary partner schools contain information about events in the secondary school and regular newsletters to the primary schools inform them about life in the secondary school.
- Secondary school newsletters contain information on partner primary schools and their activities.
- Primary school pupils from year 4 upwards have regular contact with the secondary school and will visit to play sport, take part in events put on by the secondary school (eg drama productions, carol concerts, etc). The aim is to make the buildings and its staff familiar to potential new pupils.
- Specialist secondary staff will help deliver parts of the key stage 2 programmes of study in science, information technology, technology, music, drama and physical education. This can happen in any subject area but many primary schools identify these

curriculum areas as ones that can cause them problems owing to the lack of specialist facilities, such as science laboratories, or the absence of specialist staff. Secondary staff in these subjects will gain information about what has been covered in the primary school and what needs to happen next to present a challenge to excited new pupils eager to learn.

- There will be regular visits to the primary school by secondary pupils involved in the buddy scheme so that new pupils have older pupils to support them. They normally work with the Year 6 pupils to build up friendship groups and reassure them about the myths that surround the move from primary to secondary school. However, buddies may also write and illustrate stories, taking them to read to nursery and reception classes. They may also work on numeracy with young pupils.

- There will be specialist insets delivered to primary schools by secondary experts and vice versa. Primary schools have smaller budgets than secondary schools and in the summer term, when years 11/12/13 are involved in external examinations, primary schools and secondary schools can combine to share valuable resources. This builds up an important loyalty bridge.

Combining to share resources

Below are examples of the kind of strategies currently used by some schools to ease transition.

- Primary colleagues will deliver inset to secondary teachers on the use of key skills in their everyday classroom teaching and the varied teaching methods used at primary level that could be used at secondary level.

- There will be an open day at the secondary school for all interested pupils from any school.

- There will be induction days for all potential pupils providing taster programmes of study.

- Teachers from the secondary school core subject teaching team will visit partner primary schools to deliver sample lessons to Year 5 and 6 pupils or to team teach. This ensures that potential pupils get to know some of their new teachers before arrival in the new school.

- Teachers from the primary school will visit the secondary school to teach former pupils now in year 7.

- Primary and secondary schools will share schemes of work ensuring that pupils are not repeating work already done but that the new school is presenting the pupils with a challenge. This is not easy when a school may take pupils from, say, 26 different schools but only six are partner schools. Etiquette is important in relationships between primary and secondary schools and finding out what is taught in a primary school that is not a partner is sometimes difficult.

- There will be information sharing about the pastoral programme and its delivery.

- There will be information sharing about school policies and school councils. If a partner school has spent a lot of time developing pupils in a certain way – for instance building up their self-assessment skills – a secondary school will wish to build on this where possible. If another school has a well-established school council and pupils coming from there could be valuably used in the new secondary school council then this is also worth knowing. Information transfer is not just about the pupil – it is about the school as well.

- The key stage 3 manager will produce a booklet for secondary staff that contains detailed information on all pupils. This includes academic achievement, medical history, attendance history, extra-curricular achievements, support needed or in place, etc. This is added to throughout the year as more information is gathered and forms the base-line information for the secondary school and its staff.

Remember that the above is the ideal and not all primary and secondary schools will put in place all of these strategies. However, many of these initiatives will be common in transition arrangements. In addition to the above, all primary schools will use their pastoral programme to discuss issues that arise on transfer such as making new friends, preparing for change and making decisions.

See the website for the transition case study from Bishop Gore School

Thus the pastoral programme is used to support pupils through this transition. Many secondary schools stagger the start of the new academic year. They may have only Year 7 and Year 12 pupils in school and put on a specific induction day for each group. This enables form groups to get to know each other and for the Year 7 pupils to get to know the school when it is not full.

One primary school wanted to deliver a full-day African drumming inset that would have cost them £400. This information came to light in a scheduled meeting between primary and secondary senior staff. Their partner secondary school had a music teacher who was an African drum specialist and offered to deliver the course for free.

Bridging the gap

How do you bridge the curriculum gap when your intake comes from 26 primary schools? In order to ensure that teachers are provided with useful information about new pupils, one school provides all new pupils with a bridging pack. This pack contains work in English, maths, science and history. It also has free coloured pencils, pens, a rubber, ruler and pencil sharpener and a free exercise book that has ruled pages and blank pages. Pupils also receive Basic Skills Agency cards with the times tables on them and information about spelling rules. The Parent Teachers' Association (**PTA**) in the secondary school pays for the packs that replace some of

Case Study

the curriculum bridging that would normally occur but cannot when so many schools are involved.

All pupils are given these packs to take home on their induction day in July and the work has to be completed over the summer holiday. The work is differentiated and pupils get merits for its completion, its quality, etc. The tasks include the type of work that has been done in the primary school and should ensure that skills are not lost over the six-week break. Pupils are expected to keep a diary of their summer holiday and they are encouraged to include postcards or pictures in their exercise book and to illustrate it in any way they wish. Pupils' work is marked using diagnostic marking sheets. For instance, English teachers use a marksheet similar to the extract shown below. To make things simple they put a name at the top of each marksheet and tick the relevant boxes. A class summary sheet is provided at the end.

☐ Can this pupil punctuate accurately using full stops, commas and paragraphs?

☐ Can they spell simple words?

☐ Complex words?

☐ Can they structure their writing and sustain it?

☐ Have they got a mature vocabulary?

☐ Is their handwriting legible?

☐ Are there causes for concern?

This enables the teachers to determine where individual pupils are on a learning continuum and they can then differentiate work for the classes that they are teaching from the outset. This school was inspected within one week of the beginning of the autumn term and inspectors were impressed at how quickly Year 7 pupils were settling and progressing within these subject areas.

Supporting pupils making choices

Transition occurs throughout a pupil's school career and the next large move is from key stage 3 to 4. It is at this point that pupils will need to choose the subjects that they will study to GCSE level. Although pupils normally remain in the same school the transition from one key stage to another is a very important one, determining the next stage of learning. Many schools put in place a lot of counselling for pupils around this time and careers advisors and staff, through the pastoral programme, will stress the importance of making sensible choices based on interest, aptitude and present attainment in subjects. In some cases where subjects offered are new schools will often put on taster lessons. The following suggests the types of strategies that may be used to ensure that pupils and parents are informed and that pupils make sensible well-informed choices:

- Options booklets are given out to all pupils and contain information about the courses on offer both in school and in other establishments. Increasingly schools use outside providers for certain courses such as construction, hairdressing, catering and electronics.

- Careers teachers and the pastoral team deliver a series of PSHE lessons that focus on making choices and careers advice – 'WHICH WAY NOW?'

- An options fair is held in the school with visitors from outside industries, the army, navy, and careers advisors. Parents are also invited.

- Parents are invited to meet teachers to discuss their child's progress in the subjects that they are thinking of opting for.

- Parents attend a meeting with pupils and the senior staff involved in curriculum planning and the options are discussed. Parents are free to ask questions.

- A series of taster lessons is put on for pupils who want to start new courses that were not offered at key stage 3. Visits to colleges are arranged for some pupils.

- Pupils' choices are scrutinised to ensure that they have chosen a broad and balanced range of subjects and that they are within their capability. Where staff have concerns, pupils are interviewed to ensure that they are making an informed choice. For instance, a very able child may want to take triple science GCSE but is equally able across the board and has no career in mind as yet. In this case they may be better advised to take double science at GCSE. This enables them to take another subject other than the third science. If in future they decide to take A levels in biology, chemistry and physics this is still possible. This allows the pupil time to make a more definite choice about a future career and allows them to take a broader range of subjects that may open up a wider career choice for the future.

Finalising choices and administration

Pupils are usually given a school deadline of the start of June to finalise choices. Once this is done class lists will be drawn up and resources for the courses will need to be ordered by subject leaders. The take-up for courses can vary dramatically from one year to another and a course that attracts 16 pupils one year may have 30 another and this has stock and resource implications. In addition, some courses offered may not attract enough pupils and decisions may need to be made to withdraw that subject option. Running courses costs money and these days courses need to be cost effective if they are to run. All this occurs at the end of the summer term and therefore sufficient time between making final choices and the official end of the summer term needs to be allowed for all administration to be completed. Most schools now complete a timetable on computer and class lists and pupil timetables will be generated from the computer system. When pupils start in September they will be given an individual timetable with the subject, teacher and classroom clearly stated for each lesson.

Sixth form transition

Pupils who have studied to GCSE in a school may now stay on and enter the sixth form if the school has one. In some cases pupils will be attending an 11–16 school and will progress on to tertiary education provided by colleges. Whatever the situation, the transition process starts again with pupils being given clear information about the next step for them and the options available. The pastoral team and programme will once again fully support this process.

A sixth form produces its own prospectus that outlines in detail the subjects offered for study. Some may be traditional A and AS courses but others may be alternative qualifications that are unfamiliar to many pupils. Sixth forms often offer a wide range of subjects like psychology, law, sociology, photography, media studies and business that may not have been available to pupils before. They will also put on subject fairs with current sixth form students attending to explain what life in the sixth form is like. Many schools have a day set aside in year 11 for transition where pupils meet a range of advisors, sixth formers and the pastoral team to discuss their options. In the case of an 11–16 school the subject fair may take place in the colleges and pupils will visit the ones that they may attend after GCSEs.

Some schools have now combined to deliver certain subjects that would not be viable if they were to teach them alone. These schools often produce a consortium prospectus. In most cases, they offer a core of subjects in their individual schools but will rationalise the delivery of minority subjects (ie those that will not attract ten or more pupils). Funding is crucial in sixth forms and is often dependent on a subject being seen to be viable, thus explaining why schools try to rationalise delivery of some subjects. In order for this to work, schools ensure that timetables are consistent and certain afternoons or mornings will be blocked off for this rationalisation to occur. The obvious benefit is that courses are protected, along with small sixth forms, that may not be viable without this provision and would cease to exist. One of the disadvantages is that pupils like to stay in their home school and do not always like to travel to other schools to attend the odd course even when transport is provided free and door-to-door. Another disadvantage is that schools may lose the expertise to deliver an A level in a certain subject if this happens year on year. One way around this problem has been for schools to decide who will deliver subjects on a biannual basis and then the provision is moved to another school. This is a little more difficult to arrange but does allow all teachers the opportunity to deliver A level courses at some point. This can be an incentive for some staff who particularly enjoy the challenge of A level teaching.

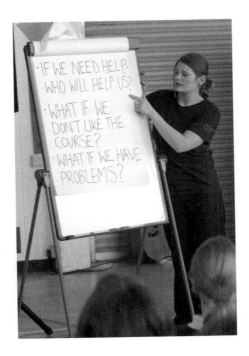

Transition to further and higher education

For some pupils there will be another transition that the school also plans for – the move on to further education. The pastoral team of the school will work closely with careers advisors to ensure that pupils are well advised as to what options are available to them. Pupils will be supported in attending open days, filling in application forms, applying for financial support, writing personal statements for Universities and Colleges Admissions Service (**UCAS**), preparing for interviews, studying for examinations, etc. The school's pastoral programme will also focus very clearly on preparing pupils for independence, living away from home, managing money, health, and so on. This is especially true of the move from the sixth form to the world of work or university. In many schools a dedicated team of staff will be on hand the day the A2 results are received. Their role is to ensure that pupil transfers from school to university are assured and where difficulties arise they will contact universities to support their pupils' entry.

A planned approach

In all these cases the consistent theme is that the transition is planned and pupils are well prepared and therefore able to make informed decisions about their next move. The pastoral team play a huge part in the transition and transfer processes that occur throughout the life of a pupil. Senior staff in all schools will have a clear overview of the process and are very much involved at a strategic level in helping to plan the pastoral programme. It is the senior team in a school who will ensure that days are set aside in the academic calendar for transition and transfer issues to be covered with potential new pupils at whatever key stage.

The best schools are those whose academic subject and pastoral teams are equally strong and where as much thought goes into the planning of the pastoral scheme of work as it does into the academic scheme of work. It is important that the delivery of the pastoral programme is monitored and evaluated, and regularly reviewed. Those in the best position to judge how well it has gone - the pupils - should always be asked to evaluate the effectiveness of the transition.

Time to reflect

Think about the school you are currently working in.

✔ What strategies are in place to induct pupils into the school?

✔ Who is in charge of this?

✔ Is there a team involved?

✔ What transfers occur from key stage to key stage?

✔ What data is transferred and how is this done?

✔ Who monitors, evaluates and reviews its effectiveness?

✔ What booklets, if any, are used to support the transfers?

✔ What meetings are held and who are they with?

Chapter 20

Attendance, Child Protection and Anti-bullying Strategies

![apple] **What will you find in this chapter?**

✔ Attendance – a key inspection issue.

✔ How does the Educational Welfare Service work?

✔ What strategies are in place?

✔ How schools use project workers.

✔ The role of the child protection officer.

✔ Anti-bullying strategies.

This chapter examines the issues that can prevent children learning. In order for pupils to learn they need to be in school: new teachers will be shown the strategies used to improve the attendance of those at risk. This chapter is also about child protection: at some point in every teacher's career they will come across a child who is at risk for some reason. Schools usually work closely with other organisations and adopt a multi-agency approach to this area. Every school has to have a child protection officer and their role is clarified. Further, the problem of bullying is considered. Every school has to deal with it at some time, both supporting the victim and dealing with the perpetrator and the cause. There has been a lot of success in counteracting bullying and in adopting overt measures to eradicate it as far as possible.

In order for pupils to succeed in school they need to attend. Figures are collected for attendance and schools are expected to achieve at least a 90% attendance figure over the course of a year. The reasons for pupil absence should also be recorded and where this occurs this is termed an authorised absence. Where no reason is given this is recorded as unauthorised. Pupils are expected to attend school unless there is a valid reason for non-attendance. Valid reasons include illness, a medical or dental appointment, attendance at a family wedding or funeral, or participating in extra-curricular activities. Although some pupils go on holiday in term time this should be an exception not the rule.

There may be reasons that are not immediately apparent for a pupil's non-attendance in school and this chapter explores some of these as well as looking at how pupils can be supported by various strategies.

Attendance – a key inspection issue

LEA performance for attendance and the recording of authorised and unauthorised figures are audited by respective national governments. LEAs are subject to inspections, like schools, and attendance is a key issue for inspection. To have a successful inspection report an LEA must provide evidence of the following:

- robust policies and strategies for improving attendance
- well-established multi-agency approach to tackling truancy and attendance issues
- advice provided to schools for improving the attendance of minority groups like traveller children and of pupils absent due to bullying
- regular sharing of good practice regarding attendance
- systematic use of legal powers available to Education Welfare Service (**EWS**) (policies for prosecutions in place and truancy sweeps used)
- monitoring and reviewing of effectiveness of attendance strategies
- attendance a key issue for self-review in every school
- rigorous monitoring of child employment
- improving rates of attendance in line with those of other authorities
- cost effective service.

How does the Education Welfare Service work?

In every one of the four nations there is an EWS whose job it is to ensure that pupils attend school regularly and that they get the best out of school. The EWS works on behalf of the LEA in ensuring that parents fulfil their responsibilities and get their children to attend school on a regular basis. The EWS may also be involved in monitoring child employment and ensuring that working children are of legal age and that they work no more than the maximum amount of hours permitted. In most counties one of the educational welfare officers (**EWOs**) will have a responsibility for this aspect of the provision. The EWS will also prosecute parents who fail to ensure that their children attend school. One person, normally the head of the EWS, will be the named person who has the jurisdiction to do this.

The parent of every child of compulsory age shall cause him/her to receive efficient full-time education suitable to his/her age and aptitude, and to any special educational needs he/she may have, either by regular attendance at school or otherwise.

(Western Education and Library Board NI, the equivalent of an EWS for Northern Ireland)

The EWS is made up of EWOs who may be regarded as educational social workers or advisors but they also work closely with schools to identify pupils whose attendance is giving cause for concern. In some counties they are called education and social welfare officers and they are a part of the social services provision for that county. Some large schools may have a full time EWO but many will share the services between a cluster of schools. In some areas the ratio is one EWO per 2,700 pupils.

The EWO visits homes and works with families and schools to ensure that attendance issues are, where possible, resolved. They investigate the reasons for absence and can advise families about specialist support services. In primary schools the EWO may work with a deputy headteacher or a teacher with overall responsibility for attendance. In a secondary school where there are pastoral coordinators for all year groups each may alert the EWO about pupils whose attendance has been poor. However, there will be a senior member of staff with overall responsibility for attendance. This could be a key stage manager, an assistant head or deputy headteacher. They will take the lead in monitoring, evaluating and reviewing the whole school strategies employed to maintain the high level of attendance or improve it where necessary.

All schools should have an attendance policy and many have strategies in place for monitoring and improving attendance. Though there has been much debate about the level of absenteeism despite interventions, many educationalists feel that the measures have been in part successful and without them the numbers failing to attend would indeed be higher.

What strategies are in place?

Many schools have an attendance policy. The policy will identify how the school ensures that attendance is targeted and how individual pupil attendance is monitored. It will also identify key personnel who are responsible for this task. In some secondary schools registration is electronic and pupil attendance is carefully monitored throughout the day through the use of lesson registrations. Pupils who fail to turn up for school are registered as absent. In some systems a phone call home is generated automatically, alerting parents to the fact that their child has failed to turn up for school. In other systems a person in charge of attendance (called an attendance officer) will ring home to find out the cause for absence.

In all schools parents are encouraged to ring the attendance officer/school before 8.30 a.m. to give a reason for a pupil's absence. This is then recorded on the system with a code being entered for a medical absence or illness. An attendance officer, who is usually a member of the administrative staff, enters the codes centrally. Each subject teacher takes a lesson register throughout the day. It is easy to see when pupils have failed to attend a lesson and this form of 'electronic tagging' of individual attendance has helped to reduce internal truancy figures. In addition, this type of system has been extended in some schools and is linked to an automatic system that generates a phone call home when a pupil who was present suddenly shows up as absent with no coded reason having been entered.

The electronic systems are on the whole successful but are subject to human error and if a teacher forgets to register a class then unnecessary phone calls may be triggered. Fully electronic systems that have a call system built in are also extremely expensive to run, rely on a stable database and working IT equipment.

In primary and secondary schools teachers with a responsibility for attendance will track individual pupil attendance and focus on those pupils where it falls below the norm. Initially teachers will look to see if there is a pattern to absence. Children may be missing school on particular days or at particular times. This may coincide with times when pupils have a particular subject or teacher. Discussions are held with pupils and parents to discover the reasons for absence and interventions are put in place. Where a school has the services of a good EWO then they can be used to work with the family to support them. Other interventions include amending the school week for some pupils who are bordering on being school refusers. This might mean encouraging pupils to attend for mornings or part of the week only until they build up their confidence and can cope with attending full-time. In some cases pupils refuse to attend for other reasons; they may have problems outside school related to drugs or crime. In cases like this the EWS or the school staff may work with outside agencies like the Youth Offending Team and agencies that support pupils with addictions. In other instances, parents, for a number of reasons, collude with pupils and give reasons for absence that are untrue. It may be that they are ill and need support at home and the child provides this level of unpaid help; or could be because the older child is useful in helping to look after younger siblings. Dealing with absences caused by parent collusion is difficult.

There are also pupils who fail to attend for no significant reason other than that they do not want to come to school and no amount of persuasion or coercion can make them do so. In cases like these parents are still responsible for their children's attendance and are liable to prosecution when their children persist in the non-attendance. Parents are usually given an opportunity to improve the attendance of their child but if an improvement is not seen in a short time then court proceedings can be instigated.

EWOs also take part in truancy sweeps supported by the police who have powers to pick up pupils found truanting but not to arrest them. Pupils are then taken to a central location or back to school.

The Learning House – helping children to attend

In some authorities strategies are provided centrally for pupils who are school phobics or lack the social skills and confidence they need to manage in a primary or secondary school. In some LEAs Learning Houses have been set up and schools nominate pupils who would benefit from this type of intervention. Pupils will attend the Learning House for a set number of days a week and will spend the rest of the time in their 'home' school. The intervention lasts for a term and at the end of this time pupils return to their school on a full-time basis. These strategies can be successful. However, some children who flourish in the protected environment of the Learning House, where pupil numbers are very small, often need very intensive support when they return to school on a full-time basis. The Learning House experience is normally shared between a number of schools and they can be used for primary or secondary pupils depending on the designation of the resource. Teachers and teaching assistants permanently staff the house, not only delivering subject-based learning but also concentrating on improving the social skills and confidence of the pupils they are working with.

The role of project workers

Project workers work on specific projects. Their brief is different to that of EWOs and they take on tasks that an EWO would not normally be able to accommodate in their working week. Project workers are also funded by the LEA through funding that is applied for and that comes from outside the normal funding streams.

Project workers usually have training in counselling and may have social services training. They will always work with children who are identified as being at risk of non-attending or of being excluded. They may, for instance, work on transition projects with pupils who are moving from the primary to the secondary school. The pupils they work with may lack confidence and be at risk of non-attendance on transfer. The project worker works with individual pupils, spending time with them to gain an understanding of their concerns and worries. They can take them on visits to the new secondary school and can also offer rewards like taking pupils on a special visit or trip. Project workers are usually shared between a number of schools and work with a number of pupils over time.

The role of the child protection officer

> **A disclosure means** when a child has revealed that something has happened to them that is inappropriate. Disclosures include information about physical or sexual abuse, or risk at home due to negligence for a number of reasons, including abandonment.

Every school has to appoint a designated child protection officer (**CPO**). These are usually senior members of staff. In secondary schools it is usually a deputy headteacher who is responsible for pastoral teams within the school. In a primary school it may be the headteacher but this can cause problems if an allegation is made against a member of staff. In such cases another member of staff usually investigates and presents the information to the headteacher who then makes the ultimate decision about how to proceed. It is not usual for the same person to both investigate and decide.

The CPO will have an overview of pupils in the school that may be 'looked-after children', ie those in foster placements or in a children's home. They will also know who is on the child protection register. All these pupils will be subject to regular reviews involving representatives from a range of services, including the school where the representative may be the CPO or someone delegated by them. The CPO is also the person who takes charge if a child in the school makes a **disclosure** to another teacher, adult or fellow pupil.

The CPO must work under the direction of the headteacher and therefore must keep the headteacher informed at all times. In extreme cases of disclosure the police and social services need to be involved. All action will be in accordance with local child protection procedures. The CPO will also take the lead if a child is thought to be at risk for some reason.

The CPO has clear guidelines about what procedures need to be followed in a number of scenarios and if unsure can ask for support from the LEA, social services or the police. However, if the CPO feels that a criminal offence has been committed then they must alert the police. In addition, if they feel that the child is at serious risk if they go home then they have to call in other agencies to support them. Every CPO has a file provided by the LEA with contact numbers and in all cases if the CPO is not the headteacher then they must keep the headteacher informed about all current child protection issues.

CPOs keep detailed records on the children they deal with and these should be regularly reviewed and updated. All relevant meetings and information must be filed appropriately and when inspections of schools take place the work and effectiveness of the CPO is reviewed.

Anti-bullying strategies

In 1988 the Scottish Office pioneered the first government-sponsored research into bullying in the UK. The project was carried out in ten secondary schools with a sample of 942 pupils who were between 12 and 16 years of age. The research showed that 6% of Scottish pupils had experienced bullying at some time or another and 4% admitted that they had bullied others. The research showed that more boys were involved in bullying than girls. The research also showed that some schools were far more successful at containing bullying than others. Further research suggested that some schools, despite the lack of anti-bullying policies, had for some reason managed to curb bullying to some extent in their schools. The location and social class of pupils or their parents were found to be insignificant. However, what the successful schools did seem to have in common were strategies that had been used in other countries where bullying was being tackled:

- These schools had been honest about bullying and admitted its existence.
- They openly discussed bullying and its causes.
- Teachers, pupils and parents were involved in putting together anti-bullying strategies and policies and were interested in making these work.

Since 1999 LEAs have had specific duties to combat bullying. Schools *must* have anti-bullying policies and LEAs must ensure that their schools comply with their duties. In

December 2003 the Department for Education and Skills published an anti-bullying pack entitled *Bullying: Don't Suffer in Silence*. This was intended to give schools helpful guidance. Surveys of children and young people suggest that bullying in schools is more common than most adults seem to think.

A report by Ofsted in 2003 suggested that although schools had policies in place which varied in their coverage and depth, they were generally good. Their effectiveness tended to depend on the commitment of the headteacher and staff to keeping the issue high on the agenda and making the policies work in practice on a day-to-day basis. It was generally found that schools with the most successful approaches to bullying took full account of pupils' views and ensured that curriculum and tutorial time was given to discussing relationships and issues like bullying. Other features tended to include checking the school site frequently and ensuring that there were safe play areas. In some primary and secondary schools for instance areas are set aside that are strictly for younger pupils or, in secondary schools, for Year 7 pupils new to the school. These are in central areas where teachers are visible and accessible.

Where schools were successful they also had sound procedures for the reporting and investigation of bullying and spent a lot of time investigating when concerns arose. Communicating with parents was also a part of the process. In many schools the circle of friends, peer counselling, learning mentors and outside agencies were used to support the victims and ensure that their confidence was rebuilt. These groups were also used to modify the behaviour of bullies.

It is important that schools take seriously their responsibilities with regard to pupils. If a pupil feels that they are being bullied and reports this then the school has a duty of care to respond. The perception by a pupil that they are a victim is enough and means that the school has to act to support that pupil and investigate the circumstances carefully. The pastoral team in any school plays a vital part in this and some members may have had training in how to identify and deal with bullying. It is important that all incidents of bullying are logged and that detailed records are kept of the intervention strategies used. Witness statements, where possible, should also be included and most schools keep named files on pupils who have been the victims of bullying.

At the time of the Ofsted report there were no firm national statistics of reported or proven cases of bullying in schools. Childline and other organisations have figures that indicate the numbers of young people who have contacted them about being bullied. Bullying was the biggest single reason for young people to contact Childline and in 2001 the victims of bullying made over 22,000 calls.

The effects of bullying can be extreme with victims suffering from depression and anxiety. This can also result in their missing prolonged periods from school which is itself counterproductive as they lose their friendship groups and this makes them more vulnerable as individuals to bullying.

What do you do if a pupil alleges that they are being bullied?

All teachers should be familiar with the school policy on bullying, child protection and other important policies and these should be re-read at the start of each academic year.

✔ Take as many details about the incident or incidents as you can from the victim. Always date information of this kind. Tell the victim that you will see them later in the day when you have discussed this. If you feel the victim is at risk if they leave you, then your duty is to keep them with you for safety. If it is the end of the school day and the victim is going to be at risk when they travel home then you need to ring a parent to come and get them and pass on relevant information to them. You must explain that you are taking it seriously and will, with advice, investigate the allegations.

✔ Try to work with a more experienced member of staff and discuss your findings with them. They may suggest you proceed alone but if you do not feel confident ask if you can shadow them and learn for the future.

✔ If the victim has given you the names of witnesses then you or another member of staff will need to interview them. Follow school procedures ensuring that interviews take place, where possible, in the presence of another member of staff or in an appropriate location. However, in sensitive cases like this witnesses may want to remain unknown to the bully or bullies and discretion will be necessary. You may need to find an office that is available and allows some privacy.

✔ If there is insufficient evidence and no witnesses then ask the pupil to keep a log of what is going on. This can be a small notebook that they record in so that you build up information against the bullies.

✔ If you think it is necessary you will need to contact the victim's parents if you haven't done so already and keep them informed about your investigation.

✔ When you are sure that you have enough evidence you will need to interview the bully. If there is more than one this needs to be done individually. It is good to get them to own up to their crime! Dealing with pupils on a one-to-one basis makes this more likely.

✔ Look at the school policy and seek advice as to how the bully should be punished. It may be that an exclusion is needed or some form of serious sanction. Warn the bully that you do not want them involved in any form of intimidation again. You will need to warn them that you do not want their friends involved either. Some bullies will pass the baton to a friend to carry on the bullying, others may be stopped at this point.

✔ In many cases this should put an end to the problems but some bullies are persistent and encourage others to carry on where they left off.

✔ If the bullying persists it may be that you will need to use other resources. Some schools have trained mediators or counsellors and in serious cases outside agencies like the police will need to be used.

✔ The LEA will also have people who can support you.

✔ To be wholly successful and to eradicate as many of the causes of bullying as it can, a school has to state overtly and repeatedly that it is against bullying and that it will not be tolerated!

Schools that are successful in combating bullying take the issue seriously and investigate cases and causes rigorously. They also record incidents of bullying so that patterns can be analysed and keep records of both bullies and victims. These schools also have a very good buddy system in place and a lot of extra-curricular activities going on. This gives vulnerable children a place to go other than the playground.

As I quickly learned when I became a head, dealing with bullying is a never-ending process and one that needs to be proactive rather than simply reactive. It's about being vigilant and taking every opportunity to develop a school ethos that rejects stereotypes, values everybody for his or her own unique self, and promotes the ability to empathise. Achieving and maintaining that fundamental shift in attitudes and behaviour is hard work and it has to involve every member of staff all the time.

(Ofsted, 2003: 8)

In many of the successful schools another key feature is the willingness to involve pupils in the process. School councils are involved in discussions and many schools undertake repeated surveys as a basis for a discussion about the issue. These surveys provide valuable information about the most vulnerable groups of children, the extent of the bullying and the range of intimidation that went on. Staff training is another important element. It is important that all staff are united and refuse to allow intimidation in their classrooms, ensuring that no put-downs of any kind are allowed. In this way staff present a united front in refusing to allow intimidation and overtly state that the ethos of the school is one that does not allow bullying of any kind.

Time to reflect

Consider the following questions.

✔ Ask to read the school policies on attendance, child protection and anti-bullying. Are there any strategies used in the school that have been mentioned in this chapter?

✔ Who is in charge of attendance and has the school got the use of an EWO?

✔ How many days a week is the EWO available to the school?

✔ How does the school support pupils who have problems attending?

✔ Who is the CPO?

✔ Ask the CPO about some of the issues they have to deal with.

✔ Has the school got a school council?

✔ What training have the teaching and non-teaching staff had over the last three years in tackling bullying?

✔ Is there a safe zone in the school for young or vulnerable pupils?

✔ How successful is the school at preventing or dealing with bullying as and when it arises?

References and further reading

Ofsted (2003), 'Bullying: effective action in secondary schools', HMI 465.

Western Education and Library Board, **www.welbni.org**, Services for Parents, Students and Youth.

Scottish Action Against Bullying, **www.scre.ac.uk**

Every Child Matters, 'Change for children', **www.everychildmatters.gov.uk**

Part 6

School Improvement and Continuing Professional Development

Chapter 21

School Inspections: What Makes a Good School?

What will you find in this chapter?

✔ What makes a good school?

✔ The inspection framework in the four nations.

✔ What is the purpose of an inspection?

✔ Self-evaluation in schools.

✔ How should you prepare for an inspection?

This chapter looks at the elements that make up a good school and discusses how you should prepare for inspection – an event that causes anxiety in many schools.

What makes a good school?

In reality the most important aspect of any school is the quality of teaching and learning that goes on there. When the teaching is of a high quality, is differentiated appropriately to the needs of the pupils and complies with national programmes of study then pupils will engage with the teaching and progress. However, pupils are complex beings and good-quality teaching and learning needs to be supported by a strong discipline structure and a strong pastoral team. Inspectors will look for these aspects among others.

> See Chapter 20 for the roles of project workers, EWOs and attendance officers.

Attendance is another key issue that can affect pupil performance: in order to do well pupils have to attend for at least 90% of the school year or the school is deemed to be failing in this crucial area. Schools have a team of staff to ensure that strategies are in place to maximise pupil attendance and that interventions are put in place to ensure this occurs. This team could comprise **project workers, EWOs and attendance officers**.

Good schools are self-reviewing organisations and this self-review is evident at all levels within the management structure. There are common themes that run through the school development plan and these are also evident in departmental development plans. Monitoring is regular and rigorous and all plans are evaluated for their effectiveness – the school is data-rich *and* knowledge-rich. The school knows if pupils are achieving in line with expectations and results are evaluated. When issues arise strategies are put in place to address them.

Organisations that are successful are also consistent in the application of strategies. To ensure that this happens the school has clear written policies that all teachers are expected to follow and this is monitored by key personnel in the school. They will set numerical targets and will, through departmental development plans, be able to see how the whole staff can work to ensure that targets are met. These schools have clear strategies in place to monitor, evaluate and review their development plans. They also build in success criteria, like that of school A below, to ensure they have something clear to aim for.

Clear aims and targets

School A: teaching and learning is our number one priority

Over the next year we want to:

- Improve the percentage of lessons that gain a grade 1 or 2 instead of a 3, when lessons are observed by senior staff or heads of department, from 50% to 75%.
- Ensure that all departments include in their scheme of work lessons that have more innovative methods of teaching and appeal to auditory, visual and kinaesthetic learners.

- See written evidence of this in schemes of work and evidence when monitoring classroom teaching.
- See a bank of innovative lessons develop in the staff library of resources.
- See a reduction of at least 5% in poor behaviour and fixed-term exclusions as a result of this.
- See an improvement in results (+5% over predicted outcomes) of those pupils gaining three level 5s at the end of key stage 2.
- See evidence in all subjects of teachers helping pupils to understand how to learn and teaching them to learn skills.
- The present teaching and learning policy will be revised in the light of this work and the evidence. This will be done in consultation with all staff.

In education these are often called **SMART** targets, meaning that they are:

- **S**pecific
- **M**easurable
- **A**ttainable
- **R**ealistic
- **T**ime related.

Good schools are also well-managed and the senior team and all managers have a clear, shared vision for the future. Staff and pupils feel valued and the teaching and non-teaching staff have access to good-quality professional development and recognition of their hard work. The school is fully inclusive and all pupils are provided with equal opportunities; the vulnerable are supported and the able developed. The school is well-resourced and the budget is managed efficiently. Links with outside agencies are strong and the school has an established relationship with partner schools and organisations, and this is consistently managed.

Results are consistently above the national and LEA average and the school is in the upper quartile for benchmarking. The school has many additional awards such the as the Basic Skills Quality Mark, Investors in People, Curriculum Awards and Careers Awards. The school is oversubscribed and staff turnover is low.

The inspection framework in the four nations

Inspections are conducted in primary and secondary schools throughout the UK, but there the similarity ends. The amount of warning schools are given, the time inspectors will be in the school, the time lapse between one inspection and another and the focus of the inspection all vary according to which nation you happen to teach in.

Schools in England get a maximum of five days warning of an inspection and will be inspected once every three years. In Wales, schools have approximately half a term's warning and will be inspected every five years. Scotland and Northern Ireland are also inspected approximately every five years and get three weeks' notice. In some countries the inspection teams are made up solely of inspectors who are employed by the department of education in that nation. In England and Wales inspection teams tender for inspections and the team is made up of people who have undergone training to become team inspectors or registered inspectors. Most of the trainees will be teachers from all forms of educational background.

The reality is that in order to be sure about the inspection framework within your own nation you need to keep up with ongoing developments. For instance, it is likely that the lead time for inspections in all nations will be dramatically reduced so that schools have less time to prepare as this has proved to be successful in England. The advantages are obvious. Teachers and pupils have less time to get stressed about the intrusion into their working space and inspectors feel that they are getting to see the real school rather than one that has had time to prepare artificially.

What is the purpose of an inspection?

The purpose of any inspection is to ensure that standards of teaching and learning in the school are sound. Pupils should be:

Pupils are assessed on entry to a school. This assessment level determines what pupils should achieve at the end of their stay in primary or secondary school. If a pupil exceeds this prediction the school has added value. If schools do not get pupils to achieve at this level they have taken value away.

- achieving at a level in line with their potential on entry to the school; the school should actually be *adding value* to pupils
- behaving in an orderly fashion in a school which is a safe environment for them to learn in.

The school should be:

- well-managed with resources being used effectively and efficiently; governors should play an active role in its running.
- obeying statutory orders and following national curriculum programmes of study.
- a self-reviewing establishment where all levels of management regularly monitor, evaluate and review progress. It should be able to identify strengths and weaknesses, and in the case of weaknesses put in place intervention strategies to remove them.
- proactive and ensuring that current initiatives are built into its development planning. The development plan should reflect the needs of the whole school and individual departments.

- taking account of and giving consideration to parents' and pupils' points of view. The school should be a fully-inclusive organisation and provide equal opportunities for all.

- working well with partner schools and the community.

- providing an independent evaluation framework.

- keeping national government informed about standards.

- identifying and promoting good practice, enabling it to be shared with other organisations.

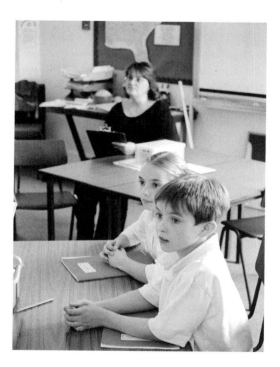

Self-evaluation in schools

Self-evaluation is important in all schools. Many LEAs have produced a self-evaluation form/school profile that schools in their area complete. The headteacher usually fills in the form online but the information is provided in consultation with other senior managers and the middle management teams. Basically, the completed form provides vital information for the inspection team. Where a form has not been completed the inspection team will ask the relevant questions once it gets to the school. It is therefore in the best interests of the school and the LEA to have completed documentation like this in place.

The form will provide a context for the inspection. It will state the location of the school, size, numbers of staff and pupils, percentage of pupils who are on free school meals, the ethnic mix of the school and the number of pupils who have statements of educational need. It will also indicate the financial income of the school and the expenditure, which will be itemised under cost headings. The curriculum of the school and the amount of time spent on specific subjects will also be specified. In addition the external results for the school will be included for a three-year period.

Many authorities have a team of statisticians who analyse the results for their schools and the form will be annotated so that trends will be identified. Where a difference in a year is significant this will be highlighted. For instance, 5% differences up or down are seen as statistically significant. If a school gets 65% of its pupils at level 3 in English one year and the following year it is 71% that would count as a significant trend and a green arrow pointing up would indicate this. This information is useful for the LEA and the inspection team. However, it is the school that needs to indicate whether this has occurred due to interventions used or whether the improvement is down to a more able cohort. In each category, space on the form is available for more information to be added. This might include details of strategies the school has put in place to address issues or hindrances that have prevented improvement.

Inspection teams have information on the statistical achievement of all schools in the four nations. In particular, they will gather as much statistical evidence about the examination performance of a school over the three-year period prior to its inspection. The use of a three-year period ensures that the inspection team is able to look at trends over time and not rely on one cohort's results. The cohort could be atypical (ie weaker or stronger than usual) and this would significantly weaken the accuracy of the team's findings. The team then looks at schools of a similar size and intake and will compare results in a number of categories for all these schools. This is called benchmarking. If a school is doing well they would be in the upper quartiles when compared with other schools.

The local education authority will want to know the same information as any inspection team. The most important way of judging how a school is doing is to assess the results that pupils attain. Pupils are assessed on entry to a school and teacher assessment and standard assessment tasks give an idea of the potential of the cohort. The aim is to ensure that pupils attain or exceed their potential. Inspection teams will also have more detailed information on results. They will be able to tell if a school is producing the appropriate percentage of pupils attaining level 3 at age seven or A*/A grades for their cohort at age 16. A school may be achieving good levels or A*-C GCSE grades for their pupils but could still be failing to extend pupils at the top end of the attainment spectrum. Similarly, the school may achieve good results for the very able and able but below-average children may not be supported sufficiently to achieve their potential.

If a school is fully self-reviewing, they will identify issues like this for the inspection team and will identify the strategies that have been put in place to improve the situation.

Similarly, a school could have an issue with a gender gap and they may be trying to improve the performance of boys in English and girls in maths. The self-evaluation form provides a school with an opportunity to show what is in place to remedy problems but it also enables schools to identify strengths that they have. When schools are reviewing performance effectively they will also identify weaknesses and the strategies that have been put in place to remedy these.

In some cases the self-evaluation form mirrors that of the inspection framework. This is because some schools have to self-evaluate taking account of the inspection framework. By the time they are inspected, the school has already prepared a form and has kept it updated so does not need to prepare a large report again. Using the self-evaluation form schools also grade their performance in each area, for instance teaching and learning, managing staff and resources, contribution to the personal, social, emotional and cultural development of pupils according to the inspection framework grading system. The forms are also useful for LEA planning and this is why many LEAs have introduced them. An LEA that is strategically managing a number of schools uses the forms to provide it with powerful information about how its schools are doing, enabling it to use resources strategically. If in one authority a lot of schools are struggling with the same problems, then resources could be effectively and efficiently deployed to support schools as a cluster. The sharing of self-evaluation data with the LEA is vital.

Before an inspection team comes into a school it will have carefully scrutinised the performance data and read the self-evaluation report of the school. Then it will devise a list of questions that it wants answered. The aim of the team will be to find the answers through practical observation of teaching and learning, looking at past work in pupils' books or through questioning the staff and pupils, asking for further evidence.

How should you prepare for an inspection?

Ensure that:

- all pupils' books are marked and ready for viewing by an inspector
- lessons are well planned and lesson plans are available.

Most teachers, no matter how experienced, plan lessons. However, for an inspection revert to what is common on teaching practice and prepare lessons more fully. A lesson information sheet is shown in Figure 7.2 on page 77. This has been used in many schools when they have been inspected.

Read an NQT's personal experiences of inspections online.

Inspectors will also want to see evidence of past work that pupils have done and will be interested in classroom displays. It is important that where possible all pupils are up-to-date with their work and that missed work has been copied up. Inspectors believe that underachievement is initially the responsibility of the class teacher. This means that the class teacher should have supported any pupil who has missed a considerable amount of work or who is having problems in some way. It is important to be able to show the strategies that have been used and if these have failed what other strategies or teachers have been involved. If a school is fully inclusive then there will be strategies in place to support pupils who have missed a considerable amount of work due to absence and all teachers will use these strategies.

Inspectors are also keen to know if pupils understand the level they are working at and if they understand how to improve the standard of their work and move onto the next level or grade. They will observe lessons and look at books, as well as question pupils about their learning. They will also want to know how class teachers keep records on pupil achievement and what information is used to inform parents, either face-to-face or in written reports, about progress.

Class teachers are expected to form a part of the self-reviewing process and to understand all data available on their pupils. They will be expected to monitor and evaluate progress and assess whether their pupils are on track to achieve their potential or not.

Inspection teams expect to see copies of all documentation in a school and these should be made available to them. Each school has a school handbook that contains detailed information about the school itself, the day-to-day running routines and policies that a school has to have in place. Most schools put all their policies into this to ensure that all teachers have up-to-date copies of all relevant material.

Where there are large lead-in time to inspection this material will be copied and sent to the inspection team beforehand. In England, under the existing framework there is not enough time for this to happen so that this documentation will need to be ready for the team to view. Inspection teams work a long day and can be in a school at 7.00 a.m. reading through information. They will often leave late in the evening, taking more material away with them.

Most new teachers are responsible only for their own classroom teaching and their form or tutor class. However, it is common in primary schools for teachers to have additional management responsibility. If this is the case the documentation will need to be in evidence for that as well. You are not expected to contribute to the school handbook unless you are responsible for a policy (literacy, numeracy, etc) that is used across the school but you may have to produce a departmental handbook.

A school/staff handbook

This could contain:

- staff and governors' names
- day-to-day running information
- job specifications
- roles and responsibilities
- lesson times including breaks and lunch
- important whole school policies and procedures
  - child protection
  - anti-bullying
  - teaching and learning
  - assessment
  - equal opportunities policy
  - routines for organising school visits
  - health and safety guidance
  - attendance
  - behaviour.

All this will be available in your school and is normally in one file or booklet.

All staff must know the contents of this handbook well as inspection teams will want to ensure that the school is working as a team and that policies are being delivered consistently. This will not happen if some staff are unaware that the handbook exists and are not familiar with its policies.

A new teacher may be expected to produce a SOW for a subject where they are the only specialist teacher. However, if there is more than one person involved in the delivery of a subject it is now common to produce a handbook to accompany the SOW as this ensures consistency of delivery and standards.

A departmental handbook

This is common in primary and secondary schools where one person has responsibility for a subject and others are involved in delivering that subject. It will contain information about:

- the departmental development plan
- staffing
- location of resources
- schemes of work for all year groups and levels
- policies on marking and assessment
- cross-curricular dimensions (some schemes of work, for instance science, link into PSHE)
- monitoring and how it is managed
- lesson observation
- monitoring of pupils' books and how pupils' work is moderated to ensure that assessment levels are being correctly awarded
- a resources stock list that is checked annually
- copies of ordered materials.

A departmental development plan shows two distinct things:

1 The improvement you wish to make within your own subject area.
2 The improvement you intend to make in your subject area in response to the needs of the whole school.

In order to document what you are going to do to fulfil point 2 above you will need to read the school improvement/development plan (SIP/SDP).

What is the school improvement/development plan?

This is the whole school document produced in consultation with all staff, especially those with responsibility for curriculum, pastoral and whole school management. It may also respond to the governor, parent and pupil voices of the school. The SIP/SDP may identify an issue for improvement, eg the performance of boys at key stage 1. Although this goal may be stated in the SIP/SDP, each individual development plan should show how it will be addressed and identify how it will ensure this whole school aim is achieved.

See Chapter 3 for a SOW template.

New teachers may be expected to produce SOWs early in their career and can even be plunged straight into an inspection. Some schools adopt a standard format for SOWs and others allow teachers autonomy in this. Storing SOWs electronically makes updating them very easy and time efficient.

This chapter has put forward suggestions for how best to be prepared for an inspection. However, good teachers do not need an inspection to ensure that they prepare good lessons, mark pupils' work using detailed diagnostic comments or have the administrative materials in place to perform their role effectively. Good teachers do these things as a matter of course. Finally, inspections are nothing to fear. During my career I have been involved in at least five full inspections in three different schools. This does not take account of the many other times when inspectors have visited my departments or have been auditing specific areas of school life for which I had responsibility. In most cases the relationship between the inspector and the teacher is one of mutual respect where a meaningful dialogue can be held about the work that is on-going in the classroom. Inspections allow a teacher to showcase their work and that of their pupils and most cases are positive and profitable experiences for all concerned.

Time to reflect

✔ Think about the school you are in at present. Obtain a copy of the school handbook, the area/departmental handbook, the school development plan and the departmental development plan.
   🍎 Look at the development plans and see if there are any issues that are common to both.
   🍎 Look at the results for the school you are in and then compare them with the results for the rest of the area and nationally.

✔ Get a copy of the last inspection report. Look at any aspects that the inspection team picked out as being weak.
   🍎 How is the school addressing these issues?
   🍎 What strategies have been put in place?
   🍎 What strengths have been identified?

✔ How does your school self-review? Ask your mentor or line manager what monitoring is in place, who is involved and how often it occurs.

✔ What awards has your school got?

✔ What professional development has your mentor or line manager been on recently? Why?

✔ Do you think that the school is an orderly place to work in?

✔ Are the children well managed and is behaviour good?

References and further reading

Inspection reports are in the public domain and are free to download.

🍎 For England go to **www.ofsted.gov.uk**

🍎 for Scotland go to **www.hmie.gov.uk**

🍎 for Wales go to **www.estyn.gov.uk**

🍎 and for Northern Ireland go to **www.deni.gov.uk**

Reading through these gives you a good idea of what inspection teams are looking for and what they think makes a good school.

Chapter 22

Applying for a Job, Preparing a Lesson and the Interview

🍎 **What will you find in this chapter?**

✔ Looking at job adverts.

✔ How to write a CV.

✔ The letter and application form.

✔ Planning a lesson as part of an interview.

✔ How to prepare for the interview.

This chapter shows you how to go about getting that all-important first post. You may think you know how to write a CV and a letter of application, however, even if you feel confident it is better to read this chapter first! And, once you are over the first hurdle and have been short-listed, how do you arrive at the interview ready to impress? We look carefully at how to plan an impressive lesson and analyse potential interview questions.

Teaching posts are advertised in a number of ways, in the local or national press, within LEAs via a regular bulletin or on their own intranets or on the Internet. The *Times Educational Supplement* is published every week on a Friday and is widely used to advertise teaching vacancies. Most vacancies tend to be advertised in the spring term from January onwards but there is a regular supply of job vacancies advertised throughout the year.

Looking at job adverts

Read the following advertisements. Figure 22.1 shows one for a job in the primary sector and Figure 22.2 for one in the secondary.

Fielding Primary School
Wyndham Road
Ealing
London
Tel 020 8567 *****
Fax 020 *******
E-mail: admin@topschool.com
Required from September 2006

NEWLY QUALIFIED TEACHERS (TWO)

Are you talented and creative?
Have a sense of humour?
A team player?
Support others and be supported by colleagues?
Share?
Like children? Ours are delightful!
Enjoy good personal and professional relationships?
Then our school is for you.

The governing body, as part of a new staffing structure, has created these vacancies for classroom teachers. Following our successful Ofsted inspection in May 2004, Fielding was described as a 'good school with many outstanding features'.

You will be well supported by your colleagues and will have a clear induction programme in a friendly, structured environment.

Applications are welcomed from newly qualified teachers to join this friendly, three-form entry school. Telephone for further details and application forms from the Headteacher, or write/e-mail. Visits to the school are welcome and can be arranged by telephone. Closing date: Friday, 22 April 2006 at noon. Interviews will be held in the week beginning 2 May 2006.

What do you see in an advertisement?

The address and contact details are clearly given.

The type of post is clearly stated. It is suited particularly to those newly qualified and means you will not need to compete with already experienced teachers.

The rhetorical questions give you some good information about the type of person they are looking for and why. This could be useful for your application letter.

The school is successful and proud·of its recent inspection. The school seems supportive of new staff.

They are happy for you to look around before applying and seem to have nothing to hide.

The school has already fixed the time scale it is working to, suggesting good organisation.

Figure 22.1 Job advertisement for a primary school

The City of Leicester College

A specialist Business and Enterprise College

Downing Drive, Evington, Leicester LE5 6LN

Required from August 2006, permanent full-time

TEACHERS OF MATHEMATICS

(MPS) (2 posts)

Our mathematics faculty is looking for well-qualified, enthusiastic and ambitious teachers of mathematics.

As a specialist Business and Enterprise College we are actively developing enterprise through all aspects of the curriculum. In the mathematics faculty we have a dedicated set of laptops, interactive whiteboards and all staff have their own laptop. These posts would suit an NQT or an experienced teacher seeking a new challenge. A level teaching is available for suitably qualified candidates. There is an established induction programme and professional development is fully supported. Informal enquiries or visits are welcomed and encouraged.

For application pack including more details please call the job line on 0116 *******. For any further enquiries please contact The head of mathematics 0116 ******* or e-mail office@cityleics.sch.uk. Initial closing date for applications is 29 April 2006.

What does this advertisement tell you?

Two posts are available at a specialist college. Do you know anything about specialist colleges of this kind? If not you need to get researching quickly.

The mathematics faculty is well equipped but high-level IT skills would seem to be essential. Do you have them? If unsure take up the offer and speak to the head of mathematics directly. Never waste time applying for a post for which you lack essential skills.

NQT applications are welcomed and there is the added bonus of A level teaching if you are able to offer it.

New staff are well-supported and staff development is a high priority.

Visits are welcomed and this suggests that the college is open and has nothing to hide. The head of mathematics is empowered by the college and is approachable. The college shows trust with this task and respect for management skills.

Figure 22.2 *Job advertisement for a secondary school*

Having studied the advertisements you will need to contact the school or college for an application pack. This will contain some or all of the following:

- a school prospectus
- details about the area the school is situated in
- details about the department you would be applying to join or the area of the school the job is relevant to
- a job specification
- a person specification
- an interview time-scale
- requirements for the application – a letter, CV and completed application forms.

The information in the pack must be used to inform your letter of application along with information about your teaching experience and **vision** for this teaching post.

See the rest of this chapter for more on **vision**.

How to write a CV

A curriculum vitae (CV) is in essence a life history with only relevant details. It should be word processed so that it can be kept up to date. It should be current, there should be no gaps in the time-scale, and it should be true!

You'll find a sample CV template on the website.

The curriculum vitae

A typical CV should contain the following elements:

- Name
- Address
- Date of birth
- Marital status
- Contact numbers (including mobile number and e-mail)
- Schools attended in chronological order
- Qualifications obtained. Dates and grades are useful. (However, as you progress up the career ladder the dates are useful but the grades you obtained in GCSEs 20 years ago becomes less so! Other later qualifications obtained while teaching will be more relevant – in the case of a senior manager having the National Professional Qualification for Headship for instance.)
- University attended
- Undergraduate qualifications obtained, level and date (if some are pending state this)
- Postgraduate qualifications obtained or pending. (The date and level is important.)
- Other relevant qualifications. These could include sporting qualifications for refereeing, first aid certificates, life-saving awards, music exam qualifications, etc
- Work experience or teaching placements if you are training or are entering the profession from another area of work; post details if you are already in post. These should all be in chronological order. (It is important to avoid time gaps and any present must be explained. If you took a gap year then explain what you did in this time, likewise if you were at home looking after children, etc)
- Courses attended relevant to the post. This may not apply to new teachers but when you apply for future posts this should cover a three-year period prior to the application. Keeping accurate details is important
- Hobbies and interests
- The names and contact details of two referees.

The CV is an important document so spend time on it. Insert a header with the school and post details and make a cover for it with your name on the front. This may seem excessive but first appearances really do make a big difference. If a school employs you from NQT to retirement age they might, by the time you finish, have invested over £1 million in that post and you in particular. This investment has to be carefully considered. You will need to prove to the team that you are worth every penny.

The letter and application form

The letter is a formal one and should follow that format. It should begin 'Dear Sir/Madam' unless you know the name of the headteacher. You should end with 'Yours sincerely' if a name is used and 'Yours faithfully' if a title is used. All of this may seem rather trite but having seen hundreds of applications over time, it is not! At least 20% of all applications for posts will fail because too little time and attention has been paid to filling in an application form, presenting a sound CV and writing a detailed and accurate letter.

Fill in the application form ensuring that all parts are accurate and that spelling is correct. Remember that all posts are now subject to a police check and a medical.

In the letter you should clearly state:

Find sample letters on the website.

- the post you are applying for and where you saw the advertisement

- the experience you have had on teaching placements or in a post that you feel is relevant to this job

- the vision you have of education and for this post in particular.

What does the word 'vision' mean - it is used a lot in organisations today. It is a word used to encompass a person's individual philosophy about how pupils should be taught. It should also encompass any ideas a person may have about the specific job/role being applied for. It means that you answer questions that are not asked. *How important is marking/ using data/ use of praise in a classroom situation/ promoting high expectations/ target setting/ lesson planning?* Your letter should contain words such as *'I believe', 'I think it is important ...', 'I believe my placement at ... has taught me the importance of ...'.*

You may also want to state your vision for your own future. *'I would like to consolidate my teaching expertise and in the future would like to think I could ...'.* Being ambitious and having a clear career plan is a good thing.

The letter should also build up a profile of you as a person. If you are committed, hardworking, a team player and have a sense of humour then say this in your letter. All these characteristics help a school to gain a picture of what makes you an individual.

In addition you need to think of:

- Any extra-curricular talents you have that a school may find useful. Primary schools always need people with musical or sporting ability to support their extra-curricular programme.
- Any additional qualifications such as those gained for special educational needs, dyslexia as a specialism, etc.
- Any experience in the world of work that is relevant and makes you more useful to a school.
- Any other subject expertise that may be useful.

Schools these days require staff to be multi-functional. Staff are an expensive commodity and the more skilled you are the better. Being able to coach sport, begin a new club in an area that you have expertise, produce a school play, offer musical support, run a business enterprise, coach a public-speaking team, produce a school newspaper, run a science club or teach swimming in addition to your subject or class role are all useful skills to flag up to your future employer. Do not be afraid to sell yourself as no one else can do this for you.

The letter, application form and the CV pave the way to an interview. The references will come later, usually at short-listing stage.

Ensure that your letter is well-planned and free of grammatical and spelling errors. Schools rely on staff to communicate via reports with parents. If you are unable to send in a *perfect* application form they will query your communication skills and your commitment to perfection that is needed in a school organisation. Your letter can be handwritten if this is requested but word-processed letters are now standard practice. The letter should be produced on good-quality paper and contain two addresses, yours and that of the school you are applying to. Letters are normally addressed to the head-teacher unless you are otherwise instructed.

Your letter should be at least two-and-a-half sides long. This allows you sufficient space to sell yourself, explaining how your qualifications, experience and vision will benefit the school.

Planning a lesson as part of an interview

Many schools now insist that all prospective teachers 'teach' a lesson. The school will give you clear guidelines about the age and the ability of the class and the length of the lesson. Some schools will actually tell you what they want taught. In a modern foreign language lesson they may ask you to teach the past tense of the verb 'to be' for instance. Lesson duration will be short, 20–40 minutes, to allow time for all short-listed candidates to teach a lesson and be observed. The lesson is observed by the line manager or head of department or a senior member of staff in the school such as the

PUPIL EVALUATION FORM

Name of pupil .... Lesson ....

1 Was the lesson interesting? Why?

2 Were you interested all of the time? If not, why not?

3 What did you learn during the lesson?

4 What part of the lesson did you most enjoy?

5 What part of the lesson did you least enjoy?

6 Was this lesson
   Excellent   Very good   Good   Fair   Poor
   (Underline or circle one of these only)

Thank you for helping us to choose your new teacher

Figure 22.3 *Example of a pupil evaluation form for a lesson*

> **A printable version** of this form is available on the website.

deputy head teacher. In many schools now pupils are being 'included' and 'empowered'. They may therefore be asked to complete a simple evaluation form such as the one shown in Figure 22.3.

Planning a lesson

✔ Re-read Chapters 7 and 8.

✔ Look closely at the age and ability of the class the school wants you to teach.

✔ Look at the programme of study for that age and subject. Decide carefully on a topic (if you have a choice) ensuring that it will enable you to differentiate the lesson and show off your skills.

✔ Think about the lesson aims and objectives carefully, preparing a lesson plan that you will present on the day to the observers. Ensure that copies of resource material are also available for them. You may want to put this together in a pack with your name on it. Ensure that you have enough copies for the class and that it is free of errors.

✔ Plan to use a range of activities to encourage class interaction.

✔ Make sure that the pupils will have learnt something concrete by the end of the lesson and that there is proof of this through oral, written or practical assessment.

✔ Close the lesson appropriately by summing up what has been taught and learnt in the form of a plenary-type session. Even though the lesson duration is short the introduction and conclusion of the lesson must be obvious to those monitoring it.

Delivering a lesson

✔ Feel confident when you enter the classroom and ensure that you look around and make good eye contact with the pupils.

✔ Give out name tags if they do not have them on. Take sticky backed labels with you and give them to a pupil to give out. Names give you power. For instance, if a pupil is talking when you are, stop what you are saying and say 'Thank you [name the pupil]', and maintain eye contact for a few seconds. Then carry on with the lesson but every now and then ensure that that pupil sees you are watching them. Do not let them repeat the offence. If they do move them. (Note that you do not really need to say 'stop talking'. They will know what they have done.)

✔ Introduce the purpose of the lesson clearly and get someone to distribute materials for you. Keep an eye on them while they do this. Do not assume that the pupils present will have books with them, this could well be a group that has been brought together for this purpose alone. Make sure that your worksheets have space for written work.

✔ Ensure that the activities you have prepared are carried out well and that all pupils are on task. Think about providing activities for the class that will ensure this.

✔ Look at different teaching activities that are suggested by experts like Paul Ginnis in his *Teacher's Toolkit* (2002). How could you adapt such activities to suit your lesson?

✔ Watch the time and ensure that you synchronise your watch with the person observing so that you are sure to have enough time to finish your planned activities.

✔ Allow enough time to conclude the lesson efficiently. Sum up the learning outcomes and ensure that pupils understand that they have completed the learning objectives that you clearly outlined at the beginning of the lesson.

✔ Ensure that you have differentiated the materials and that if anyone finishes the work you have something else prepared. Ensure that it is an extension of the work and not just more of the same. Your aim is to enrich the most able and challenge them, not just keep them occupied.

How to prepare for the interview

The school or college will write to you explaining the format for the day. Make sure that you read this carefully. What you wear is a matter of choice and if you teach a practical subject and are going to teach a lesson this may influence your choice. However, first impressions do count so try to choose wisely.

Below are some questions that may be similar to those asked in an interview. Think about how you might answer them:

- Tell us about your teaching experiences to date.
- Tell us about a successful lesson or series of lessons that you have taught recently.
- What are the challenges facing teachers today?
- What strategies would you use to enhance learning?
- We work as a friendly, close-knit department/school. Do you view yourself as an adaptable team player willing to integrate and contribute?
- How important is classroom organisation in creating a well-disciplined learning environment?
- How would you create a welcoming, learning classroom environment?
- What strategies would you use to cope with a pupil disrupting the lesson by constant calling out or low-level disruption?
- Is assessment target-setting important?
- What data are you familiar with using and how do you use it?
- How would you create a welcoming, learning classroom environment?
- We have a policy of sharing teaching materials in the curriculum area/learning area. What skills could you offer for the production of these resources.
- How do you see the role of ICT, whiteboard, PowerPoint in teaching today?
- What do you feel makes you particularly suitable for this job?
- Is there anything else that you would like to add that you haven't had a chance to say?
- Many staff in our school offer extra-curricular activities for our children. What extra-curricular activities could you offer us?
- What range of strategies or activities would you employ to attract and hold the attention and interest of potentially disaffected and less-able pupils?
- What would be your vision for the teaching of your subject? How would you promote your subject in the school?

For each of these questions the interviewing panel will have a list of points that it wants to hear as part of your answer. These will be scored and a comparison made between candidates. In some interviews candidates may also be asked to prepare a presentation based on questions that are given to them beforehand.

Time to reflect

✔ Look at the questions above and think about how they might be adapted to your subject or area of the school.

✔ How would you answer the questions?

✔ Look at your CV critically to check that it is detailed enough.

✔ Try writing an application letter for a job that you have seen advertised. Think about how you would impart your vision for education to the school and how you get across something of your personality in the letter.

References and further reading

Ginnis, P. (2002), *Teacher's Toolkit*, Crown House Publishing: Carmarthen.

Chapter 23

Continuing Professional Development

What will you find in this chapter?

✔ Career entry and development profiles.

✔ NQT induction.

✔ Continuing professional development.

I f a teacher were to stay in a school for the duration of their career over the 40 years or so of employment that school will have spent over £1m on that individual! A teacher is therefore a valuable resource who needs to be updated at regular intervals on the latest developments in their chosen profession. This is done through a schools inset/training budget. However, it is vitally important that teachers keep detailed records of any training that has been received and that teachers think carefully about what their own development needs might be. This chapter looks at how teachers can progress most effectively, developing valuable skills along the way and how they can do this whilst being supported by their school and in some cases by national teaching councils.

Career entry and development profiles

One of the things that the four nations have in common is the requirement that new entrants to the profession should have a career entry and development profile. The aim of this is to ensure that new teachers are encouraged to think about their professional development at key points. It is structured around transition points that occur at:

- the end of initial teacher training
- the beginning and end of the induction process.

The purpose of the profile is to ensure that new teachers make links between the training that has gone before and the reality of working on a day-to-day basis in a school. It is intended that new teachers should reflect on individual achievements and be able to set goals and realistic targets based on this reflection. Each new teacher should be assigned a professional mentor. Part of the mentor's role is to lead this discussion and encourage the reflection so that new entrants can determine what their training needs might be. For instance questions might include:

- What do you find the most interesting and rewarding aspects of teaching to date?
- What do you consider to be your main strengths?
- What aspects of your teaching do you need to develop further or require further training in?

NQT induction

Newly qualified teachers involved in the induction phase of their career are not involved in the performance management processes. In addition they are expected to have more non-contact time and in many cases do not have the responsibility of a registration group. They also have a designated mentor who will observe them teach on a regular basis and meet with them to discuss progress. In the first year of teaching, specific funding is made available for training purposes and this is ring-fenced for individual training only. Many LEAs run their own induction training programmes, which all NQTS will attend.

Many schools encourage new teachers to keep a portfolio of evidence. This builds on the professional development record. Keeping a record of evidence is a good habit to get into and it should contain:

- reports on your progress and teaching
- reports on lesson observation
- examples of lesson plans
- records of objectives individually set or set in consultation with a mentor or induction tutor

◢ individual reviews of progress towards qualified teacher status and evidence of course assignments.

Throughout a career, many teachers have a lot of opportunities to take on specific tasks and roles. Keeping evidence of this involvement is important. It enables a person to track their own career development as well as build up information that can be incorporated into an up-to-date CV.

Induction arrangements

For information on the induction arrangements that exist in your region access the information below by typing the key words into a search engine and following the links.

In England

DfES (2003), *The Induction Support Period for Newly Qualified Teachers*, London.

In Northern Ireland

Department for Education for Northern Ireland (1999), *The Teacher Education Partnership Handbook*, Belfast.

In Scotland

Scottish Executive (2003) *Teacher Induction Scheme*, Edinburgh.

In Wales

The National Assembly for Wales (2003), *Induction for Newly Qualified Teachers in Wales*, Cardiff.

Continuing professional development

All schools have a training budget for the continuing professional development (**CPD**) of all staff. This was originally used to train only teaching staff but as the numbers of teaching assistants employed in schools increases, the training fund is used to provide CPD for all staff who come into contact with pupils.

Staff development in schools is managed by a school development officer (**SDO**); this might be a deputy headteacher. The inset budget is normally allocated under different headings, which include induction, and the SDO manages the budget: ensuring that all teachers' training needs are met. The way the budget is spent is determined by three criteria:

◢ the school development plan and the training that is needed to realise it.

- the needs of individual departments and areas of the school, and the individual plans that have been written to vision the future in these areas

- the needs of the individual and their performance management targets.

Funding is provided in the case of the NQT. However, the SDO has only a limited budget and has to ensure that the funding is used strategically and fairly throughout the school. Teachers who go on courses are encouraged to evaluate the quality of training and, where possible, to report back to others. The competing needs of those of the school, specific areas and individuals need to be met. In England and Wales the General Teaching Councils provide additional funding for teachers to undergo specific training. The amount of funding varies and in some cases teachers can form groups to carry out joint training. The provision of funding depends on certain criteria being met and all teachers who are allocated funding by these bodies have to submit a final report on their training. The report outlines how the training has provided CPD for the individual concerned. When teachers attend courses it is important to keep the training materials safe and to file them under recognisable headings where they can be retrieved easily. This is a useful habit to get into, as are the following:

- Ensure that you have copies of your career entry profile and that you review your progress with your mentor.

- Keep documents that prove your qualification status safe. Schools often photocopy degree certificates, etc and place these in your staff file.

- Ensure that you regularly self-review your progress. Assess your strengths and weaknesses. Use this to determine your own training needs.

- Keep your CV up to date by keeping a detailed record of all training you have attended. File data from courses carefully.

- When you are subject to performance management arrangements, ensure that you have some idea of what CPD you require.

Time to reflect

Having read this book you should be much better equipped to face the challenges confronting teachers today. You will have a good understanding of

✔ How schools are organised for learning.

✔ How to plan differentiated lessons and manage the behaviour of your pupils.

✔ How to use data effectively to track the progress of your pupils and set meaningful targets.

✔ How to mark effectively and manage your time.

✔ How to manage an area of responsibility in a school.

✔ How to contribute to the pastoral team of the school.

✔ How to apply for jobs and manage your own professional development.

🍎 And finally . . .

This book is intended to be a reference book and therefore should not be set aside like a novel that you may never read again. Instead it should be used as part of your own reviewing strategy. For instance if you find that a class of boys you are teaching are under-performing in line with their potential, you may wish to refer back to the material in Chapter 4. The same class may also have behaviour issues that need addressing and again the chapters on behaviour management may be of use. In fact from my own experience I predict that there will be many times when information from this could be a life-line for a new teacher. I firmly believe that this book with its mix of practical advice based on 25 years in the profession coupled with the theoretical information will be invaluable. If I had started my own professional career with this knowledge I think the journey would have been a lot smoother and the climb a lot easier. Finally, I love the job I do and for me every teacher should be in the classroom to make a difference. You are entrusted with this: good teachers really do make a difference. The acknowledgements at the front of the book are my own testament to this.

Index